RADIANT BEAMS

100 Bright Stories Of God in Our Lives

SUSAN DARST WILLIAMS

Scripture is taken from the King James Version of the Holy Bible.

First published by Dog Ear Publishing
4011 Vincennes Rd.
Indianapolis, IN 46268
www.dogearpublishing.net

ISBN: 978-1-4575-4144-5

This book is printed on acid-free paper.

Printed in the United States of America

To my Keeper.

Contents

Preface

Stories with a deeper meaning are the best. I crave stories that give me tingles or make me laugh. It is so good to read about situations that illustrate Bible truths and show how fun Christian living really is.

When things happen that touch you, and give you new insight into how God works in our lives, it's as if He is shining a ray of truth toward you. That's why I call these stories "radiant beams." They light your path and warm your heart in a world that's often dark and cold.

Radiant beams are crazy coincidences, moments of truth, and mini-miracles that come out of nowhere to solve problems. When you're at the end of your rope but something happens to save the day, or when you get a flash of inspiration or a jolt of encouragement, you've just experienced a message of love from God.

I hope you enjoy these 100 stories that show Him active in our everyday lives. Some will make you laugh. Some will bring a tear to your eye. The best will do both. Many will remind you of the compassion and insight that are ours to give and receive through a personal relationship with Jesus Christ. Bask in His glow! And pass it on!

Let's celebrate the joy of living, blessed by the sweetness and warmth of the Light of the World.

—Susan Darst Williams, Mount Laundry, Nebraska

1. Double D's

Trust in the Lord with all thine heart; and lean not unto thine own understanding.

— Proverbs 3:5

The number of ways that people can misunderstand each other is endless. Luckily, God's communication is flawless. Here's a little story to keep you (ahem) abreast of what I mean:

This friend of mine was driving her married son, 22, to pick up his car from the shop. It was a lovely morning. They had the windows rolled down in her car. The sunroof was open.

They were rumbling across a big bridge. It was so noisy in the rush-hour traffic they practically had to yell. My friend was talking about a former co-worker of hers, age 49, whom the married son had met, but didn't know very well.

It seems this lady had had both of her knees totally replaced the week before. They had both taken a tremendous amount of abuse over the years. Arthritis had apparently finally finished them off.

This lady had wanted both of her knees replaced at the same time because she only wanted one insurance hassle. She also did not have enough disability recovery time to have them done separately. So she had a "double."

Now, it was really, really noisy on that bridge. They were in heavy traffic, with the windows wide open. So when my friend said that the woman had had her "double knees done," her son thought she said her friend had had her . . .

. . . "double ***D***'s done."

As in, he thought the lady had a large bust with size D-cups, and had had breast reduction surgery!

But he didn't say so, being a polite young man who loved his mother, even when he thought she was giving him just a WEE bit Too Much Information about someone he barely knew.

And so the conversation continued, both clueless about the misunderstanding. The mother was convinced her son was one of the most compassionate, caring young men in the whole world. He was asking all kinds of questions about the procedure.

He shouted back to his mom: "Really???? REALLY???? She had double D's? I did not know she HAD that problem. I never really noticed, I guess."

His mother shouted back, "Yes, and she did not have enough time built up to take two medical leaves. But she sure didn't want to wait 'til January for the second surgery. The pain would be the same, virtually, to have them done together."

"Gee, does insurance PAY for that, Mom?"

"Sure, Honey. But there was some talk that they might not, if it was deemed a pre-existing condition."

"Well, wouldn't it be pre-existing? I mean, how could it NOT be?"

"Yeah, I sure would think so. She had scars on both sides already, so there has been one surgery already done. Sounds pre-existing to me, too."

As he absorbed this information, the mother continued. "She blew me away the other day when we had coffee. I couldn't believe she had just returned from participating in a regional bowling tournament in Tulsa. You'd think they'd have interfered with her bowling game!

"Then she had played golf, and had walked to the tennis court to play a few games with her daughter . . . all just before the necessary surgery!

"And when we walked to our cars, HERS was in a handicapped stall! I challenged her right to park there, and she only shrugged.

"Those activities HAD to be harder on her knees than walking into Panera's for a bagel."

"Yeah," the son agreed, although his perplexity was mounting.

"So . . . the weight of her double D's was too much for her knees? Yet she could still swing a golf club, serve a tennis ball, and BOWL around her double D's?!?"

The mother stared at him. "What are you saying? Her knees ALWAYS hurt. That's why they just REPLACED them."

The son pondered this revelation. "Ohhhhhh."

Then he burst out: "Double 'KNEES'? Did you say 'KNEES'?!? I thought you said 'D's!

"I thought you said 'double D's' back there on the bridge in the noise!!! As in, bra size!!! As in, a D-cup bustline!!!"

That interfered with her BOWLING?!?

That was a pre-existing condition?!?

That enabled her to use a handicapped parking spot?!?

They laughed 'til they cried. As they replayed the conversation with the double entendres, it became even funnier.

The moral of the story is: speak clearly and listen well. Or you'll get yourself and others into . . . double trouble. †

2. Stiff Upper Lip

***Consider the lilies of the field, how they grow;
they toil not, neither do they spin:
and yet I say unto you, that even Solomon in all his glory
was not arrayed like one of these.
Wherefore, if God so clothe the grass of the field,
which to day is, and to morrow is cast into the oven,
shall He not much more clothe you, O ye of little faith?***

— Matthew 6:28b-30

We were going to Hawaii. We were leaving at O Dark Thirty. We had never been, and we were very excited. To top it off, it was cold and snowing in our Midwestern city. HA HA HA HA HA!!!!

But, as usual, I had run myself into a tizzy getting all the Top Priority Must-Do Tasks done so that we could get out of town. You know, the Top Priority Must-Do Tasks that are suspiciously like sane people's Bottom Priority Who-Cares-Hakuna-Matata-Que-Sera-Sera-Let-It-Go Tasks. Somehow, it's in my DNA that I've got to do all this prep, or I won't have fun on my trip. Meanwhile, I spend the whole trip recovering from the frazzle of getting out of town. It's a cuckoo situation.

Anyway, I needed to do something about my unwanted facial hair. See, when Aunt Flo stopped coming around any more, I started getting Nuclear Power Jolts on weird places like the insides of my elbows. But the worst midlife crisis came when I noticed one day, looking in a mirror in the sunlight, that I was suddenly sporting a Fu Manchu moustache!

AAAIIIEEE!!!

I now had an easier time growing facial hair than my Beloved. His one errant attempt at growing a lush, manly moustache ended badly. He grew a nice patch on the left side, and a nice patch on the right side. But there was a stubborn one-inch gap under his nose that refused to sprout even one wisp of hair. He looked like the Morse Code of hair – dahhh dit dahhh! So he quickly shaved again, and resigned himself to a bald upper lip for life.

But mine, ironically, was amply fuzzy, but unwanted. The fact that I am female made having a Fu Manchu moustache a bad thing. It made me say . . . fu-ey.

I couldn't let my Beloved spend that kind of money on a second honeymoon in Hawaii, imagining Brooke Shields running toward him on the beach in her bikini . . . and instead he gets me, in a Fat Lady muumuu with a Fu Manchu!!!

So I went to get waxed. The stylist was of Asian descent. I tried not to let it bother me when she said, "I going to WHACK you."

The room she led me to looked suspiciously like a morgue. At least it had a lot more comfortable bed. I didn't realize that to get waxed on just my upper lip, I would have to lay down on the bed like a surgery patient. I took off my shoes and socks, and lay there, awaiting my fate, with cold feet – a signal to which I should have attended.

Here came the happy, peppy, positive Wax Mistress, ready to whack me, wielding her Whack Pot. Did you KNOW there's such a thing as a Whack Pot?

She loaded up heavy, warm wax on both sides of my upper lip and down the sides. It felt like warm, heavy bricks. She waited a moment. It was ominous. Just as I was wondering if I could move my lips enough to say, "I CHANGED MY MI. . . ."

RRRRRRRRRRRRRRRIP!!!!!!!!

She yanked a long strip on the right up and away, with tiny hairs visible in the wax. A pelt from Beauty Shop Hell.

I saw my bare feet rise up off the foot of the bed, toes spreading out wider than I thought possible. Hmm. Wonder why my feet are doing that?

Then YOWSA! I felt the PAIN!!! My nerves must be shot, if my feet felt the pain in my upper lip before my upper lip did.

No sense trying to organize my lips into telling her I changed my mind NOW. If I did, I'd have to go to Hawaii with one side lustrously Fu Manchu, and the other as bald as a baby's behind. So I braced myself, and sure enough:

RRRRRRRRRRRRRRRIP!!!!!!!!

There went the pelt on the other side. Holy schmoly! Ouchie oochie!

Then she plucked and pulled out about 50 more little dollops of wax-speckled, deep-rooted hairs, here and there and everywhere, all the while making pleasant small talk. So that's what it feels like getting whacked. O . . . K. In shock, I paid the money and walked out into the cold, my now-hairless, totally numb lip icing up like a slick airplane wing.

Within a day, the numbness gave way to blisters and a few little sores. I think she accidentally whacked off a few sections of the skin of my lip, too.

Darn! It didn't look THAT bad, before. Now it was eye-catching, like a strawberry milk moustache.

Our daughter Eden helpfully pointed out that the irritated and brand-new skin would be much more likely to sunburn. If you sunburn fresh, new skin, you get a permanent scar. So here I was, going to bright and sunny Hawaii, planning to be outside every day for 11 days!

"A SCAR 'STASHE!" she chortled. "You'd better wear a thick layer of sunblock with the highest SPF on your upper lip the whole time!"

So now my Beloved is going to have his Brooke Shields running toward him in a Fat Lady muumuu with a Santa Claus moustache!!!

Oh, why didn't I leave well enough alone? Why do I always try to improve on the looks God gave me? They should be good enough, since they're from Him. Shouldn't they? Sigh.

At least the Whack Mistress gave me SOMETHING to bolster my flagging self-esteem. As I was leaving the beauty shop, she said, "You whack well."

Heyyyy! I whack well! That's something! Look out, Hawaii! Here we come! †

3. That Sinking Feeling

Nay, much more those members of the body,
which seem to be more feeble, are necessary:
and those members of the body,
which we think to be less honourable,
upon these we bestow more abundant honour. . . .

— I Corinthians 12:22

She was on a first date with a very attractive young man. He took her out for a romantic picnic on the Missouri River on his flashy speedboat. It was his pride and joy. He had a bottle of wine and some munchies. He impressed her a great deal with his skill in maneuvering the boat trailer and launching the craft. Off they went.

Ah, boating! Such a relaxing hobby! The wind whipping through your hair! The hum of the powerful motor! The delight of leaving the cares of the world in your wake!

But not ALL of the cares. . . .

A few miles down the river – or, in her humorous re-telling, when they were definitely UP the river – he suddenly realized that he had forgotten a key thing. It was highly, highly important. But it was very, very small:

The plug!

He had forgotten to put the plug in the boat! She didn't even KNOW there was a plug in a boat. She knows now. Even though the plug is very, very small, she now knows: it is highly, highly important.

So THAT'S why the boat was dramatically planing more toward vertical than horizontal!

Yikes! His suave and debonair, relaxed demeanor transformed him immediately into A MAN OF DESPERATION!!!

Instead of impressing his date, he now focused on staying out of Davey Jones' Locker. He'd heard that if you have left the plug out, but you keep going fast enough, your boat won't take on as much water. So he plunged the throttle forward like the last lap of a NASCAR race, heading back for the dock as fast as the boat could go.

Meanwhile, she risked her life over every bump, leaning out over the back of the boat at that breakneck speed, trying to get the cork from the wine bottle from their cute little picnic into the little bitty hole where the plug was supposed to go.

Bump! Bumpety bump!

She couldn't get it in.

Plan B was for him to swing by the dock ramp, slowing down just enough to allow her to survive the leap onto the dock. Meanwhile, he would keep the boat moving quickly to keep from taking on more water. She could dash up to his truck, start it up, and back it down partially in the water on the ramp, so he could run the boat up on the trailer before it sank.

She listened to this plan, wondering if her life insurance was up to date.

Where's the *America's Funniest Home Videos* camera when you need it?

He zoomed by the dock. She leaped from the boat and lumbered up the steep boat ramp to the parking lot. He ran the boat in circles, still at breakneck speed.

Being a South Dakota farmer's daughter, you'd think she'd have the mechanical skills to operate a truck and trailer. But after several pitiful attempts, she failed to get the trailer cranked around and backed down the ramp. It's hard! YOU try it!

Embarrassed, she ran down to the dock and tried to holler at her date over the roar of the motor. He was still out circling around in his speedy little boat, and couldn't hear her. Resorting to gestures, she waved her arms and shook her head back and forth, "No!"

Oh, the look on his face. . . .

On to Plan C: He would swing by the ramp and slow down just enough for her to jump back in the boat. Then he would zoom up to full speed again as soon as possible to get rid of some of the water they took on when he stopped long enough for her to jump back in. Next, she would get a 15-second lesson on how to drive a boat. She would circle the boat at full throttle in the middle of the fast and treacherous Muddy Mo on her first experience driving a boat, while he ran for the trailer.

It worked! He backed his rig down onto the ramp, and somehow, she maneuvered the boat back close enough without demolishing the dock or sinking the boat. He leaped back in the boat, took the wheel and ran a couple more full-speed circles around the river to get some more water out. Then he turned toward the ramp and rammed the boat up onto the trailer. Finally, he leaped out of the boat one last time, raced around to the truck, and drove the trailer laden with the waterlogged boat up the ramp to let good old gravity drain it for a good, long while.

During that good, long while, they exchanged a good, long glance, panting in their drenched clothes and messed-up hair. And they started to laugh. And laughed some more. And zzzzzzing!

It was love.

How could it not be? After an experience like that, they were a team.

They've been married now for 18 years. I don't think they took any more boat rides on the river after that. But there's a moral to their story:

Little things mean a lot. It's not the size or strength of something that makes it important. Same thing goes for humans.

Like that little boat plug, you are part of the whole. If you're not in place, you'll be missed. Bigtime!

Everybody and everything counts. That's the way the Big El Capitano in the Sky charted our course. It's how the human race stays afloat.

Oh, yeah, and have a bottle of wine handy at all times. You may need a few swigs of the contents if you get into trouble. And the little bitty cork might just come in handy! ✝

4. Why I Pinched the Principal

(W)e glory in tribulations also:
knowing that tribulation worketh patience;
and patience, experience; and experience, hope:
and hope maketh not ashamed. . . .

— Romans 5:3-5a

I blame the whole thing on Maddy's harmonica.

EEEEE-AAAAY-EEEEE-AAAAY-EEEEE-AAAAY. . . .

She found it among some old toys, loved it immediately, and refused to be separated from it, 24/7.

EEEEE-AAAAY-EEEEE-AAAAY-EEEEE-AAAAY. . . .

Our 2-year-old's two-note serenade rang out all over the house, on every car ride and in my dreams. She kept one hand on it while she ate, so that Mommy couldn't "lose" it the way Mommy "lost" the permanent markers and the finger paints.

She was like a reverse Pied Piper at the shopping mall, which emptied in our wake, as normal consumers out ahead of us heard the harmonica coming and ran for their lives.

We went to a restaurant with hopes of finishing an actual sit-down meal in public for the first time in months. But Maddy spent the whole evening standing up on the seat, leaning over to the next booth, and playing her harmonica with all her might into the faces of the would-be diners on the other side.

EEEEE-AAAAY-EEEEE-AAAAY-EEEEE-AAAAY. . . .

Most people smiled mildly and cut us some slack. One guy, however, shot us a dirty look. My husband planned to get his phone number, make a recording of Maddy's incessant serenade, and then call him up every night at 3 a.m. and play it for him:

EEEEE-AAAAY-EEEEE-AAAAY-EEEEE-AAAAY. . . .

We thought about contacting the military and offering her for top-secret mind control, propaganda and torture maneuvers against foreign terrorist leaders. You know, set up loudspeakers outside their camps and, night and day at high decibels, drive them crazy:

EEEEE-AAAAY-EEEEE-AAAAY-EEEEE-AAAAY. . . .

Then we remembered: terrorists are already crazy. We were just getting that way one brain cell at a time.

Miraculously, my sister called to invite Maddy to a movie at the same time one of our older daughters was playing in her high school softball team's district championship. Yay! A place to park Maddy so I could enjoy the game in peace! I had been worried that Maddy's constant harmonic-izing in the stands would get our team disqualified or at least make the ump grumpy.

Plus, the exciting lure of going to the movies was the perfect excuse to get Maddy to hand over the harmonica at long last and then "lose" it. You can't have one in the movie, Honey. They won't play the movie if anybody has one. Really. Let Mommy pry your fingers off your 'monica, now. Come on. It can take a "nap" while you're at the movie with Aunt Robin!

She bought it! Hallelujah! She bought it!

So I was delighted. I could go to the teenager's softball game and see every play. I wouldn't have to haul the stroller, diaper bag, jacket, sweatshirt, mini soccer ball, treat bag, juice box, Binky, Blanky, Bunky and assorted books and toys like an overloaded pack mule.

I wouldn't have to miss the whole game because I was busy serpentining after the thundering sneakers of a 2-year-old track star down either sideline and past the outfield.

I wouldn't have to sustain eternal vigilance so that she wouldn't be kidnapped, conked by a foul ball or cause an oncoming train to derail with her antics.

I wouldn't have to spend the whole time at the s'ingset, schlide and teeter-totter at the playground all the way across the park. I wouldn't be relegated to peering back toward the field trying to see the game.

It was heavenly to drive there in blissful silence, pop the keys in my pocket and, for once, walk someplace without a mountain of paraphernalia and a toddler tornado in tow. I didn't miss the 'monica at all.

In fact, I barely knew what to do with myself. My brain, so used to being assaulted by the two-note serenade of the harmonica, searched about for stimuli in the unaccustomed serenity.

I sauntered up to the bleachers containing our team's fans, including my husband. He was sitting on the end, several rows up, in front of a bevy of beautiful teenage cheerleaders. The sun was in my eyes, but I saw his red golf cap. He had planned to come to the game right after his golf round.

In the carefree spirit of the afternoon, feeling light-hearted and frisky, I walked over to the side of the bleachers right next to him in his trademark khaki slacks. Saucily, I reached my hand up, and took a meaty chunk of his flank between my thumb and finger. I gave him a sexy little pinch to playfully let him know I was there. Tra la!

And he looked down at me. But it wasn't my husband.

It was the school principal!!!!!

EEEEE-AAAAY-EEEEE-AAAAY-EEEEE-AAAAY. . . .

Same posture, same glued-on red golf cap, same khakis . . . but it wasn't him. Too late, I spotted my Beloved, two rows over, engrossed in the game.

The principal's face slowly broke into an enormous smile at the stricken look on my face. He knew exactly who I thought he was. Principals have a tough job. I was glad to give him some comic relief. Thank goodness he was such a good sport and laughed it off. The cheerleaders behind him saw the whole thing and got a big laugh out of it as well.

Thank goodness our team's color was red, since my entire body, especially my face, radiated that color for hours.

Thank goodness we won. Everybody was happy. I dodged a sexual-harassment lawsuit from the principal. My husband said he'd postpone the divorce one more time. Our teenager promised that she won't feel it necessary to go around with a bag over her head for the rest of her high-school career, on two conditions:

(1) That Mom looks before she pinches, next time, and

(2) that Mom loses Maddy's harmonica, before Mom loses "it." ✝

5. Oh! *THAT* Red Durango SUV

But the very hairs of your head are all numbered.

— Matthew 10:30

It's a good thing we have a perfect God. He can keep us all straight and keep track of who's who 'til we get up to heaven. It's not quite that way here on Earth.

Take what happened to my Beloved. He's a conscientious, law-abiding captain of industry. He is owner and president of his company. He is prudent, careful and wise. That's why it was a surprise when one of his employees burst into the office one day and exclaimed, "There's a cop downstairs looking for you, and it sounds serious!"

AA-OO-GAH! DIVE! DIVE!

It seems my Beloved's red Durango SUV had been spotted bashing into a mailbox on 29th and Douglas Streets in downtown Omaha a little over an hour earlier.

The business manager at the scene of the crime had jotted down the license-plate number of the red Durango SUV and called 911. A policeman had tracked the car to my husband's company. Now he wanted the facts. Just the facts.

"But . . . but . . ." my husband sputtered, "I wasn't anywhere NEAR 29th and Douglas today. I know I'm getting old, but I THINK I would have remembered running over a mailbox."

Hmm. The facts didn't square with the report from the scene of the crime. The policeman asked, "Could someone have been using your vehicle?"

"No, I was in it, all through the lunch hour," my Beloved replied. "I parked it back here just about 20 minutes ago."

The policeman squinted at him, no doubt thinking: "Suuu-uuuure you did. We've got you dead to rights, you closet vandal. You're goin' DOWN!"

Oh, these white-collar criminals! They think they can get away with anything!

They went outside and looked at the Durango. Whoops! There WERE a few chinks on the driver's side door. The officer said they would be "consistent" with the mailbox caper.

"Whaaat?!?" my husband protested. "Those are 'consistent' with the fact that this car has 80,000 miles on it! I didn't do it, I tell you! It's a bad rap!"

Sigh. Law enforcement duties can be tedious when dysfunctional suspects live in a world of denial.

"OK, then, let's go to the scene," the policeman said . . . adding silently, no doubt, "you lying scumbag."

The . . . "SCENE"? This cop was serious! My husband was perplexed. Was he going crazy? Was this a nightmare? Or some kind of practical joke?

Upon their arrival, a bunch of people came out of the building to glare at the dirty, rotten scoundrel who had viciously attacked their poor, defenseless mailbox and snapped that $10 post in two with his red Durango SUV.

There it was! The weapon of mail destruction, which was also the getaway car.

They were lining up the crunched mailbox with the tiny chinks on the driver's side door. My husband's anxiety and out-of-body experience was at its peak. Finally, the business manager came out and said:

"Nah, that's not the guy. The driver was Hispanic-looking."

WHAAAT?!?

Could a Hispanic-looking guy have stolen my Beloved's car, rushed over and purposely bashed this mailbox on a mission from Diablo, and then returned the car to my Beloved's office parking lot, leaving without a trace?

And if so, WHY?!?

It was an orgy of head-scratching.

Finally, the breakthrough came. The business manager had jotted down the license plate number of the red Durango SUV on a scrap of paper. She read it off for the cop.

Eureka! Two of the digits had been accidentally reversed! The 911 operator must have recorded it wrong.

Dyslexia happens . . . but what a coincidence! What are the odds? That meant there must be ANOTHER red Durango SUV in town with a license-plate number nearly IDENTICAL to my husband's. Just two digits reversed.

Ohhh! So he WASN'T the dirty, rotten scoundrel, after all.

Nevvvvver mind. My husband joked with the policeman that, if anything ever happened to HIS mailbox, he'd know who to call. Off the cop went on the fresh, new trail. Shaking his head, and hoping his employees would believe this wild tale, my Beloved went back to work.

The afternoon was uneventful until the drive home. My Beloved was stopped at a red light, ironically just a few blocks from "the scene." Suddenly, he heard the sickening sound of brakes squealing behind him. WHAM!

A truck rear-ended a car, which rear-ended him!

The damage would be slight. But he still sat there for an instant in shock. Then he smiled.

What if the policeman who came to THAT "scene" was the same guy who had been involved in the mailbox caper?

And what if. . . .

He was almost afraid to turn around.

If it was a red Durango SUV with a strikingly familiar license plate and a Hispanic-looking guy at the wheel. . . .

Theme song: "Twilight Zone."

But whew! Different car. And new cop. This time, it was clear my husband was the innocent victim, not the perp.

At least it was only a fender-bender . . . not a mind-bender. †

6. Principessa

(D)early beloved and longed for, my joy and crown, stand fast in the Lord, my dearly beloved.

— Philippians 4:1

She was a sweet, lovely teenager from a small town outside Omaha, and she was deathly ill.

She had a heart that didn't work very well.

The oldest of three children, she united family and friends, hospital staff and clergy, schoolteachers and neighbors in the battle against what a sick heart will do to a young body.

You talk about a challenge. You talk about a burden.

In recent months, her steps were slower and her energy was dwindling. Her parents talked over her worsening situation with the doctors. They did diligent research, prayed, and finally decided to take a bold step.

They took their daughter to San Francisco for a very difficult surgery by world-renowned specialists. The odds weren't great, but the potential benefit was powerfully attractive. So they went for it.

They left, to great fanfare and exhortations. People sang, "I Got My Heart Fixed in San Francisco" and made silly posters and things. But the minute the plane took off, out came the worry beads among those who loved the family.

The situation was serious. Very scary. What would be a way to help them get through this?

The dad's coworkers hatched a wonderful plan. They fanned out and bought all kinds of little gifts: funny, sweet, inexpensive, practical and impractical ones.

They got together and wrapped them all up in brightly-colored papers with crazy, glittery bows that a young girl would like. They sent them off to her in one great big box, with instructions that she could open one gift a day.

Her hospital room might have been in fabulous San Francisco, but it was decorated in Designer Drab. Beige and blah. So when the box arrived with the tissue paper and colorful gifts, and the fun and anticipation of those daily surprises, it was a big hit.

As the days dragged on before her surgery, she got a lift from opening a little bottle of lotion or a funky color of nail polish. One day, her feet were cold, and surprise! Her gift was a pair of embroidered footies.

Every day, she got a touch of love from home. Every day, she had something to look forward to, something to take her mind off what was ahead.

The surgery still loomed. The fear was building. A big question mark hung over her hospital bed.

Her parents still acted strong and confident in front of her. But at night, in the hotel, they would huddle close and cry a little, wondering if they were doing the right thing.

Every day, the girl enjoyed the attention of the medical staff. This was an international teaching hospital. Faces came before her in all colors, and voices in all accents. Most had never met anyone from Nebraska, so that made her feel special.

One of her favorite doctors was from Italy. His bedside manner was unforgettably grand. He would come into her room, throw his hands up into the air, and in his warm and booming voice call her the Italian word for princess: "Principessa! How are you today?" She loved it.

The day before surgery, her Italian friend had come and gone. The room was still. Feelings of fear and dread started creeping back in. She could feel herself sinking.

Her dad saw. He quickly brought over her gift of the day. She opened it.

It was a princess crown, a dimestore tiara from the folks back home. Her parents' throats tightened and their eyes filled with tears.

A crown for the "principessa."

It linked her support network from near and far in a sweet, crazy way that defied the limits of coincidence . . . with the perfect timing that comes only from heavenly airmail.

She put it on, smiled at her mom and dad, and winked.

It was a turning point. Now that she was a principessa, she was ready. The time came. The surgery went well.

And on her bedpost hangs the rhinestone tiara, a special and meaningful souvenir. It came to her by way of friends of the Great Physician . . . the One we crown with many crowns . . . the King of Kings. †

7. Hambone

Behold, I show you a mystery:
We shall not all sleep, but we shall all be changed.

— I Corinthians 15:51

My nephew Mark is adorable. He has sparkling brown eyes, blond hair, and a smile that just radiates charm. Once when he was little, he got a magic set for his birthday. With all his little toy props, he set up a grand performance for us.

After each magic trick, we'd give him riotous applause. His goofy grin would just grow and grow. He was such a ham that day that his grandfather nicknamed him "Hambone." It was something special, just between them.

Recently Mark, now a computer engineer, had to do one of the hardest things of his life: say goodbye to our family's summer cabin on a wilderness lake in northern Minnesota.

The great-grandparents who built it are gone. The grandfather who called him "Hambone" and nurtured him and the other grandchildren up there also is gone. The deed to the property is gone, too: it was taken though the power of eminent domain by the federal government to become part of Voyageurs National Park. There was nothing we could do to stop it. It was a done deal.

Mark had accepted the change. But he was sad. For his final stay, Mark and four friends "batched" it for a week at the cabin, hiking and boating and fishing, making lifelong memories in the spot Mark calls "the most beautiful place in the whole, wide world."

"Everything tastes better up there," Mark says. "Everything smells better. It's so quiet and peaceful. There's no phone, no TV, no cars going by. Nothing can disturb you. You sleep 10 hours a night."

He said it's priceless to stay in a place that has been in your family for four generations, to see bear, deer, eagles and beaver, and to know all the family lore and inside jokes built up over the years. Like the deep outhouse hole dug by a guy named Puny. And the brick under a certain bush by a certain rock — it has his great-grandfather's name etched on it, and nobody knows it's there but us.

He remembers the morning he and his grandfather went down to the dock and caught enough walleyed pike for breakfast for the whole family.

There's a picture of Mark in an orange life jacket as big as he was, eager to go out in Grandpa's boat. He can remember Grandpa holding him on one knee and his sister Julie on the other. Grandpa was telling them Minnesota tall tales on the cool screened porch.

Holding each other close: that's what family summer cabins are all about.

But now those days were over. At week's end, packing up was "the saddest moment of my life," Mark said. It felt as though a vital connection to his past was being chopped off with one of the old lumberjack axes in the cabin's workshop.

This was where he had grown to love his grandparents. This is where he experienced nature. This was where he felt closest to God. This was where his family rested and renewed.

Would the memories fade? Would he ever feel so good, anywhere else?

Grandpa, this is so hard! What can I do? Help!

As the boat pulled away from the dock, he couldn't look back. "I just thought to myself, 'This is the most beautiful place in the world. Remember it.'"

Tears welled up in his eyes. His friends understood. They loaded the car, and started down the road. Mark was getting choked up.

He had brought a newspaper to pass the time. Maybe that would help. He looked down at a word puzzle on the comics page, folded on his lap. He saw:

BONE – HAM

As in, "bone minus ham." The puzzle's solution was "boneless ham." But Mark is slightly dyslexic. To his eyes, it said:

HAM – BONE

The nickname Grandpa gave him!

Mark and his friends were in awe. The timing of it! Hambone . . . of all the words in the English language. . . .

Through some profound mystery, Mark knew that his grandfather was still alive, still loving him, still encouraging him . . . he was just in a different form now, that Mark couldn't see.

Ah, but like anything that you truly love, even if you can't see it, you can always "feel" it. Always.

It was enough to convince Mark – logical engineering student that he was – that eternal life is for real.

Mark has framed that puzzle, and plans to keep it forever.

Did the experience deepen his faith?

Mark's a man of few words. He just smiles a Hambone smile. It's a smile as wide as a walleye, as bright as the Minnesota midday sun . . . as deep as the sky-blue waters of the most beautiful place in the world. †

8. Bread and Roses

And Jesus said unto them, I am the bread of life: he that cometh to me shall never hunger; and he that believeth on me shall never thirst.

—John 6:35

My friend Carol, a cleaning lady, was driving to a client's house. It was just an ordinary day. She wasn't thinking about much of anything as she drove through traffic.

Suddenly, she got a strong urge to stop off and buy a loaf of gourmet bread for the client whose house she was going to.

"Bread? That's odd," Carol thought. She never made splurges like that for herself. She didn't have much cash in her purse. So she ignored the impulse.

She drove on, and pulled into the client's driveway. But the urge came back, even stronger.

No. Don't go in yet. First, go buy the lady a loaf of bread.

OK, OK, OK, she thought, smiling quizzically. She has gotten these little urges before, you see.

She pulled back out of the driveway, drove to a gourmet bakery, picked out a gorgeous loaf of honey wheat, and came back to the house.

She rang the doorbell. When the woman answered it, Carol held out the loaf of bread, and with a big smile, said:

"God told me to bring this to you."

The woman took one look at the bread, and burst into tears. Tears of joy, that is.

Carol was amazed. The two women hugged, and the story poured out.

It happened to be the lady's birthday. It was one of those big, bad birthdays, with a high number that sends most women kicking and screaming to the store for the Oil of Olay.

Not only that, but the woman was newly divorced and newly employed. She was under a lot of stress with her new job, struggling to make ends meet, dealing with her teenaged children, embarrassed by her messy house, drained by the recent divorce. She was feeling very blue to be having a birthday without a man at her side, her first like that in many, many years.

But she had Jesus.

And she had a deep understanding with Him. She told Carol she trusts Him to provide everything she needs, through thick and thin, divorce and loneliness, even on big, bad birthdays. He will see to her physical needs. He will see to her spiritual needs.

Life is both physical and spiritual. Both require nourishment and sustenance.

"Bread and roses." That's what the lady calls His promise to meet all the needs of her life. The practical needs, and the heart needs. All from Him.

Yes, she had been sad when she woke up on that birthday. But then, before Carol arrived, a friend had surprised her by showing up with a bouquet of flowers.

Now here was Carol . . . with bread.

Bread and roses. Everything she needed.

The two women hugged and cried. Carol was glad she had obeyed that urge to buy the bread. If not, she would have denied that woman — and herself — a big blessing and faith-strengthener.

See, Carol is a divorced mother, too. As a cleaning lady who doesn't earn much, her budget is very tight. She understands anxiety. She gets stressed out, too.

The following Sunday after church, another lady called Carol over to the trunk of her car. Turns out the lady works at a bakery. Her trunk was full of all kinds of bread — day-old, but still delicious. She urged Carol and her kids to take as much as they wanted. They filled their arms, and later their freezer. It would feed them for a month. What a wonderful blessing for this struggling young family!

What made her call them over? Turns out that lady paid attention to little urges that came out of "nowhere," too.

Payback! Carol still smiles about the brand name of the bread that she had bought for the lady that day: "Great Harvest."

That's for sure. When you're working for the Bread of Life, the "dough" is downright heavenly. †

9. Bows Up

And the Lord shall be seen over them,
and his arrow shall go forth as the lightning. . . .

— Zechariah 9:14a

One of my Great Moments in Ignominy was a day in Rocky Mountain National Park. I decided to maximize my leisure-time enjoyment by taking a class in archery.

It wasn't very leisurely because I was terrible at it. Ah, the slings and arrows of outrageous misfortune that significantly reduced my self-esteem. William Tell, I ain't. Cupid's job is safe. If I were a Native American, my family would starve.

I wasn't even strong enough to pull back the bowstring and stand still at the same time. The bow and I both wobbled as if we were drunk.

My fingers wouldn't stay in place, even after the instructor arranged them manually to hold the arrow shaft — twice. The arrow clattered against the wobbling bow like an unlatched storm door in a strong spring wind.

I wasn't nearly coordinated enough to aim properly. Spectators were backing away discreetly as we practiced our stance all along the firing line.

Finally, here came the instructor's cue: "Bows up!"

Then: "Loose!"

All of us beginning archers shot our arrows with a mighty grunt of effort.

Most everybody else's zinged forward and sank precisely into the line of targets. Mine plopped uselessly on the grass about five feet in front of me, sadly off course to the left.

I could have thrown it farther and straighter.

I never expected to be so bad at something that people have been good at for so many centuries. It looks so easy in the movies. You know: the captain says, "Bows up!" and all the archers snap into position with nary a wobble in the bunch. Then, "Loose!" and there go all these beautiful, snazzy shots with zing and precision.

How do people get so good at things like that? It was beyond me.

Well, several years later, archery was the theme of a miraculous daydream that changed my life. It was one of those waking dreams – a vision – or epiphany – or flash of inspiration, whatever you call it — where you experience something so real and yet so unusual, it can't have been a dream. And yet it can't have actually happened, either. It was over in a flash.

I was on an archery range. But instead of a traditional target, all of my loved ones were standing a distance away from me. I knew this had something to do with how I was supposed to try to win them for Christ. I was standing there with a bow and a quiver of arrows, but the arrows weren't weapons. They were words of love. Somehow I was supposed to aim and shoot at my family with them.

But I was LOUSY at archery! What was up with this?

The whole point was to waken my loved ones' hearts and kindle the flames of faith. It was as if they were my evangelism assignment, which, come to think of it, they are. But I was lousy at archery. This would not go well.

Suddenly, in this vision, my bow grew enormously in height. It stretched from over my head to the ground, eight feet tall. Its girth widened to the size of a tree trunk. No way could I handle that bow. No way could I shoot with that thing.

I tried to aim it, anyway. It wobbled in one hand as my other hand fumbled with the first arrow. This was going to be a disaster.

And then, all of a sudden, the bow was perfectly steady. I could feel it pull backward, perfectly straight, with no effort on my part.

Miraculously, the arrow was being aimed in perfect alignment. I knew that once it was released, it would fly straight and true.

That's when I realized that there was Someone standing right behind me, like a golf pro helping a beginner with the right form. I sensed warm arms around me, strong hands covering mine, and overall, a steadying influence.

I was filled with joy, boldly releasing the arrows with total confidence that they'd find their marks.

And then poof! The moment was over.

I was sure that, in my dream, that "Someone" who came up behind me, steadied the bow and aimed the arrow was Jesus. He was showing me that I didn't have to go it alone, that if I tried my best, eventually, I would succeed. He was expecting my effort, not perfection. And He would always be right there with me, helping me, especially when I reached out to others about faith matters.

It was a thrilling encouragement. I resolved to be bolder in evangelism. I didn't have to be eloquent or bowl them over with logic. I just had to trust Jesus! He would hold my bow and aim my arrows.

Years passed. Then, the other day, the lesson was brought back to me in a special way.

I was driving to meet a close friend who was very distressed. She was in big trouble with some ongoing issues, and in need of comfort and a listening ear. She was a nominal Christian, but in a fairly blah, mainstream church, and not quite "all in" to the life of faith.

On the way there, I was praying for the right words to say, special words that would really help her, console her, support her, and point her toward answers. I really wanted to love on her with all my heart. I really wanted her to come to know Jesus, and seek His wisdom and guidance in solving her serious issues.

I'm kind of a stumblebum at times like these, clumsy and tongue-tied. I was wondering how I was going to do this dear lady any good.

Suddenly, I saw the license plate on the car ahead of me:

"BOWS UP"

Bows up? Like from that archery dream?

Tears sprang into my eyes. My throat choked up.

The sense of support and purpose all came flowing back to me. Hey! I didn't need any special ammunition or skills or magic words. There was Someone right behind me, with strong arms around me, Who would aim my words like arrows of love, straight and true, into my friend's heart.

That's exactly what happened, too, at that lunch date. I didn't have to think or choose words carefully. I just opened up my mouth and the right things came out. I could see it in her face. It was helping. It was awesome.

"Bows up! Loose!" the Master had commanded. It didn't matter that I was a lousy archer . . . because His aim is perfect, and He was holding the "bow."

She laughed. She nodded. Her eyes sparkled. Color returned to her cheeks. Her shoulders unslumped. It was one of the best experiences of my life, watching her regain hope and feel better.

No matter what the target is, no matter where you aim, no matter who is involved, you will succeed if you will just remember the Archer who is there with you on the firing line. Lean in to Him. Let Him act through you.

Don't worry about having the strength and skill, or the money, or the perfect words. Just put yourself in position. He will do the rest.

Bows up, everyone. Bows up.

Loose! †

10. Satan's Pepperoni

Catch for us the foxes, the little foxes
that ruin the vineyards, our vineyards that are in bloom.

— Song of Solomon 2:15

We know a couple who really live out their faith. They are always doing things for others. They are poster children for the Golden Rule. Recently, something happened while they were on a mission of mercy that pulled back the curtain a little on the spiritual warfare that's going on all around us in the supernatural plane.

You know how God works in mysterious ways? Yeah, well, his little pizza-faced adversary, Satan, has moves, too.

It seems a middle-aged man in a motorized wheelchair was in dire need of some temporary household help. A quadriplegic, he was affiliated with a well-known religious cult. But apparently, because he was not baptized, they wouldn't help him. A kind Christian minister had been coming daily to bathe him and do his dishes, but he was going to be out of town. So our friends volunteered to fill in.

At the door, the man said briskly: "Do the kitchen dishes, change my bed and remake it, scrub the kitchen floor, vacuum everywhere and scrub the bathroom!"

O . . . K. They split up the tasks and got to work.

The man wasn't all bad: he was on call duty for a human services hotline. They overheard him being compassionate and helpful to several callers.

The husband finished first, and sat down eyeball-to-eyeball with the man. He asked, "So, what's your story?" The two connected like long-lost brothers, comparing notes on war experiences and such.

The wife joined them. They settled in for a nice, long chat.

The man went on and on about his religious feelings and beliefs, which were definitely off-base, as far as the Christians were concerned. Gently, but firmly, the husband was correcting a misstatement the man made about Christianity, when . . .

BBBRRRING! The phone rang. It was some drunk, wanting to order pizza. The man politely told him that he had the wrong number, and hung up.

They got back into their profound discussion. The husband was doing a great job refuting the man's misperceptions about what the Bible really says.

BBBRRRING! The phone rang again. The man had to answer it, in case it was from the hotline. But it wasn't; it was the drunk again, wanting pizza. The man repeated that it was a wrong number, and hung up again.

They resumed their talk. The man's cult teaches that you have to do "works" to qualify for heaven. But that's not what Christianity teaches. The man and wife were there doing a good deed for him because they WANTED to, not to get "brownie points." Salvation, they explained, is a free gift to all believers. All believers get to go to heaven. The man looked intrigued, and then. . . .

BBBRRRING! The drunk again. Now it was getting comical.

The conversation went on for two hours. The drunk called trying to order pizza probably 20 times. It was distracting — very tough to keep their concentration and stay on track.

The wife said she is pretty sure all those calls were Satan's attempt to block that conversation, and get them so frustrated that they would give up and leave.

But they didn't. They hung in there, even though the man wheeled out of the room a few times in confusion, and the phone interruptions kept coming.

Eventually, though, they gave him a New Testament, a booklet for seekers, and some candy. They explained that, just as easily as he accepted those small gifts, he could accept the eternal life that Jesus bought for him on the Cross.

He said he was ready to do that – to acknowledge Jesus as the Ruler of his life.

He agreed with them that nothing else besides belief in Jesus was necessary for salvation.

Thrilled, they led him in a standard prayer of the born-again believer. They listened as he prayed a really sweet and obviously meaningful personal prayer.

From the moment he opened his mouth on that prayer, the phone was totally silent. No more calls.

Ha, ha!

"Somebody" gave up when that soul was won!

Hell may have no fury like a pepperoni scorned . . . but God's Delivery Service always comes through. †

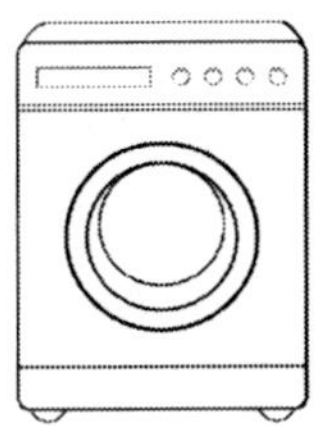

11. Love in the Laundromat

Love . . . thy neighbour as thyself.

— Luke 10:27

A friend of mine had a sleeping bag that was too big to wash in her machine at home. So she went to a place that was a little bit out of her comfort zone: the laundromat on the other side of town.

You know: people smoking, tattoos, children with dirty faces running wild, stacks of old magazines, and worn-out, cheap carpet.

As she and her daughter put their quarters into the machine, a man suddenly shouted:

"I TOLD YOU TO SHUT UP AND SIT DOWN AND QUIT BOTHERING ME!"

Her shoulders cringed. She turned around. It was a man yelling at his two sons.

The man was stocky, red-faced and dripping with sweat. The boys looked to be about 5 and 8. They were having a hard time just sitting there with nothing to do.

The younger boy stood up and moved his chair to the farthest end of the table, away from his father. The older one had a black eye. My friend couldn't help wondering how he got it.

From the looks of their clothing, they were poor. Very poor.

Where was their mother? Did they have one?

She kept one eye on a magazine and the other on the belligerent man. Again, loud bellows pierced the room:

"QUIT BOTHERING ME! JUST SIT STILL AND QUIT MOVING AROUND!"

Those were impossible requests for most children, especially boys without anything better to do.

Stony silence. Then more misbehavior. More threats. She got up from her chair, pretended to look at the dryers, and then sat down in another chair closer to the sweaty man. Maybe if he knew someone was listening, he'd tone it down.

No such luck. He yelled some more, and the boys slumped. He gruffly rustled his paper and went on ignoring them.

Maybe he had worked the graveyard shift and was exhausted. Maybe he was out of work. Maybe the wife had just left him. Maybe his father had been a bear, too, and he didn't know any better.

The washer stopped spinning. She put the sleeping bag in a dryer and motioned to her daughter. They left.

They had planned to go to a restaurant. But mother and daughter talked, and their plan changed. They went instead to the nearest discount store. Their smiles started in the parking lot.

They filled their shopping cart with beanie babies, spiral notebooks, jumbo crayons with a built-in sharpener, a plastic bat and ball, a travel-size Trouble game, and a Barrel of Monkeys game. They spent nearly $50, a good-sized chunk out of their weekly budget.

They returned to the laundromat, pulled out the clean and dry sleeping bag, put it in the car, and came back inside with the two big bags of toys.

My friend stood before the seated man. Her voice quavered. "Sir, we were wondering if you would accept these toys as a gift to your little boys."

He stared at the bags, then her. Long silence. Finally, defensively, "Why?"

The words poured out: "I just noticed your boys were having a hard time sitting still and they were getting on your nerves and I know how hard it can be when you're stressed so we just hope you will accept these toys as gifts."

"Why?" he repeated.

"We just felt like helping someone today," she said, throat tight. "Please."

His face softened. His eyes filled with tears.

He stood, shook her hand and introduced himself. "Thank you, Ma'am. You didn't have to do this."

He looked down at her daughter. "You're one very lucky little girl."

The boys started taking things out of the bag. "Can I keep this?" "Look at this!"

She said to them, "You can help your dad by showing him what big boys you can be."

The little one shook her hand, just as his father had. "Thank you, Lady."

When the mother and daughter were pulling out of the parking lot, through the window, they could see the man and boys taking toys out of the bags together, smiling and talking. Being a family.

You know, laundromats are for fresh starts.

That day, it wasn't just the clothes that got washed good as new. †

12. The Girl in the Funny Socks

Jesus said unto him,
Thou shalt love the Lord thy God with all thy heart,
and with all thy soul, and with all thy mind.
This is the first and great commandment.
And the second is like unto it,
Thou shalt love thy neighbour as thyself.
On these two commandments hang all the law and the prophets.

— Matthew 22:37-40

If anyone so much as comes near the back of my neck, much less touches me there, I go bananas, get goosebumps, scream, and wiggle and jiggle in fear. It's all because of something that happened on the way to school when I was only 6 or 7. Someone came up behind me, grabbed the back of my neck so that I couldn't twist around to see who was tormenting me, and forced me to walk too fast to school. He broke off and ran toward his classroom when we got there, and I saw that he was a friend of my older brother. But all these years later, I'm still a bullying victim, and can't help my fearful reactions.

That "abuse" was nothing compared to what a lot of victims endure. But it shows the permanent damage that abuse of any intensity can cause. There's a lot of truth to the axiom of law enforcement, that you've got to catch and correct children who are mean to others, hurt them on purpose, intimidate them and bully them. If not, they'll grow up to do even worse things in the adult world.

We tried hard to teach our daughters empathy: how not to be either a victim or a bully. But bullying happened to them a few times. Once, a boy snuck a slit-open yogurt pouch into the pants pocket of one of our daughters at lunchtime. Then he smacked her, right in the pocket. The yogurt went flying and made a mess. Everybody laughed. The lunchroom monitor didn't see. He got away with it.

On the schoolbus home, he and another little boy smacked her on the head with their schoolbooks. There was no bus monitor on board. No one stopped it.

Our daughter made it off the bus and all the way down the driveway, stone-faced and dry-eyed. I happened to be standing at the kitchen sink. Our eyes met. I saw her face "break" about halfway to the door. She burst into hysterical tears. Whaaaat? This was a happy child who NEVER cried.

She told me all about it. I comforted her. Within minutes, she was back to her old self. I knew the perpetrator had done that kind of thing to other kids. But the teachers and other parents were afraid to discipline him because his father was a close friend of an important person in the school district. There were a few powerful families whose kids were allowed to run wild, and it was a sad situation.

I decided to give his mother a call, anyway, in a while, after I cooled down and could think about what I should say.

But before I had a chance, the doorbell rang. Our daughter answered the door. There was the perpetrator and his mother. Somebody else on the bus had come home and told HIS mother, who had called HER. She had dragged her son over to our house by his ear and forced a big, drippy apology.

I thought it was best not to enter the conversation, so I stood out of sight, glad that our daughter still had on the pants with the yogurt stains so that that mother could get the full picture of what her son had been up to. I was proud of our daughter for her gracious acceptance of the apology, offering to shake the kid's hand and forget it.

It made my heart sing that she did that. I hoped it signaled a turnaround in him. His mother would discipline him, I hoped. But I had my doubts.

So it was with a lot of uneasiness that I learned, years later, that that boy's brother had grown up to be a hunky young man, and was dating a young woman I loved. An engagement was in the offing, people were saying.

Ew, ew, ewww! Was he like his brother? Full of himself and a bully? Was she in for it? I was worried.

Then, I ran into someone else who knows all our families. She brought up the impending engagement.

Something must have registered on my face, because she said:

"You know, ever since he was in middle school, I have liked that kid. She's going to get herself a wonderful husband."

Huh???

It turns out that this old friend's daughter had a fairly serious medical problem with her legs back when she was a preteen. She had to wear ugly, old-lady compression stockings all day, every day.

This happened in middle school – ouch! – the years when kids are hyper-sensitive about dressing differently than the crowd. They can be at their worst in terms of behavior towards others.

But my friend told this story:

"Some middle-school boys were giving her a really hard time about wearing those stockings. They were teasing her and saying all kinds of mean stuff. She was on the verge of tears.

"And then he (the boy whose brother had bullied our daughter) stepped forward and stood up for her. He told them to cut it out, that she could wear what she wanted, and what business was it of theirs? They all backed off. It was the nicest thing anyone's ever done for her."

The back of my neck got tingles, this time in a good way. Maybe that moment on our doorstep really was a turning point in his family. Maybe that mother went to work and made sure the bullying stopped, once and for all. Hallelujah! I was so happy.

Thank You, Jesus, for turning that boy into a hero, a protector, a suitable mate, a good prospect for a father and business person and most of all, a friend. May his courageous behavior spread. May he be blessed a thousand-fold for choosing to do the right thing for those who needed him to – both the would-be victim, and the other boys who so desperately needed a good role model.

Which reminds me . . . wasn't that what You came here for?

We resolve to do unto others . . . as You did unto us. †

13. The Wet Windowsill

But if we hope for that we see not, then do we with patience wait for it.

— Romans 8:25

A lot of people are out of work. We all know someone it has happened to. There are sleepless nights and self-doubt, days and weeks spent in scruffy jammies. Rejection! Depression! They feel like total losers.

We all love to hear about people who nail interviews, surf seamlessly to better and better jobs, and scale the ladder of success two steps at a time.

Man! That's the way to do it! It gives each of us hope. Maybe someday, somehow, something really great like that will happen to ME!!!

But even if it never does, that's OK, too. Because often, the best "wins" don't come the way you expect. Sometimes, what looks and feels like a huge disappointment actually can lead the way to the greatest victories of your life.

I learned that on a wet windowsill one spring evening long ago.

See, I was the class clown and kind of a goofball stumblebum. I was too busy cracking jokes to take dance lessons, too engrossed in reading books to learn how to apply makeup and choose the latest fashions. But once my tomboy years were over and it was no longer socially acceptable to wear a cowboy hat with a madras shirt and polka-dot shorts, I wanted to be in the cool crowd. Everyone did.

At our school, that meant being a cheerleader or on our excellent and much-admired dance team. The girls with those distinctions were the ones the cute boys went for. They had all the status. They were "there."

So, despite my two left feet — size 8½ — crazy freckles and double chin, I foolishly signed up to try out for the dance team.

We learned the routine and practiced like crazy. Girls who had taken dance class since they were in diapers were sweating bullets. It was a big deal.

At the high-pressure tryouts, I looked around the gym and realized I had no business even being there. I was Rodney Dangerfield in a herd of gazelles. I grinned like Howdy Doody; they smiled like Miss America. I marched like an East Prussian border guard; they glided like Swan Lake.

When it was our group's turn, I stumbled awkwardly into the girl in front of me, grinding my toe into her heel, when everybody took a rhythmic half-step backwards . . . everybody, that is, but me.

The judges had their hands over their mouths, and it wasn't in concentration.

But my beautiful, graceful and popular big sister was already on the squad. Surely, through her, I had "pull." Never mind that there were so many other girls who were better than I was. The pity vote was mine! I clung to hope.

That night, the girls on the squad were going to drive around in a big, noisy caravan. If you heard cars honking in your driveway, screams, and the doorbell ringing, you knew you were off on a teen-dream adventure. You had "made it."

Had I? Would they come for me?

I lay on my bed and peered out the window, cranking it open into the warm spring night so I could hear the instant the caravan approached. My heart pounded.

I sucked in my breath as the caravan sped down my street, each car honking, radios blaring, girls laughing and yelling. But the caravan passed our driveway, and went a block south. Distant screams of delight wafted over the treetops.

Horror of horrors, they were all gathering at the home of a dance team member who lived a block away. The party was on, but I wasn't invited. I realized, finally, that the caravan was finished picking up the new members, and no, I wasn't among them.

I hadn't "made it."

My throat choked up tight. A frown froze on my freckled face. I left my chin on the windowsill like a hound dog begging for a bone that would never come. I started sobbing. Tears streamed down my cheeks and pooled up on the windowsill. I wallowed in misery.

It hurt. It really did. Rejection: ooooooh, it's tough to take.

But you know what? Here's a secret: Rodney Dangerfield never cries for long.

The first little smile came when I realized that I'd better wipe up that windowsill or my tears would warp the wood.

Stop crying, you moron! You SUCKED! At least you had the guts to try. But hold your head high – that dance team was just not your thing. You can't dance, but you can write, you dumbie. So go for broke with your writing. Get over this. Tra la! Sis boom bah!

No way are you going to show up at school tomorrow with puffy, giveaway eyes, either!

Get up off of that thing . . . take a shower . . . eat chocolate. So I did.

Within a few days, I had been named the associate editor of our nationally-renowned high-school newspaper. It was a big job, a big honor for a junior-to-be. There's no way I could have managed to do that job well, along with Drill Squad.

The following year, I advanced to editor . . . and managed to pull in several journalism honors my senior year . . . which led to a college scholarship . . . and my lifelong career.

Not only that, but soon after the tryout debacle, I had my first date with my Beloved, now my husband of over 35 years. He was the kind of a guy who wouldn't want to be with a girl just because she was "cool," but preferred one who was warm . . . and fun, and comfortable in her own size 8½ shoes.

Ohhhhhhh, Lord. Now I see. What seemed so bad was really for my good. No, I hadn't "made it" . . . but my time and energy had been "made available" for something better. Something more "me." Something more like what You designed for my life.

That wet windowsill wasn't a place of mourning. It was a launchpad, thanks to God's plan.

So to all those with job woes or any other kind of major disappointment right now, listen up. Quit feeling like you're a big loser, a stumblebum, a Rodney Dangerfield. There's a place being made ready for you where you will be a gazelle. Hang in there. Keep trying. Keep hoping. Trust. Believe. Soon, it'll come.

While you're at it, wipe that windowsill, would you? Dry up that grief. The only thing in your life that should be warped is your sense of humor.

Drill Squad, Schmill Squad. With God as your dance coach, you can "make it" anywhere. †

14. Put Your Hands Together

Jesus answered and said unto him,
If a man love me, he will keep my words. . . .

—John 14:23a

One of my Great Moments in Parenting started during an archaeology dig in the baking cupboard. I found a half-used sack of nuts from 1982. Since my DNA molecules spell out "c-h-e-a-p," I opened it to see if they were any good.

Out flew two dozen little bitty moths.

Ewwwww!

Just then, the girls came walking up the driveway from the schoolbus. They saw me through the kitchen window, running around clapping my hands in the air, first left, then right. To the busload of their peers, it looked like Mrs. Williams had been hitting the cooking sherry again.

"Geez, Mom," the girls said.

I told them I was swatting the moths. They were skeptical.

They spotted the long, tan, ugly cleome pods on the kitchen counter. Pink, purple and white cleomes (klee-OH-mees) are my favorite flower. Tall and fragrant, they are known as the Queen of the Garden. I collect the seedpods in the fall, store them in the freezer, and in the early spring, put a few pods back in the garden.

When warmed by the springtime sun, they burst open and spread the seeds. If you don't collect and dispose of most of the pods in the fall, next spring there would be so many seeds you'll have cleome boldly going where no cleome has gone before.

It was early spring. I had just taken the pods out of the freezer. The pods were near the ingredients for that night's entrée, Cafeteria Surprise.

"Geez, Mom," the girls said. "Moths and pods, right by our food. Ewww!"

Well, "pod-on" ME!

I'm just TRYING to have a LIFE here! I'm SORRY if my cooking, cleaning and gardening get in your WAY!!!

Geeeeeeez.

At dinner, the kids raved about some new teen idols who had skunk mullets, tongue piercings and wretched songs that oozed angst. Oozed, I say!

And they're giving me slack about my pods? THESE are their heroes?!? Bah! I sprang into counter-attack:

"Have you ever heard of William Wilberforce, the Englishman who convinced the western world to get rid of slavery? He should be your hero! He lived in England about 200 years ago. He really must've loved Jesus, and lived out his faith with a lot of courage.

"He was short and sickly, but he was rich. He got into Parliament, and devoted his life to ending the slave trade that was going on through British ships sailing out of Africa.

"There was so much money in slavery, powerful people wanted to keep it. He got beat up, ridiculed in the press, took death threats and had to have a bodyguard. But he was a devout Christian, and knew slavery was wrong. So he hung in there and got the job done. Persistence, girls! Determination! Three days after slavery was finally outlawed, he died — a happy man!"

They stared at me, listless, perplexed about some dude who probably couldn't even sing. Their dad just kept chewing.

Just then, I saw another one of those itty bitty moths overhead. From my seat, I extended my hands high in the air trying to get it, talking all the while. It fluttered just out of reach.

"So that's why. . ."

CLAP!

". . . your heroes ought to be guys like. . ."

CLAP!

". . . William Wilberforce!"

CLAP!

They didn't see the moth. They thought I was losing it in my excitement over this antique guy, clapping ecstatically for him, like at a rock concert.

Jordan spoke for them all:

"Geez, Mom. PUT YOUR HAAAAAAAAANDS TOGETHER FOR WILLIAM WILBERFORCE?!?!?!?!"

Like, at a rock concert?

They all burst out laughing. Mom's so weird!

We stared at each other . . . across the generation gap.

Just then, from the kitchen:

POW!

KAPOW!

BANG!

KAPOW!

POW!

BANG!

Everybody hit the dirt.

But it wasn't a band of terrorists machine-gunning the kitchen. My Cafeteria Surprise wasn't THAT bad.

No, the cleome pods had simply chosen that moment to burst. Instead of the springtime sun, they'd been warmed by the nearby kitchen oven, and literally burst into action.

Thousands of round, dark seeds were bouncing all over the counters and floors, while a flock of those itty bitty moths danced overhead.

A nightmare scene. Oozing angst!

You know, you work your fingers to the BONE to give kids Christian values, empathy for the downtrodden, and admiration for positive role models who live for God. And THIS is the thanks you get?

Geez, Lord!

Wonder if William Wilberforce ever got into the cooking sherry? Hmm. They say he died a happy man. †

15. For a Rat, From a Rat

Vengeance is mine; I will repay.

— Hebrews 10:30

Has anyone ever done something to you that was so mean, you wanted to grab their upper lip, pull it far forward and use it as a trampoline?

Have you ever wanted to let 1,000 cockroaches loose in their kitchen minutes before their big party?

Or sneak into their house when they're sleeping, put super glue on their index fingers and carefully, gingerly, place those fingers in their nostrils?

Noooooo, you say. I'm a nice person. Nice people never get angry and want revenge.

Right.

Liar.

There's a fine line between seeking justice and seeking vengeance. Lots of times in my checkered past, I didn't restrain myself. When I got bonked, I bonked back.

But one time, with the help of a gerbil named Fudge, I managed to take the high road, didn't seek revenge, and let justice win out in a wonderful way.

Here's what happened:

A person I had known all my life was doing me dirt behind my back. She was one of those people who always had to feel like she was on top. She had done mean stuff to me in the past behind my back, while treating me very nicely on the surface. One time she sent me an invitation to a big party at her house with the wrong time "accidentally" written in. So I arrived an hour after everyone else had left, and looked and felt like a dummie. Passive Aggressive City.

A while later, I decided to run for the local school board. Politics was definitely out of my comfort zone. But I could see a number of things that needed to be improved in our district. I wanted to get in there and try to melt away the groupthink. However, some of my campaign planks, such as cutting spending and tightening the focus back onto the 3 R's, were seen as threats to the powers that be.

This troublesome person was their go-to girl. I'm not going to reveal the details. Just know that there were political "black ops" going on against my candidacy And she was the perp, I knew for sure.

I found out all about it on the day of the vote, too late to straighten things out. Naturally, I lost. WAH!

My mom ran into her at a store the next day, and mentioned the rumors and dirty tricks that had been employed against me, how unfair they had been and how much they had hurt me. Instead of saying how sorry she was to hear that, this troublesome woman leaned forward and murmured, "Does she know who did it?"

Wow! The guilt was seeping out of her pores.

I wanted to pay her back, bigtime. I wanted my pound of flesh. Make that a ton!

But darn. I couldn't. That turn-the-other-cheek thing. To seek revenge would lower me and not uplift her. I was known around town as professing to be a Christian. I couldn't turn to The Dark Side. I had to forgive and forget. I had to grin and bear it.

But then, to make matters worse, she sent me flowers.

She didn't do it because she was sorry for what she had done. She sent the flowers to rub it in that I had lost. To kick me when I was down. To gloat. Her nearly-sarcastic, condescending sympathy note made that clear.

Oooh! The nerve! But again, I couldn't retaliate. She had been "nice" enough to send flowers! If I called her up and told her I knew about the rumors and dirty tricks, what I really thought of her, and what she could do with her flowers, it wouldn't change a thing. I would just look like a sore loser.

So I pouted. The flowers sat on the counter all day, reminding me of the whole sad, strange mess.

On top of everything else, our gerbil, Fudge, had died, one day shy of his (or her) third birthday. We planned to bury him (or her) in a little white box in the back yard. It was freezing out, and there was snow on the ground. But we thought we could at least dig a hole and say a few words over him (or her). The memorial service was to be that afternoon.

The kids came home from school. They knew I was depressed and feeling like a loser. They saw the flowers, and read the card. They knew this person was not really my friend, and that the flowers were more about assuaging her own guilt than making me feel better.

Suddenly, the phone rang. It was our minister. He was just making his yearly check-in call. (What a coincidence, eh?) I was glad for his spiritual support and this perfectly-timed shot in the arm.

How were things going? Was there anything he could pray about on our behalf?

The kids were standing right there, so I couldn't tell him how I had been hurt or what I was really feeling. Instead, I told him we were all sad about our dearly departed gerbil, Fudge. Would he conduct a brief funeral service via telephone before the burial? His prayer made us all feel better.

Then the oldest one got a sparkle in her eye. She suggested demurely that we place the flowers outside, on Fudge's wintry grave. Yes, the flowers would turn ugly and brown after just a short while in the cold. But at least Fudge would feel honored and memorialized.

My heart leaped. Flowers, from a rat, for a rat!

The girls and I exchanged glances.

Elegant! Justice would be served!

It was the happiest funeral I ever attended.

It was nice to model how to deal with hurts without striking back, but not coming off as somebody's doormat or a wuss.

Eventually, I was able to forgive the woman, trust God to deal with her in His own way, and put it all behind me. Riiiiiiise above, Sister Susan. Riiiiiiise above.

But gee, it was fun to watch her gosh-darned, unwanted, insincere, passive-aggressive flowers turn black and crusty out on that cold little hump in the snowy back yard that day.

Thanks to Fudge, may he (or she) rest in peace, I learned something important:

Revenge may be sweet. But God's justice is sweeter. †

16. Waking Up at Funerals

First be reconciled to your brother,
and then come and offer your gift.

— Matthew 5:24b

Dead people come back to life at funerals.

Not the ones in the caskets, silly. The ones who come to mourn and really listen to what's being said.

They come looking for comfort, listening for love, feeling that vicarious self-pity that, unchecked, can be downright scary if all's not right in your world. Could I be next? Would anyone care?

Funerals make you realize that life is short and sweet. There's no time for fusses and feuds with the people you love.

Once in a while, and you can feel the brush of angels' wings when this happens, a funeral makes somebody realize that what they should do is revive their dead and dying relationships and bring them back into the land of the living, while they still can.

Reconciliation: it's one of the most important disciplines of Christian life. Ironically, sometimes it takes a death to make you realize what your duty is.

Take my friend "Wally." I call him that because he looks like Beaver Cleaver's big brother.

Wally has a funny uncle, a delightful "junior geezer." He is Wally's mother's stepbrother. Not exactly a blood relation, but kinfolk nonetheless.

He also is Wally's godfather. They share a birthday. He lives far away. Wally just loves the guy. The feeling's mutual. So somehow, they manage to spend a lot of time together.

That is, they DID, 'til the stinkbomb went off.

It was a family feud — a grudge — an icy impasse. Like all grudges, it was over something small and stupid.

Here's what happened: Wally's wedding was coming up, and this favorite step-uncle and aunt were flying in for it. They were coming from halfway across the country, so travel arrangements had to be made well in advance.

A few days before the wedding, though, Wally's mother's father died.

Because it was a stepfamily, the deceased was no relation to Wally's step-uncle. He was from the other side of the family. But the two men knew each other.

Well, because of the death, the family went into a tizzy, but held Wally's wedding as planned that Saturday. They set the funeral for the following Monday.

Wally's step-uncle and aunt arrived for Wally's wedding and participated fully. But they didn't stay for the other relative's funeral on Monday. Their plane tickets were for Sunday. So they used them.

Oh, boy. Here it comes:

Wally's mom blew her cork. She took offense that they "skipped" the funeral.

She confronted her stepbrother via telephone, but just got madder and madder when he refused to apologize.

Her feelings hardened into rock, then ice.

She didn't speak to her stepbrother for 13 long, cold years. It was as if he were dead to her.

Her unforgiveness spread. People took sides. Anger festered and paralyzed almost the whole family. Their get-togethers were strained and tense, or not scheduled at all any more.

But Wally didn't let it ruin his relationship with his favorite step-uncle. He felt guilty about calling him and visiting him from time to time, but kept doing it out of love. For years and years, they had a good, but quiet, relationship. Wally thought that's how it would be for the rest of his life, kind of sneaking around behind his mother's back to see the old guy.

He never dreamed that his mother would have a change of heart . . . much less where.

But one day, Wally's mother was sitting at a funeral. The priest read Bible verses about love, grace and forgiveness. In his homily, he talked about how final death is. Once someone dies, it's too late for second chances. That's it! Time's up! Game over!

And suddenly. . . .

No, the clouds didn't part. A lightning bolt didn't strike her in the head. She didn't see a big, wagging finger or hear angels sing.

But she did see the light.

Into her brain came this thought:

"We're not getting any younger. It's wrong for me to stay mad for 13 years. It's time for me to make up with my step-brother."

It was the strongest revelation she had ever had. It shook her to her girdle strings.

Soon thereafter, Wally got a surprise phone call out of the clear blue sky that brought tears to his eyes:

"I had the greatest talk today," his favorite step-uncle said, "with your mom."

His voice was so full of joy and excitement that Wally couldn't even speak.

But the two of them had made plans for the in-person visit that would cement the reconciliation.

Now, Wally doesn't seem like the real religious type. But this was a big deal to him. He kept praying through all those years that the situation would change. Knowing how strong-willed his mother is, though, he never expected it to happen.

It's sweet to see how he still gets choked up when he talks about how it felt to see that long-overdue hug and kiss between brother and sister, and their big smiles as they looked into each other's eyes. Sweeeeeeeeet!

So, if someone you love is in a family feud . . . or if YOU'RE in one . . . persist in heartfelt prayer, ask for a break in the ice and the restoration of the relationship, and believe that prayer will work.

Because it will.

And the next time you're at a funeral, do something unusual in that setting: smile. Look around.

Chances are, you're in a spiritual delivery room. Somebody in that room might just be on the verge of a big, beautiful revelation, and deliverance is on its way.

Even in the face of death, despite all the tears and black clothing and solemn hymns, a funeral can also be a place of joy.

That's because when God's Word is spoken, and, more than that, heard, it's going to do its job. And that means hallelujah! Somebody's heart is coming back to life. †

17. So, So Busted

And the tongue is a fire, a world of iniquity:
so is the tongue among our members,
that it defileth the whole body,
and setteth on fire the course of nature;
and it is set on fire of hell.

—James 3:6

He's a prince of a guy, a great husband, father and grandpa. He tells great stories. He's a Minnesotan with a delightful way of saying he's going to put his "booooooot" in the water. He gave his life's work to young people as a school counselor and now is enjoying a vibrant and active retirement.

But I'm here to tell about the time his gift of gab got Ed so, so busted.

He had been chomping at the bit to get started on a long-awaited trip with his son Ben. They were going to go from the Twin Cities all the way down to the Grand Canyon. But they had to delay the start of the trip until the little matter known as Ben's high-school graduation ceremony took place, first.

St. Paul is populated by tightwads of universal repute, and so naturally, every high school in town scheduled graduation on the same day. They used the same hall, same caps and gowns, same podium, same flowers and apparently even the same graduation speaker. Different ceremonies were scheduled bing, bang, bong. Parking was a nightmare. Ingress and egress were a mess.

Ed and family had to sit 'way in the back, 'way up high. The acoustics were terrible. Their son Ben's head was just one mortar board among millions. They never did actually see him.

Worst of all, the graduation speaker just droned on and on and on. Ed couldn't hear much of what he was saying. That which he could hear didn't exactly set his heart ablaze. And he was just itching to hit the road on the big trip, anyway.

The kid got the sheepskin and boom! Next morning they hit the road, and started their adventure.

They drove all through southern Minnesota, through Ed's native Nebraska, and all the way into a tiny Colorado town. They finally stopped for a bite to eat at an exotic local establishment, an ice cream and burger joint called "Zesty's."

They hadn't spoken to another soul since they left St. Paul. So they were pleased when the counter guy noticed the Minnesota license plates on their car. He asked how the weather had been up there . . . eh?

"Oh, drizzly," Ed replied, "kind of like here."

"Oh," the man commiserated. "You should have been here yesterday. It's been beautiful all week, 'til today."

Ed answered, in his friendly, talkative way, "Yeah, well, we WOULD have been here a lot sooner, but we had to stay up in St. Paul so my son, here, could graduate from high school. And what made it really bad was that we had this graduation speaker who just droned on and on and on, and made no sense, and was just horrible, and I can't believe that a fine school system like St. Paul's can't get a decent graduation speaker. . . ."

The counter man interrupted. "Was his name Paul Johnson***?"

Ed was stunned. "Why, yes! How did you know?"

The man replied, "Because he's my brother."

BUSTED!!!!!!!!

So, so busted.

The guy was big, too. Gulp.

Ed apologized profusely. But the counter guy winked. He said he agreed. His brother WAS a little long-winded and boring. Mainly, though, he was delighted to have this new, primeau razzing material drop in out of the clear blue sky. He couldn't wait to "get" his brother with this.

Ed and his son choked down their Zesty's and hightailed it out of there.

Ed knew what God was doing. Lesson learned. He swore that he would never, ever tell another "story" again, as long as he lived.

That lasted about a day. And we're glad; we would have missed out on so many laughs. His wit and wisdom just have an extra dose of thoughtfulness now, that's all.

His son wasn't the only one who graduated that week. Ed became a Phi Beta Kappa . . . of tact. †

***Not his real name.

18. The Other Other Woman

And forgive us our debts, as we forgive our debtors.

— Matthew 6:12

I was trapped at a party with someone who had recently been The Other Woman, but now was The Wife. It was a-w-k-w-a-r-d. I knew that she had been a low-ranking employee at her place of business but had bird-dogged the boss at their workplace, gone out to the bars with him after work using co-workers as decoys, rubbed up against him openly in front of everyone, and stuck that knife into the first wife's back and sent her floating downstream on the bloody river of d-i-v-o-r-c-e, taking the air out of the kids' water wings in the process.

But it was all water under the dam now. I had prayed for them all, hoping God would make it all work out, especially for the kids involved. MYOB.

So we chatted. Then here came a friend of mine.

Good. She didn't know this Other Woman or the whole sordid story. We could have a light, party conversation.

This friend is gorgeous, with a face like Bambi: huge eyes, delicate features. She has great kids, and a popular, successful mate. They'd been married forever.

To my shock, she said, "My husband and I are in the process of a divorce, and it's really, really hard."

I was having an Out of Body Experience, since The Other Woman Now Wife was listening and could hear the pain in her voice.

My friend said, "I'm pretty sure there's another woman."

It moved to an Out of Planet Experience.

She continued, "They work together."

Out of Galaxy!

"He's gotten an apartment and he won't give me any money. The kids are really suffering. My life is a mess. I can't believe this is happening."

Out of UNIVERSE.

I put my arm around her and our eyes locked in solidarity. I'm pretty sure my OTHER set of eyes locked onto that Other Woman Now Wife, and my brain telegraphed into hers:

"See how people like you hurt nice people like this, and their kids?

"See? See?!? SEE!?!?!"

Suddenly, I knew God had placed me between them for a reason.

Not for them. For me.

Inwardly, I was like one of those lizards which, when riled, erects a sheath of warty skin around its head and shoots poison out of its eyeballs!

I wanted to yank The Other Woman's upper lip over her head and twist it into a tight knot!

Judo chop!

Powerful knee into overactive groin!

I was like that cartoon character in MAD Magazine, who acts normal . . . but his SHADOW is doing all sorts of antisocial things to show how he REALLY feels!

God was saying, stop it! Who are you to act this way? Where did all those ugly thoughts come from? How rotten my heart was. My anger, resentment and unforgiveness were dirty and sinful. They were just as repugnant to God as adultery.

I was the OTHER Other Woman — in rebellion to God just like the adulteress. I'd sinned plenty in my time. I'd just done a better job of hiding it.

Confused and ashamed, I hugged the hurting Other First Wife, made an excuse, and escaped.

A while later, I attended a Bible study on King David, and finally "got it."

We learned how the adulteress Bathsheba went on to have a son by King David, and that son, Solomon, became king, the richest and wisest man ever, an ancestor of Jesus Christ.

Well, this other First Wife in our group spoke up. She had recently been jilted by her husband, who'd run off with an adulteress. She had lost most everything in the divorce. It was hard for her to see this Biblical adulteress living on Easy Street.

She told us she had snapped, and went off on God.

"How COULD You? Why should SHE live happily ever after, while the GOOD women like ME get the SHAFT?"

She raged on in anger and pain.

Finally, she told us, a strong, authoritative and incomparably tender Inner Voice spoke to her:

"Child, which of YOUR sins should I not forgive?"

She stopped. And thought. The anger subsided. Tears dripped down her face. She bowed her head in repentance.

As she finished her story, I bowed mine, too.

Judo chop . . . on myself, Lord. People get themselves into enough trouble and anguish all by themselves. They don't need me to "pile on."

No more reptilian venom spurting out of my eyes on someone who's sinned a biggie.

From now on, Lord, let it be Your grace and forgiveness coming out of my heart and through my eyes, instead. †

19. Sweet, Sweet Cherries

Now, our Lord Jesus Christ himself, and God,
even our Father, which hath loved us,
and hath given us everlasting consolation
and good hope through grace,
Comfort your hearts, and stablish you
in every good word and work.

— 2 Thessalonians 2:16,17

My very good friend has a very good friend who went on a Christian women's retreat. It was at a very special place. It was one of those deals where you didn't know anybody else when you got there, but afterwards, you had a whole new set of BFF's. You had incredibly strong ties forged in the fires of Christian love and understanding. (And maybe a little wine after hours . . . but I digress.)

Anyway, there were a dozen women, all strangers. They put on their nametags, stood and chatted at first, and then the leader had them sit down. At each chair were 12 pieces of paper and a pencil.

The leader asked them to get into a quiet mode, and then think about each participant, one by one. Look at that woman. Pray about that woman. Ask the Lord to give you a word, or a Bible verse, or a phrase, anything at all, as a message to that particular woman, even though you don't know her at all.

My friend's friend did her very best. She gazed at the other women, prayed, and wrote down whatever came to mind. Most of the messages made sense, and had to do with encouragement or praise.

But for one woman, what came into her mind puzzled her. She just kept seeing images of cherries. Sweet, sweet cherries on a tree.

Cherries?!? What kind of spiritual wisdom is there in cherries?!?

But she wrote the word down because the impetus to do so was so strong.

So they started going around the room, reading what was on the papers. Everyone seemed pleased and blessed.

It came to her turn. She read off her little messages, and came to the one with cherries.

"I don't understand this at all," she said across the table to the woman it was for, "but the word for you is 'cherries.'"

The woman's face flushed, her eyebrows raised, her hand flew to her mouth, and tears filled her eyes.

She said:

"My grandfather died a month ago, and I've been having a really hard time with it. I loved him so much. He was the only one who really thought I was special. I miss him intensely. But do you know what I remember most? Picking cherries with him."

Jaws dropped. Gasps sounded. The two women got up, ran to each other, and hugged.

What a blessing, to receive such consolation!

What a blessing, to have the privilege of delivering it.

That's our Lord – our sweet, sweet Lord – just doing what He does best:

Reminding us time after time that life is just a bowl of cherries. And the after-life, with Him, is the sweetest of all. †

20. Jatara's Flock

Who are these that fly as a cloud,
and as the doves to their windows?

— Isaiah 60:8

Jatara was tall. Beamer was short.

Jatara's hair was curly chocolate. Beamer's was glistening honey.

Jatara's skin was African expresso. Beamer's was Danish mocha.

They were friends, back in the day. When they played together, you didn't hear two separate, clashing melodies. You heard harmony. Music. Not separate tunes.

They weren't self-conscious members of two different ethnicities, trying to get along. They GOT along. They didn't need to make a big deal about their skin color differences. They were much more alike than different.

They found out a precious truth, that life is sweeter and tastier when you mix the flavors.

They both loved stories, and they both did well in school. Jatara could recite Maya Angelou's "And Still I Rise." Beamer won the third grade Continental Math Medal. They played soccer on the same team, and both loved animals. They both loved to talk and tell jokes.

On Jatara's last visit before her family moved all the way across the city, Beamer got a stomachache from laughing so hard for so long.

It was sad when they couldn't be together in school every day anymore. After the move, they were more than 200 blocks apart. Jatara was in the inner city, and Beamer was 'way out in the suburbs.

They had a few play dates before the distance just got too overwhelming.

When Beamer first went to Jatara's neighborhood, I worried. It's not exactly Nob Hill. There was a lot of traffic. There was graffiti, and junk in the yards, and tall weeds in empty lots. Parked cars dotted the streets. The houses needed paint. Even the dogs looked and sounded tough and scary. The fences didn't look strong enough.

Don't misunderstand, there were lots of fun things to do at Jatara's: sidewalk chalk, her toys, the park, basketball. Still, I worried: is my daughter safe down there, where everybody's poor . . . and some might be desperate?

Then one day, I saw how rich the inner city really is. Just rich in a different way.

I was in the 'hood on my way to pick up Beamer at Jatara's. Suddenly, a big flock of birds, hundreds of them, rose up majestically from an enormous old cottonwood.

I gasped. It was like something out of a nature film from Africa.

Then, in a perfectly-choreographed arc, the birds flew as one, darting first to the left, then right, then sweeping upward, noisily moving together, in perfect choreography and syncopation, all the way out of sight.

A cloud of birds, literally.

So many, and yet they flew as one. It was astounding.

How did all those birds rise up at the same time, with no apparent signal? How did they stay the same distance apart? How did they know to turn at the exact same instant? How did they fly so fast and change directions without bumping into each other?

I realized that these were pigeons, "city doves." You don't see them out in the matchy-poo suburbs, with designer stick-trees that are hardly bird-worthy. Only in the inner city, where the trees are big, do the doves of the city fly as a cloud.

That sight beat anything you could see in more advantaged neighborhoods. It was a spectacular example of God's perfection. He created birds that know how to fly in sync, powerfully united. It was a reminder of the blessings God has provided for the poor, blessings that the rest of us don't know about. Maybe because we haven't looked.

So I did look, at the 'hood. Now, I saw it differently:

I saw the snazzy, artistic patterns of the old brick on the buildings. The close, neighborly feeling of households joined close together by sidewalks. The more interesting mix of different house colors, shapes and sizes than you can see in a newer, planned development. The gracious, old trees that spread out their shade to anyone and everyone.

Most of all, I saw the glow shared by Beamer and Jatara as they came out of the house babbling on joyfully about their time together.

That day, I learned that the 'hood is not a scary place. It's a place where birds fly as a cloud, and little girls laugh until they get stomachaches.

It's a place where good hearts can get together, and fly as one, proving that it's more fun to move together than to stand apart.

When birds of a different feather flock together, it's an awesome sight. ✝

21. Hog Wild

And to make all men see what is the fellowship of the mystery, which from the beginning of the world hath been hid in God, who created all things by Jesus Christ.

— Ephesians 3:9

We have these friends. They seemed totally conventional, out here in suburbia. And then we heard about their first date.

It's a great Valentine's Day reminder that love really does triumph and God works in mysterious ways. Sometimes the Lord of Love uses some mighty unusual kindling to fan the flames of romance.

Mighty unusual.

See, our friend started off in life as an agricultural entrepreneur. He had a cow/calf operation and also raised 150 Yorkshire brood sows with some champion boars on 800 rolling acres in Iowa.

OK. He was a pig farmer.

But he's a hunk. He cleans up nice. Somebody introduced him to her. They hit it off and made a date.

Now, she's a city girl, or as close to it as you can get out here in the heartland of America. She is the type who "gets nails" and is beautifully dressed, petite and feminine all the way.

He told her he was busy "farrowing." He asked her to come over to his place and they could go out on their date from there.

She wasn't entirely sure what "farrowing" meant. She thought it sounded very manly and hands-on and so forth, like digging "farrows" in the field in order to plant seeds. She was impressed with his masculine knowhow. She arrived at his home in the country in her flirty little tube top and white shorts with brand-spankin' new white clogs.

"Miss Prissy," he describes her now.

Well, he wasn't at the house. But the door to the outbuilding, which she later learned was the "farrowing house," was wide open. So she went in.

It's not clear exactly why she shut her eyes. It might have been the blast of methane gas that erupted onto her hair, her clothes and her skin, like a tidal wave of stinky.

Or it might have been the sight of her newfound flame . . . down on one knee with his arm all the way up a big, fat, huge mama pig's behind.

Love at first sight is not supposed to be like this.

Whatever made her close her eyes, they snapped back open as soon as she heard him ask her to come over and stick HER arm all the way up the big, fat, huge mama pig's behind.

"She's already had eight, but this one's breech, and it has to be turned," he was shouting. "My arm's too big. Will you come over here and do it?"

Come over there and. . . .

Standing there in her flirty little tube top and white shorts and brand new white clogs, she just stared at this strange man, her date. He was filthy. He was kneeling near the manure pit, up to his armpit in moanin', squealin' mama pig, and we're talkin' 500 POUNDS of moanin', squealin' mama pig.

Miss Prissy stood there, speechless, squinting in the methane cloud.

He saw that she was hesitating. So he smiled his manliest, most entrancing, most persuasive smile. It was a great, big smile. Just for good measure, he added: "I've got a glove you can wear!"

He's got a . . . GLOVE?

And . . . SOMEHOW . . . that would make it OK?!?

You know, I'd like to be able to report that she was overcome by love and devotion for him, heard bells, was struck in the heart by Cupid's arrow, et cetera, et cetera, so she ran right over there and did what he asked.

But I believe her actual response was closer to what most of us females would have retorted:

"In a pig's eye, Buster!"

Another ending to the story might have him asking the sow to marry him. He was already down on one knee, and was feeling very, very close to her, I'm sure. But that didn't happen, either.

What did happen is that our friend DIDN'T run out of there squealing like a . . . well, a . . . stuck pig. She stayed.

He tried one more time to fix the breech, and it worked. He finished farrowing all by himself, winding up with 14 nice piglets. Then he dashed inside, washed up, and left with Miss Prissy on their date, just a little late.

They had a wonderful time. I mean, they already had something to talk about. Sort of. What an icebreaker!

But he didn't need to entertain her or impress her. She had already fallen head over heels in love with him.

The pig stink and ridiculous position she had seen him in didn't matter.

It was that smile.

That hopeful, audacious, engaging smile.

That's all she saw. That's all it took.

Conquered by the smiling pig farmer knee-deep in "it" in the farrowing house. None of his friends could believe it.

They were married shortly thereafter. And no, the 14 piglets weren't in the wedding party.

OK, you men: forget the red sports car. Forget the diamond bracelet. Forget the hours in the weight room, the wine, the roses. Forget all the things you think are your best shots at wooing the woman of your dreams.

Just be you. You're enough.

I'm not saying you need to get up to your armpit in pig dip to get her attention. But I am saying the Lord works in mysterious ways.

And brother, when it comes to winning the one who's meant for you, relax. He's on your side. And He's got moves you've never dreamed of! †

22. Valentine Moon

I found him whom my soul loveth:
I held him, and would not let him go. . . .

— Song of Solomon 3:4b

He was horrible to her. He threw her around, called her a "whore," cheated on her, and made her feel small.

Some boyfriend: she got deathly sick from food poisoning, but he wouldn't take her to the hospital. A girlfriend did. Upon her release, he was three hours late picking her up, refused to even draw her a bath, and left her to go to the bar.

She tried to dump him, but just couldn't. One night, despite her better instincts, she let him stay over.

In the middle of the night, her cell phone rang, four times. She hurried to answer it.

It was blank. No one was there.

He became enraged. "WHO THE $%&@ WOULD BE CALLING YOU AT THIS HOUR OF THE MORNING?!?" All kinds of accusations ensued, even though he admitted that HE had been unfaithful to HER, just the night before.

She didn't yell. She didn't cry.

"Get out of my house," she shouted. Finally, she did what her heart had been screaming at her to do. He left, still raging. After sobbing and shaking for a while, she got a hold of herself.

Now what?

She sat by the window. The moon was really bright, really full.

Her eyes filled with tears. "God," she prayed, "I know I shouldn't be with guys like him. But I just can't find the strength to stay away from them – to be 'enough' without a guy in my life. If I'm not ready yet for the person You want me to be with, that's fine. Keep preparing both of us. But in the meantime, keep me away from monsters!"

Tears of regret and fear gushed for several more minutes, then stopped. She felt better. Finally, she slept.

Next day, a girlfriend called out of the blue, and suggested: "You've been depressed and reclusive for months. Now you're rid of him. Good! Let's go shopping, get all dolled up, and go out and have fun!"

Did I mention she's a real, live beauty queen? Like, in a national pageant just a few years before this? I mean . . . tongues hang.

So they went out together, shopped, laughed, healed, and decided to go out on the town and celebrate.

They walked in, late, to a popular pub, and the first person she saw was this very, very cute guy.

Their eyes locked.

She felt a tremendous pull of attraction. But she thought, "NO! I am NOT doing this again!"

She walked past him with her nose in the air and joined a group of old college friends. He watched her. Her friends watched him watch her. "Oh, my gosh, he's coming over here!" they exclaimed.

They ran him through a gauntlet of protective teasing. He took it, then faced her and said earnestly:

"I know something you don't know. But this isn't the appropriate place to tell you. Is there a time we can get together?"

He WAS cute. But what was THAT? A PICKUP line?!? Manipulation? AGAIN?!? She refused to give him her name or phone number. Finally, she took his. But she never intended to call.

The friends ended up back at her house for chili. They encouraged her: "That was a good guy. You should go out with him. If anything, it's a free dinner."

She debated. She procrastinated. Finally, she called.

They talked for two hours.

They went out on a date.

Kaboom! They had everything in common. They were madly in love.

After a week, she asked him, "That thing you said, about knowing something I don't know. Was that a line?"

He looked bashful. "I can't tell you," he replied. "You'll think I'm crazy."

"Try me."

"Well . . . the night before we met, the moon was really bright and really full. I was looking at it, and praying to God to prepare the girl that I'm going to marry. Because I'm ready."

He looked at her.

She looked at him. "You're not going to believe this. . . ."

He searched her eyes: "You saw it? You were praying, too?"

His eyes filled with tears.

He said, "When you walked past me that first night, my whole life passed before my eyes."

It was the same for her. They embraced. They wept.

They got married. They have two amazingly adorable sons, and a beautiful daughter.

They're teaching them this:

If you want to have love in your life – real love – just trust God with His plan. He'll work it out for you. He has ways to alert you to what's best for you, like phone calls from "nobody" in the middle of the night. Funny: those calls never did show up on her cell-phone bill. But they helped wake her up – enough to give God her dream and trust Him to make it come true.

Want love? Ask Him. Trust Him. It's so simple, it's crazy.

Ask Him for a life that's really bright . . . and a heart that's really full. †

23. Boyfriend Flap

Be anxious for nothing;
but in every thing by prayer and supplication with thanksgiving
let your requests be made known unto God.
And the peace of God, which passeth all understanding,
shall keep your hearts and minds through Christ Jesus.

— Philippians 4:6,7

There once was this worrywart mother, see. Her daughter was far, far away at college. When they dropped her off there, the poor girl didn't know a soul. Driving away from campus, this worrywart mother was all choked up over whether her beautiful but quiet daughter was going to be terribly lonely.

Didn't the college guys go for the loud and crazy, party-going coeds, and ignore the nice, quiet ones? Was there even one young man on that campus who would ask her out? Oh, Lord, please, let her make some friends.

Instantly, the worrywart mother saw an ATM. There was a young man standing in front of it. He had a spectacular skunk mullet, tattoos down his arms, and one of those long chains that swooped down from his pants practically to the sidewalk. There was a ridiculously beat-up car nearby. Furthermore, he was pounding on the ATM as if force and violence would get him money even if it wasn't technically in his account.

No, Lord! No! Not THAT kind of friend!!!!

It was one of those epiphanies of motherhood: first shock, then laughter, then relief. She knew the Big Matchmaker in the

Sky had the situation well-covered. He was just kidding her out of her fears. It worked.

A few weeks later, the daughter called from the faraway college. Hearts and flowers were pouring out of the phone. She said, "I've MET someone. . . ." Her voice was different.

Somehow, the worrywart mother knew that THIS young man wouldn't have a skunk mullet or a chain. And indeed, he did not.

The daughter and the non-mulleted young man commenced dating. They dated all school year. That summer, when they returned to their respective homes half a country apart, he constantly sent her letters. The family pretended they were "red-hot" love letters, presenting them to her wearing oven mitts, holding tongs, and so forth. In general, it was nice to know that she was having a great time with a nice boyfriend. At least he was persistent.

The next school year, they continued to date. Another summer featured lots of activity in the family mailbox from the Lonely Hearts Club far away.

When it got to be her senior year, and she was still dating this same young man, the worrywart mother began to worry anew. She had met the young man a few times, and liked him very much. But she had spent relatively few hours in his presence. Of course he seemed like the perfect match for her daughter. But how can any parent be sure?

Could he be a . . . (her kids teased her about her old-fashioned lingo) MASHER?!?!? Or a RAKE? Church-going A student by day, Hell's Angel meth dealer by night? Maybe he was an Oklahoma football fan! AAAIIIEEE!!! Not THAT!!!

She calmed down and prayed a simple prayer. God, we trust You. Please bring him on strong if he's "the one." But if he's not, please move him aside. Amen!

One night not long thereafter, she couldn't sleep. Her husband was respiring with gusto, louder than ever. Imagine the kitchen cupboard doors downstairs creaking open and shut with each of his mighty snores.

The worrywart mother slunk into her absent daughter's empty bedroom to sleep in peace and quiet. But she couldn't sleep. She was worrying about her daughter. She tossed and turned. Every possible distraction was augmented.

What was that pesky, muted sound? She snapped on the light and got up. Even though the clock radio was turned off, you could still hear the teeny, tiny voice of the late-night talk show host. Hyperactive antenna! She pulled out the plug. That fixed it.

She plunged back into bed. Almost asleep. But darn! What was that rhythmic vibration? Ohhhh. The muffled nasal jackhammering from the master bedroom down the hall was still faintly audible.

Exasperated, she jumped out of bed again and shut the door.

Ahhhh! Quiet! Finally! She buried her head in the pillow, willing herself to sleep.

Noooooooooo!!!!! Now she became aware of a tiny but persistent noise in the corner of the room. It sounded like a little piece of paper was softly flapping. It sounded like a playing card clothespinned to a bike spoke.

Every time the overhead fan spun by, some little flap of paper was being almost-imperceptibly moved. But to her postmenopausal hyper-ear, it sounded like a PELICAN taking flight.

AARRGGHH!!! One more time, she leaped out of bed, snapped on the light, and stomped over to the corner of her daughter's room.

She had never noticed the cardboard box wedged beside the chest of drawers. On top, there was a piece of paper, tri-folded as if it had been in an envelope. It was hanging over the edge of the box. It must have been making the flapping noise.

She turned the paper over.

It was one of those red-hot love letters that the boyfriend had mailed home during those long summers of separation.

She prided herself on maintaining her children's privacy. She would never snoop on purpose. But after all her worrying, she just couldn't help herself. She read the letter.

Her throat clutched up tight in the first sentence. The tears started in the second.

The letter was beautiful, loving, respectful: exactly what a mother would want a suitor to say to her daughter.

The romantic words of love that the boyfriend expressed revealed him as a young man of tremendous character who was head over heels in love with her daughter.

He wrote that he would do anything for her, would give anything to be with her, and would always be there for her. He wrote that he was miserable without her, that he tried each day to figure out how to express his love for her, and could only come up with the letter, and hoped it was enough.

How refreshing, in this cynical world. His sincerity and ardor shone through. Not a single coarse word.

He was expressing love in a guy-like and yet highly romantic way, that was respectful and adoring, tender and funny – the kind of a letter that you would clutch to your heart and hold there for a long, long time.

The worrywart mother knew that the Lord had engineered the whole episode, world-record snoring, annoying flapping noise and all, so that she would read that letter and stop worrying.

She chuckled and wiped her tears. She put the letter back, tucking in the corner so it wouldn't flap.

She went back to bed, and fell asleep instantly, dreaming of a beautiful wedding which, indeed, has come to pass, with non-skunk mulleted grandchildren expected one day, too.

So let this be a lesson to all you worrywarts:

Our Lord knows how to communicate with us, any time, in countless ways. If you have any doubts about anything at all, just send a little p-mail – PRAYER! – to the Big Matchmaker In the Sky. Don't worry: He'll answer.

He knows how to open our eyes to true love. It's His favorite thing to do. He gets a kick out of revealing love to us in all its forms. His timing is always perfect.

And the messages He sends always bear His unique, unmistakeable, incredible stamp of love. †

24. 125,000 Houses

Ask thee a sign of the Lord thy God; ask it either in the depth, or in the height above.

— Isaiah 7:11

Once upon a time there was a princess who was blonde and beautiful. She got a "5" on the Advanced Placement Calculus test. She could hit a powerful drive with a graceful little fade around tall trees using her hybrid club. The other ladies in her golf league went "Wow!"

Despite her beauty, intelligence and great golf swing, this princess was the kind who was not that much into herself. She was reserved and ladylike. She followed the Queen Mother's command: "Don't chase boys."

As she and her friends hit their 20s, the friends started getting married. One wedding. Two. Forty-seven. The bridesmaid's dresses were crowding out the regular clothes in the princess' royal closet. But that was OK. She followed the Queen Mother's other command: "You are complete in yourself, with Jesus living in your heart. Just trust Him, and see what He brings your way."

Or, more specifically, who.

One day, the princess attended a birthday party for a close friend. She met a smiling young prince named John. They stayed after everybody else left, and played pool. She won.

One year later to the day, he won. He got down on his knees and asked her to marry him. He offered a royal-size rock, and that winning smile. She was surprised, she wept, she said yes.

Then she sat down and ate a piece of the chocolate cake that he had arranged for, along with roses and candles, as secondary inducements, just in case.

He is, you see, the type who plans ahead. He is a computer engineer. Oh, sure, her blonde beauty was compelling, and he loved it that she could beat him at golf, pool and just about every other game. But what sealed the deal, it seems, is that "5" on the A.P. Calc test. To a brainy computer guy, that's like . . . well, not exactly porno . . . but it's attractive.

Turns out the prince had humbly and manfully asked for her hand a whole month in advance. So the King knew. But the Queen did not. That is because of the Queen's enormous communications army. It would have spilled the beans to three-quarters of the civilized world before the princess even knew what was up.

But the prince's advance planning and respect, along with well-thought-out and sensible plans for how he would love, honor and cherish the precious princess, won him big points with the King.

The morning after the proposal, the princess came over to see how long it would take for the Queen Mother to notice the ring. Fifteen minutes! Slow learner. Tears and big whoops ensued. Later, the ladies in her golf league literally swarmed the princess, to get a look at the ring. As they do with her golf drives, they all went, "Wow!"

The King and Queen have no doubt that these two are going to live happily ever after. They have a lot in common, after all:

- They both have mothers with movie-star good looks named Susan.
- They both are the second children in families of four.
- They both have three sisters.
- They both were honor students.

But here's how everybody knew for CERTAIN SURE that these two were meant for one another:

See, after they started dating, the princess told her paternal grandparents that her new boyfriend, who had an excellent job, had also purchased a slightly rundown duplex in a midtown neighborhood. He was fixing it up. He already had tenants living on one side of it for revenue stream. He was showing a lot of ambition and initiative.

The grandparents were intrigued. Hmm! That sounds close to their old stomping grounds! What's the closest intersection? She told them.

Does the house face north or south? She told them.

Can you see a grade school right up the street? Yes. Is there a set of skinny steps up from the back patio into the kitchen of the upper unit? Yes. And the washer-dryer is in the garage? Yes!?!?!

The grandparents recited the exact address.

That's right, she responded. How did you know?

BECAUSE *THEY* LIVED IN THAT EXACT SAME DUPLEX BACK IN THE LATE 1950's!!!

They were newlyweds, with a darling little toddler, who grew up to be . . . her very own dad! They had moved away when his younger brother was born to get more room.

No wonder John had been working feverishly all summer to finish the kitchen remodeling. He wanted to propose to her in that house, where she will live after they're married, without all the construction dust around.

We called the county assessor's office, and found out that there are 125,000 houses in our county. Out of 125,000 houses, what are the odds that John would own his fiancee's dad's childhood home?!?

He was either the ultimate stalker . . . or "the one."

Let's toast our incomparable Matchmaker, who knows how to "engineer" love for each one of us in a unique way that helps you "know."

No wonder. He created happily-ever-after'ing in the first place. †

25. When Elmer Blushed

***Now these things were our examples,
to the intent we should not lust after evil things,
as they also lusted.***

– I Corinthians 10:6

Somewhere, there's a 60-something woman with a puzzled smile on her face. It's all thanks to an impromptu meeting of the First Wives' Club held in the lingerie department at Dillard's this past Christmas.

It was one of the busiest shopping days of the Christmas season. I was one of nearly a dozen women standing in two lines with armfuls of unmentionables – or, as we say in my family, "frou-frou."

It hadn't taken me long to pick out colorful new robes for our daughters and some much-needed new undergarments for myself.

There were two clerks working feverishly. I looked around, and noticed a man in the other line.

He was in his 60s. He had on a nice topcoat with well-shined shoes. That's a good sign. A man in well-shined shoes thinks well of himself. I figured him to be an accountant, a government office manager, or an insurance executive, nearing retirement.

He was about half-bald, in an appealing way, with a shiny pate that matched his well-shined shoes. He looked solid and reliable. I couldn't help myself: I mentally nicknamed him "Elmer Fudd."

He was holding a woman's robe in a thick chenille. I believe it was in a sensible dark color, maybe plum, that wouldn't show stains. It was obviously a Christmas gift for his wife. But it looked like a Christmas gift for his mother.

He had thick, long, lustrous, curly eyelashes that were very attractive, but I only noticed because he was looking down. I suspected he was embarrassed to be the only man for miles in the frou-frou department of the busiest store in town.

But he wasn't embarrassed. He was thinking.

Suddenly, he looked up, looked around, caught my eye, nodded toward a lingerie rack, and asked, shyly:

"Do you think she'd rather have one of THOSE?"

He was motioning his head toward a rack of little satin teddies: powder blue, princess pink, mint green and white. They were classy, but sexy. They were cut high on the thigh and had a little discreet fur trim along the bodice. Verrrrry niiiiiice.

I was so shocked, I didn't self-edit.

"This is for your wife?" I asked, stupidly. He nodded.

"Been married long?" "Thirty-seven years."

Diagnosis complete.

"I'd sure rather get one of THOSE than one of THOSE." I motioned my head first toward the teddies, then toward the thick robe in his arms. "Nobody likes to feel like an East German border guard. Go ahead! She'll love it!"

Elmer smiled big, and blushed.

Another woman chimed in. "Heck, yes, get one of those pretty things," she said. "What you've got looks like something Whistler's Mother would wear."

And another: "When you're buying lingerie for the woman you love, it's no time to be practical."

And another: "Go for it!"

Not just his face, but his whole head blushed bright red from bottom to top. It reminded me of what happened to Bashful when Snow White kissed the top of his head at the end of the movie. Booooooop! Bright red!

We witnessed all the sensible, conservative, mortgaged and leveraged molecules in his body transform into pulsating, determined, testosterone-crazed, hot-blooded passion molecules.

Wow! All this drama in the lingerie department at Dillard's!

I'll never forget what he did next: "By golly, you're right," he muttered. He dumped the sensible chenille robe right down onto the floor and moved manfully toward the teddies.

"But I wouldn't know what size," he mused.

We all cooed happily and helped him pick out a powder blue one, encouraging him to add a matching satin robe and luxurious satin slippers as well.

When it was his turn at the counter, the clerk said casually over her half-moon specs, "And what do you know? These JUST went on sale – 30 percent off."

Winks and smiles all 'round.

The transaction accomplished, off he went, clutching his sack. But 'ere he strode out of sight, he whipped around and exclaimed a joyful, "Merry Christmas!" with a sweet, shy look right at me: ". . . and thanks."

My heart just sang. It's still singing.

Maybe it's the pornography all around us. Or the raunchy, hypersexed TV, music and movies in our marketplaces. Maybe it's the recent scandals involving homosexual assaults on children, or the world epidemic of sexually-transmitted diseases. Or the lurid sex ed in our publicly-funded classrooms.

All I know is, somewhere along the way in recent years, the fun and the joy of God's gift of sexuality have been stolen from too many decent, married people, Yet they're the ones for whom God meant the fun and joy of sex in the first place.

In a sincere effort to separate themselves from what's wrong in our increasingly immoral, oversexed society, they've ended up denying themselves what is very, very right.

They settle for the chenille when they have every right to the satin.

God never said we couldn't be passionate and lusty. He just put a simple condition on it: holy matrimony. God never meant for sex to be a bore. He meant for it to be, well, holy moly!

So to all you married folks out there, I say let's fight back by turning up the heat. Let's expose all that's wrong with sexuality outside God's plan, by thoroughly enjoying ourselves within it.

Elmer Fudd, wherever you are, thanks for reminding us. Tell the Mrs. that the First Wives' Club hopes she likes her new frou-frou.

Go get 'er, Tiger . . . rrrrrrrrrrrr. †

26. I Know Who You Are

I am the good shepherd, and know my sheep, and am known by mine.

—John 10:14

The pharmacist had been stressed out at work lately. To make things worse, her manager had an "all about ME" attitude. All she cared about was her bonus, and whatever it took to make it bigger. Her selfishness was annoying the entire crew.

The pharmacist is a born-again Christian. But every time she mentions faith matters, the boss gets downright surly. That stuff's not scientific, or important to the bottom line. The boss wants nothing to do with anything that didn't revolve around herself.

Consequently, the pharmacist gets hammered a lot as a department manager reporting to this rather unpleasant boss. Her co-workers don't know how she takes it. Her motivation is the people she truly works for — the patients. Serving them, and encouraging them along the way, is what she's all about.

Well, recently, she marked her 33rd anniversary with the same company, an amazing achievement in this day and age. It was just another day as far as management was concerned, and she knew that. But a simple, "Hey, congratulations!" from her boss would have gone a long way.

It had been a terribly busy day. Near the end of her long shift, she had a phone conversation with a nurse about a patient who had just been dismissed from the hospital. They had to call each other back a couple of times to make arrangements for prescriptions.

Then the wife of the patient came in. The pharmacist talked with her about the medications and what to expect.

The pharmacist, ever friendly, asked the woman about her unusual middle initial, "Q," which turned out to be for "Quinn." The customer thanked the pharmacist for all the work she had done with the nurse to make her husband's meds affordable. They talked about his condition and his heart catheter. They talked about his emotional state, and hers. Then the wife left.

The next day, someone called to speak to a supervisor. The pharmacist took the call. A woman said, "I have never done this before, but I wanted to launch a compliment." How refreshing! Then the customer said, "I didn't get the pharmacist's name, but she was wonderful!!! She was short, with dark brown hair almost to her shoulders, and it was 9:45 p.m. . . ."

The pharmacist said, "And you are Marilyn Quinn!"

The caller gasped, "Was that YOU?" Then she asked to speak to her supervisor to pass on the compliment. So the pharmacist shifted the call to her crabby boss, smiling a little about the praise that would be lavished in her behalf.

During that day, she had to go into the office twice, but the boss said nothing to her. She regretted not having shifted the caller to the district office instead. The whole day passed. Not a word.

The other pharmacists were livid that the boss said nothing. She started getting angry herself, about fielding a patient compliment on her 33rd work anniversary, and no one cared, NO one. . . .

She fumed and griped to herself, walking angrily through the drugstore . . .

. . . and as she passed the cold medicines, a still, small voice spoke quietly into her heart:

"***I*** know who you are."

She didn't even break stride. She continued to rant and rave to herself about how unfair it all was . . . what is the point of trying so hard . . .

. . . and the voice repeated:

"***I*** know who you are."

By then, she was in front of the vitamins, muttering, "Yeah, sure, YOU know, but THEY don't know OR care, and it isn't asking TOO much to be told something GOOD once in a while. How about some MINOR praise in a SEA of turmoil. . . ."

. . . but the quiet voice said a third time:

"***I*** know who you are."

She stopped short.

What had just happened finally sank in.

WHOA! WAIT A MINUTE! THE GOD OF THE UNIVERSE KNOWS WHO I AM! THE GOD WHO MADE ME, AND MY BOSS, AND THE WHOLE WORLD, SEES ME AND KNOWS WHAT I'VE DONE!!!

She said out loud, "And that ***IS*** enough, Lord."

The hurt was instantly gone. Joy spread across her body. She smiled the rest of the day, even though the nasty boss never passed on that compliment or acknowledged her lengthy service.

Who cared? God knew.

There's nothing like a supernatural "atta girl" to get you back on track. Just the right medicine for a sick and tired spirit. From the Great Physician who always knows the right Rx. †

27. Pressing a Suit

Agree with thine adversary quickly,
whiles thou art in the way with him;
lest at any time the adversary deliver thee to the judge,
and the judge deliver thee to the officer,
and thou be cast into prison.

— Matthew 5:25

A judge in Washington, D.C., reportedly took a Korean couple to the cleaners to the tune of $67 million in a court case a few ago. Why? Because they left his pants out of his dry-cleaning order.

Talk about pressing a suit. I mean, you have to be really . . . steamed . . . to do something like that.

The defendants countered that they found the missing pants a week later, but the judge claimed they weren't his – though the inseam length was the same, and the ticket on the pants matched his receipt. He turned down all offers to settle, and took them to court instead.

In his lawsuit, he demanded:

- More than $1,000 for the suit.
- $15,000 to rent a car every weekend for 10 years to go to another dry cleaners, since he didn't want to go back to their establishment.
- A fine of $1,500 per violation, per day, under his interpretation of the Washington consumer protection law; he

claimed 12 violations and tripled the sum because there are three defendants.

The dry cleaners won the case of *Pearson v. Chung*. You can read all about it, and how poorly things turned out for the judge – who lost his job, got a divorce, and so on. Most people would say he had extremely overreacted, and wound up making things worse, not better. It's cited as the poster child case for the need for tort reform in this country.

All I know is, that case is an extreme example of the crying need for grace in this world. And it reminds me of the great way my younger brother handled a similar mix-up much better, years ago.

Danny had graduated from college. He was trying to find a professional job in Los Angeles. In the meantime, he was working at a pud job that he hated, in a warehouse. He wore jeans to work every day and got really grubby.

There was a great job halfway across L.A. that he really wanted. It was in a snazzy office complex. Twice before, after he had driven all the way across L.A. for the interview, the honcho had been called away from the office, and the interview had to be canceled. Danny persevered, and made one last appointment for 5 p.m. on a workday.

He went to his warehouse job that day, then fought through traffic to get to his interview a few minutes early. He grabbed his suit, which was still in the dry-cleaner's bag, and rode the elevator to the 27th floor. He popped into the restroom to change out of his workclothes into his suit.

He pulled off the plastic, revealing his suitcoat . . . but no pants.

NO PANTS?!?!?

AAAIIIEEE!!!

But he didn't freak out. He didn't rage against the dry cleaner's. He didn't file a $67 million lawsuit.

Instead, he put his jeans back on, draped the dry cleaning plastic over his shoulder, and walked into the office.

The secretary stared at this stranger in the nice coat . . . and grubby jeans . . . and told Mr. Big that the interview candidate had arrived.

Danny walked in with a confident smile, his right hand out for a shake, saying: "I want you to know that I wasn't caught with my pants down even though the cleaners forgot my pants. The bottom line is, I'll work my pants off for you."

Mr. Big liked his moxie, stood up, grasped his hand, and said:

"YOU'RE HIRED!"

That's called making the best of a bad situation. How things would have been different for that Washington, D.C., judge, if he'd done something like Danny did.

The best way to keep your life from getting stained by conflict and soiled by strife is to keep a clean, forgiving heart. ✝

28. A Screw Loose

***And he said, Go forth, and stand upon the mount before the Lord.
And, behold, the Lord passed by,
and a great and strong wind rent the mountains,
and brake in pieces the rocks before the Lord;
but the Lord was not in the wind:
and after the wind an earthquake;
but the Lord was not in the earthquake:
and after the earthquake a fire;
but the Lord was not in the fire: and after the fire
a still small voice.***

— I Kings 19:11,12

I'm hardware-impaired. Totally intimidated. If I need a thingybob or a dealie, I go to the hardware store. I survey the 5,023,742 bins and drawers containing thingybobs and dealies of every size, shape and mysterious purpose. I burst into tears, go home and use duct tape.

I once took a camera in to be fixed. "I think you have a screw loose," the counter guy said. I replied, "Yeah, but what about my camera?" Ba-bum CRASH!

My Beloved, in contrast, is Hardware Hank. He goes to the hardware store regularly to escape the hormonal storms in our otherwise all-girl, estrogen-laced household. There, he can find the thingybobs and dealies to complete his Honey-Do List. Peace and parts: he finds them both in the hardware panorama.

For us city folks, hardware emergencies are no big deal. But for a friend of mine who lives 'way out in the sticks, things are different.

Rolly is a farmer. He's frugal and can't waste time. One winter day, he was home alone running wire for the stock tank heaters. Rolly jokes that he knows as much about wiring as the next man knows about filling out a National Pollutant Discharge Elimination System report. But at least he tries.

Well, he went inside the chicken coop where the fuse box was, and studied the wiring. He walked to the power pole, then back to the coop to rearrange some things. Then back to the pole, and back.

All along, he was careful to not lose any screws. If he dropped one, he quickly watched it fall so he could pick it right back up. He had no replacements and didn't want to go all the way to town for a ten-cent screw.

Then, trying to bend taut wire, he dropped one.

He knew he'd never find it in the soft dirt of the chicken coop floor.

Ohh, Lord. Ohhhh, help me learn my lesson. Ohhhhhhh, well.

He made do without the lost screw, though it messed up his repair efforts. He finished the 20-minute job in an hour and a half. But at least it worked perfectly. Well, 90 percent.

He made a mental note to pick up a pack of those screws next time he went to town. Then it would be fixed for good. But it was going to be a while before he could get to town. Oh, well.

Two days later, on his land nearly 2½ miles away from the house, he was walking along fixing fenceposts when he looked down . . . and there on the ground was a screw EXACTLY like the one he'd dropped.

Now, to most folks, that would be just a coincidence. But how many other little thingybobs or dealies could it have been, besides the exact same screw? 5,023,741?

To Rolly, it was evidence of the power of God – a reminder of His faithfulness – proof that He is able to meet all our needs. He provides the Earth and the tides, the sun and the rain . . . and the little things, too.

If He can provide a stinking little screw, He can provide anything.

Rolly thought back to the story of Elijah, looking for God in the earthquakes, hurricanes and fires . . . like the recent tornadoes, tsunamis and hurricanes we've experienced . . . but that's not where Elijah found God.

He was in the still, small voice.

People often see God for the first time in awesome, spectacular displays. But it's in the quiet, little God-incidences, like that screw at Rolly's feet, that those who already know God see Him every day.

That's how to live: with the certainty of His presence and provision for all your needs, large or small.

That's the invisible screw that holds a well-built life together.

'Til you have that simple, strong connection, you're not quite whole. Your life will rattle around, and sometimes fall apart. You can only go around with a spiritual screw loose.

But when you look to the Lord, at all times and for all things, you can have peace of mind and everything you need . . . from His very special heartware store. †

29. Leaving the Laptop

For the mountains shall depart, and the hills be removed; but my kindness shall not depart from thee, neither shall the covenant of my peace be removed, saith the LORD that hath mercy on thee.

— Isaiah 54:10

A friend of a friend is a Midwesterner nurturing a new small business. The recent nosedive in the economy has been extra tough. He had to lay off some people, and it nearly killed him. He had to cash in his IRA to stay afloat.

One day recently was extra stressful. He'd flown to New York City for an important meeting, and then went to a restaurant to meet an old friend for dinner. He lugged his carry-on bag and laptop with him. But as soon as he got there, he got a text message from the friend saying he'd given him the wrong address. The right restaurant was four blocks away.

So he gathered back up his stuff, hailed a cab, and rode over there in the hustle bustle of the big city on a cold, rainy night.

The cab pulled up to the restaurant. He grabbed his stuff, paid the cabbie, jumped out, and headed to the door.

But just as he got there, he realized HIS LAPTOP WAS STILL IN THE CAB!!!

He spun around to see the cab rolling away in traffic. Everything went into slow motion: he ran after it, but couldn't catch it. He shouted and waved his arms:

"Hey! HEY!! HEYYYYYYY!!!!!"

But his pleas were unheard. The cab disappeared into the rainy night.

He felt sick. And not just because of the replacement cost.

EVERYTHING was on that laptop. Know the feeling? His business stuff was backed up at home, but he hadn't backed up most of the 5,000 photos stored on the laptop, including the ones from a recent family trip to London, Paris and Ireland. Those photos were precious documentation of what he had been doing with his life over the past several years. He loved looking at those pictures for a moment's respite from his business worries and financial woes.

And now they were gone. Gone! Uncharacteristically, he didn't even have a receipt or a cab number. But he was a man of action! He would get that laptop back somehow.

Standing in the rainy vestibule, he started making phone calls to cab companies, police precincts, every place he could think of. No luck. He skipped dinner, went back to his hotel and kept calling for five hours. Fruitless.

In resignation, at 1:30 a.m., he fell asleep.

A half-hour later, his hotel phone rang. It was a stranger with a foreign accent:

"Is this Mr. Shawn? You will not mind my calling at this hour. I have your laptop!"

It was the cabbie. He'd found it right away, with the hotel reservation printout tucked in the bag. His shift had ended, and he offered to bring it right over. The businessman was flabbergasted at his good fortune.

The cabbie was originally from Argentina, where the businessman's grandfather had grown up. He had been in New York City for 30 years. He was startled when the businessman gave him a great, big bear hug of thanks. And when he opened his wallet and emptied every cent he had, $130, into the cabbie's hands as a tip, he was even more surprised.

But I'm not surprised.

See, that businessman is the most wonderful, ethical, honest, hard-working, thoughtful, fastidious, generous, obedient Christian you can imagine.

And yes, his faith figured in this incident. Yes, he cried a little and prayed a lot. In fact, he says he prays all day, every day, about everything he can think of. He totally trusts God. Even if he hadn't gotten his laptop back, he would have trusted Him.

He described how he applies his prayer life to his business life: "You listen a little, and follow, and listen and follow, listen and follow."

Well, he communes closely with a God Who answers prayers by engineering solutions. And He does it in intricate detail. God fixed it so that, if this man in a moment of stress had left his precious laptop in a cab, it would "by coincidence" be the cab of an honest driver, who probably needed that $130 tip as much as the businessman needed to be reminded once again that God was with him in every way, every day.

And getting the laptop back wasn't the only encouragement. As a result of that nearly-disastrous trip, he got 10 new orders. Things are looking better for his company. He's smiling again.

No, the laptop incident wasn't life and death. There wasn't a lot of money at stake. But we've all been in those straw-that-breaks-a-camel's-back situations.

Recovering the laptop restored his equilibrium, and put a spring back in his step.

So here's the bottom line:

No matter what, a guy like that can never really lose anything. That's because the LORD has downloaded kindness, mercy and peace into him, as a believer.

He's living life in the best possible place . . . embraced by love on the laptop of the living God. †

30. Moonbeam Remembrance

Then spake Jesus again unto them, saying,
I am the light of the world:
he that followeth me shall not walk in darkness,
but shall have the light of life.

—John 8:12

He was a big shot, a big-city businessman with a big job, a big salary, and big responsibilities.

But nobody knew the truth: he felt small.

He had phones in his office, home, car, and growing out of his ear. He had a thick daily planner, a fat Rolodex, and a wide circle of business associates. He had a long job description, a long line of employees to supervise, and a long commute. He left early and came home late, coming and going, quite often in the dark.

In more ways than one.

His business associates thought he had found the path to success. But he felt like a failure, totally lost.

People thought he was a captain of industry, sailing full speed ahead. But he felt like a gerbil on a wheel, going nowhere fast.

Something was missing, and he didn't know what. It was scary, but he felt only numbness, or maybe the beginnings of chest pains. But he suppressed those implications, because he just didn't have time.

In the midst of people constantly, he felt utterly alone.

Time passed. He tried to fill the emptiness with activity. His stress, restlessness and hyperactivity grew. The clock was like a choke collar. Fifteen-minute deadlines left him no time for relaxation, reflection or rest.

He was trapped in workaholism, the way people lose themselves in booze or drugs or food or TV or sports or shopping or gambling. Too much, too much, too much. It always winds up being not nearly enough.

Doing more, more, more, but satisfied less, less, less. Feeling alienated . . . empty . . . disconnected . . . discouraged.

Then one morning at O-Dark-Thirty, long before sunrise, he dragged himself out of bed and robotically got ready for work. He didn't even glance toward his wife's sleeping form as he left their room and started down the stairs.

Suddenly, he noticed a bright beam of light coming into his dark home from the skylight up above. It was from the full moon. It was shining down through the skylight onto the stairway landing.

The moonbeam was illuminating an old Christmas decoration that was on a table on the landing – a homemade miniature church.

He'd been so busy, he hadn't even noticed that his wife had put up the holiday decorations. But coming down the stairs, his eyes locked onto the little homemade church with the roof of Ivory Snow, frosted like a cake. His grandmother had made it back in the 1940s. His mother had passed it on to him.

It was glowing with such warmth and beauty, he couldn't take his eyes away. The little bulb inside the church was not plugged in. But the small structure was fully lit from the moonlight streaming through the skylight. It seemed so real.

He stood stock still. His feet seemed bolted in place. His eyes locked onto the church.

A thought came into his head:

"Remember what you learned in this place."

He caught his breath. Who said that?

Silence.

He looked around. He saw nothing.

This place? What place?

Church? It had been ages since he'd been in a church.

He remembered sitting in the pew of his hometown church as a boy, bathed in the light of the stained-glass window his family had given in memory of his grandfather, the one he looked like. His father would put his strong arm around him, and he would sit in warmth and security, listening to the Bible stories and beautiful hymns. The light would shine in on him through that window, and he would feel loved and safe, happy and complete.

The businessman looked up, and saw how the moon completely filled the skylight, as in a picture frame. For the first time in a long time, he felt as full as that moon. Complete. At peace.

As if mesmerized, he walked downstairs and outside, to where he could see how the moon was brightening the entire back yard. He felt as though the light was shining on him and into him, deep into his heart.

He felt bathed in that light, helpless as a baby, but perfectly safe. Cared for. Tended to. Loved.

He dropped to his knees, buried his face in his hands, and sobbed, remembering what it was he had learned so long ago in that place called church.

Ohhhh, God! Oh . . . my . . . God!

He didn't know how much time passed. But he ran back inside, taking the stairs two at a time. He knelt beside his sleeping wife. He kissed her awake, held her, and told her about the church and the moonbeam, and the voice-that-wasn't-a-voice but that had still spoken directly to his heart.

He told her how much he loved her, and how things were going to change. Really change! She would see!

She cried, too, with relief and joy, and maybe a little fear that he was going crazy.

But he wasn't. Like the shepherds of old, he had seen the light. And that's all it took.

He put sanity back in his schedule. He made time to go back to that place called church, and he took his family with him. Now they're all there together, feeling safe. Cared for. At peace.

With his arm around his son, next to his wife, listening to the music and the stories, his heart full, he found what he had been missing.

It was love, the only thing he ever needed. The one thing you don't find on a things-to-do list or meeting agenda. Love! And it was there all along, waiting for him, in the peace and fullness of the Light of the World. †

31. Angel on a Snowmobile

Behold, I send an Angel before thee, to keep thee in the way, and to bring thee into the place which I have prepared.

— Exodus 23:20

SOME corporate spouses get to go to luxury resorts in the winter, for meetings in Florida, Hawaii and the Caribbean.

But *I* got to go to Canada . . . in January.

At least it was Quèbec. I speak a little French. My husband doesn't. This made for high humor. He could only smile nervously as I told people, in French, what color underwear he had on, and what pattern or cartoon character was on the fabric.

Everyone looked at him and roared with laughter. He was totally clueless. He could only smile wanly. Next time, there'd better be palm trees, Bud. Live and learn.

Well, I shouldn't be so ungrateful. We actually had a blast. On the last day, we had a recreational choice:

- Aromatherapy and a relaxing massage at the hotel (sounded great to me, but his body language was screaming that that was "wussified" and "no way");

Or . . .

- Strap on ice cleats and portage a canoe over the frozen St. Lawrence Seaway (he beamed, but I scowled – what do I look like, Sacajawea?!?);

Or . . .

- Go snowmobiling in the scenic Laurentian Mountains.

Excuse the pun, but . . . COOL! We both beamed. We signed up.

It started off badly. I slipped on the ice in the parking lot, threw up my arms to try to balance myself, and delivered a powerful uppercut to the chin of a Quèbeçois woman. The surprising blow knocked her to the icy pavement.

"CRA-ZEE A-MER-I-CAINS!!!!" she muttered as we helped her up, apologizing profusely.

"I can't take you anywhere," my husband hissed, attempting to charm our way out of an international incident.

It got worse. We had to put on these enormous black snowsuits and clumpy boots, with helmets and goggles. We looked like East German border guards.

They were putting people on the snowmobiles two by two. But my Beloved wanted his own unit, so that he could go fast with no backseat driving "advice." That meant I had to have my own, too. I was the only female driver in a group of about 20.

"Gas, *à gauche*," the helper shouted over the engine. My foggy brain reverted to high-school French. OK, gas on the left. "Brake, *à droit. Vite, vite*!"

Wait a minute . . . wait a minute! *Droit* means on the right. Right? So you stop it with the one on the right. *N'est-ce pas*? Anybody? I knew *vite, vite* meant "go fast." But I didn't LIKE knowing that, because I didn't WANT to go fast.

So much for driver's ed. Everybody roared off, *vite, vite*. So I *vited* off behind them as best I could.

We went up the mountain in the pristine forest, although everybody went 'way too fast for the goofy dame from the Nebraska Flatlands. At the top, there was a picturesque chalet, which in the Nebraska Flatlands we call a "bar." We socked down the schnapps. That part, I liked very much.

But then came word:

A whiteout had arisen from the frozen St. Lawrence Seaway.

Ahhhhhhh! muttered the Quèbeçois. *Sacre bleu*! We had to get back. *Vite, vite*.

Everybody hopped back on their snowmobiles and roared off, again too fast. I sputtered along at the end. My Beloved motioned me to speed up. *Vite, vite*!

I tried. But they kept zooming around those hairpin curves in the worsening fog. I was afraid I'd plunge over a cliff or bash into someone. I locked my eyes on the taillight of the snowmobile in front of me, and tried to follow. It wavered in and out of sight. And then disappeared.

I stopped and idled.

Hey! You guys?

The fog got thicker. I waited. And waited.

And panicked.

I was alone! They were gone! They wouldn't realize I was left behind 'til they got to the bottom! Then, with the whiteout, how could they ever get back up here and find me?

I was lost! I was going to die! I was going to freeze to death! I would be a stiff! Literally!

No, I wouldn't. I tried to encourage myself. I couldn't freeze in that enormous snowsuit. They'd find me in the morning, and I'd be fine. Probably.

Please, God! Help me! But there was only silence and whiteness.

I thought of my husband and children. I got a lump in my throat. Tears fogged my goggles and froze on my cheeks. I wasn't crying because I was going to die in my big, black snowsuit. I was crying because I was going to die and I LOOKED SO FAT!

Just then, a snowmobile appeared. Its driver motioned me to follow. My eyes jutted out of their sockets, cartoon-style, focusing on that taillight. It led me all the way back down the mountain to the crowded dressing room. I stomped in planning to bonk my husband for abandoning me to save his own hide.

But first, I wanted to thank my hero. Everyone was still in their identical black snowsuits. I went around asking, "Who came back for me? Who led me down the mountain? Who saved my life?"

Nobody would take credit. They just smiled and shrugged. Not me! Not me, either, you cra-zee A-mer-i-cain.

It must have been an angel on a snowmobile sent to save me, *vite, vite.* †

32. 666 and Cigarettes

I can do all things through Christ who strengthens me.

— Philippians 4:13

Was I an addict!

I slept with my pack of cigarettes inches away, ready for that first smoke of the day.

My hair was stinky. My clothes closet reeked.

My children were ashamed. They stole my cigarettes, smashed them to smithereens and flushed it all down the toilet so I couldn't salvage any smokeable smithereens. They posted signs all over the house, such as a drawing of a cigarette inside a circle with a slash through it, and a kid sticking out a tongue the size of a dirigible and going "Yuck."

But I liked smoking. I didn't want to quit.

The ultimate rejection came at the dentist's. We were matching colors for a ceramic crown. You know how they have lovely names for lipsticks and nail polishes? Rah Rah Red and Marvelous Mauve? Well, to match my teeth, I expected the dentist would pick a white tone like Pearly Gates. Blinding Snow. Bridal Veil.

But no. The color he picked was more like Pond Bottom Gray.

Eww! The truth hurt. It was time to quit.

I tried quitting cold turkey. It didn't go well. I was a turkey and smoked again.

I tried dwindling down. Soon, I dwindled right back up again.

I tried snapping a rubber band around my wrist to inflict pain every time I wanted to smoke. I must be one of those sado-masochistic types who love pain. I kept on smoking.

I tried putting out my cigarettes in a coffee can full of water by the kitchen sink. The butts floated in the black, smelly brine. It grossed out everybody but me.

Finally, I turned to that desperation ploy: prayer.

"Oh, God," I sobbed, in full-strength tobacco breath. "Please keep me from smoking." My entwined, nicotine-stained fingers tightened. "In the name of the Lord Jesus Christ, take this addiction away from me, once and for all!"

I really meant it this time. I dropped into my favorite drugstore and told them not to sell me any more cigarettes, even if I begged on my knees. They know me well enough to know it could happen. Figuring I was still a good profit center for them with all the chocolate I buy, they agreed.

I destroyed all my "stashes" and went to bed.

The next day, presto! I woke up, and I didn't want to smoke. Didn't want to smoke all day. Halle-LOO-jah! That was easy, Lord!

The second day, I still didn't want to smoke, and got through the day cigarette-free. AY-men!!! Can I get a witness?!?

I felt good about myself. Light-headed, but good.

On the third day, I rose again . . . and MAN, DID I WANT A CIGARETTE!!! Right here, right now! Emergency! AA-OO-GAH!!!

My eyes crossed. My head spun. My fingers twitched. My body shook. I had to have one! Had to! In my crazed, nicotine-addicted state, I hatched this scheme:

"I'll drive to a drugstore far away where they don't know me and don't know I'm trying to quit. Then I'll buy one pack. Just one! And I'll smoke one cigarette. Just one! Then I'll throw all the rest away!"

Yeah, right.

Furtively, in sunglasses and collar up like Jackie O avoiding the paparazzi, I got in the car and hunched over the wheel. That way, God "couldn't see me."

Eyes crossing, nerves jangling, I pulled out into traffic. I stopped at a red light and stared straight ahead. My eyes suddenly focused sharply, like a laser beam.

The license plate on that car!

It had a few letters, followed by "666."

WHOA! That's the number of the devil! (Revelation 13:18)

If I follow that car, go ahead with my plan and buy cigarettes after I prayed for God's help not to smoke anymore, I'll be following Satan . . . not God.

I'll not only have Pond Bottom Gray teeth and smelly clothes . . . I'd have Pond Bottom Gray teeth and smelly clothes FOREVER! IN *HELL!!!*

SCREECH!!!

I did a wheelie (well, almost) and laid scratch the other way. I went home and smoked no more. It was hard . . . but not as hard as hell. Ha.

Today, nearly 20 years later, I'm still smoke-free. That was one of the toughest challenges of my life. Health-wise, it was a no-brainer, but if you've ever been an addict, you know: uff da, it's hard to quit such an ingrained habit. But boy, am I glad.

And what do you know? My teeth are beginning to look less like a pond bottom, and more like the pearly gates. †

33. Ransoming Sunshine

***For the Lord hath redeemed Jacob,
and ransomed him from the hand of him
that was stronger than he.***

—Jeremiah 31:11

She was born with red hair and white feet. A little ornery, but very good bloodlines.

You guessed it: she's a horse. A very special horse. She gave a friend of mine a chance to show the rest of us what true love is all about. The story goes like this:

My friend, "Annie," lives in a small town in eastern Nebraska. She has loved horses all her life. She's great with them, and they return the favor. When things aren't going well in her life, she can always make herself feel better by mucking stalls, cleaning tack, grooming the big, warm bodies, and best of all, feeling the power and joy that comes from being a good rider on a good horse.

She has spent a lot of time at the different barns around the area, just hanging out, pitching in, and observing people and horses, not necessarily in that order. Annie has become a bit of a horse whisperer or equine psychologist. She loves figuring out why horses act the way they do, and what to do about it.

She came to know a pretty little filly, "Sunshine," in one barn. Sunshine was a flashy sorrel with white feet. Lots of potential there for a show horse. But Annie saw that the filly was nervous around people, especially big men with booming voices. Like her, the young horse was skinny and skittish.

One day, Sunshine was old enough for her feet to be trimmed for the first time. The farrier came to do it. The filly didn't like the sharp tool that was suddenly biting into her hoof. So she bucked and kicked and refused to cooperate with the shoer, a big man with a booming voice.

He is by no means a bad man or a mean man. He just does things "the cowboy way." That means get a little rough. Sunshine's owner was OK with it.

The farrier wanted to teach the young horse a lesson. So he tied her up with her chin tight to the wall, and proceeded to beat on her with a big, rough, metal file called a rasp.

Well, he beat her and beat her. All four of the horse's legs were sliced open. Her hips had welts on them. Her shoulders gleamed red with blood. But still, she fought him. So he led her out onto the concrete, and flipped her.

That means he made her rear back so that she fell on her back. Then he stood on her. Again, the intention wasn't murderous: it was to establish dominance and exert discipline. "The cowboy way."

Annie watched the whole horrible, nightmare scene, her heart in her throat.

The big farrier stepped off the horse. But Sunshine didn't move. Her eyes rolled back in her head. Blood pooled beneath her.

"Aw, ________," he yelled. "I killed her!"

Annie rushed to the horse and did cardiopulmonary resuscitation. Yes, you can do that for a horse. Someone called the vet.

Sunshine survived. Annie, shaken and furious, arranged to buy her on the spot. She didn't have the money, but made a few calls and sold things and scrounged around to come up with it.

Yes, it was an impulsive reaction. But a meaningful one.

You see, Annie has been beaten, too.

Shoved, kicked and punched, and some other terrible things. She knows what physical abuse feels like, and how it's wrong and unfair, brutal and frightening.

Did she buy the filly to ransom her away from a violent situation? To save her life, deliver her from evil? Like Jesus did for all of us, on the Cross?

Sort of. Annie says she just wanted the horse to be safe and happy. Who wouldn't? Maybe she wishes someone had done something like that for her, to spare her all that pain and horror. Again . . . who wouldn't?

But Annie did more than most of us would. She even went to farrier school in another state, to learn to shoe horses for herself. Now she's able to handle them "the cowGIRL way" — gentle, understanding, and yet plenty effective.

"Shoe" unto others as you would have them "shoe" unto you. †

34. Saved By the Toilet

(F)or he hath said,
I will never leave thee, nor forsake thee.

— Hebrews 13:5b

I have this friend who is so witty, she makes my cheeks hurt from an excess of laughing. I scold her for being so hard on my face. That's the last thing I need at my age.

I can remember laying in a hospital bed after giving birth, with her standing at the foot of the bed making wisecracks, most of them extremely graphic and highly inappropriate. I remember laughing so hard I thought I was going to give birth again.

She's super-smart, super-organized, capable, competent, sensitive and thoughtful . . . the last person you'd expect to become a desperate alcoholic on the verge of suicide.

But she did.

It's a long, sad, familiar story. Stuff went wrong. Real wrong. She got down on herself. She slipped into self-destructive habits. The wit and wisecracks left her.

She put up a good front for years and few people knew, but her private hours were black and blue. She pushed her friends away. She felt all alone in the world. She ate and ate and ate, and drank and drank and drank.

Then one terrible night, she tried to kill herself.

I still can't believe she did this. Throughout history, millions of people have put up with things far worse than what was wrong in her life. There are so many better, smarter ways of dealing with life's problems. Being stupid is just not like her. But boy, can anybody become stupid, as the suicide statistics show.

The whole thing is sobering. If it can happen to her. . . .

One night, she hit bottom. She was done with life. She drank a whole bottle of booze, swallowed a whole bottle of pills, and stretched out her body on her lonely bed in her apartment.

She had had it. This was the end. She was going to die.

But she forgot about one thing:

The female bladder.

She didn't know how long she had been laying there. She just knew that all of a sudden, she had to "go."

It never occurred to her that, if you're planning to die in a few minutes, you might as well wet the bed; people are going to be really, really mad at you already.

But nooooo. Ever the perfectionist, she had to get to the bathroom. She was in a stupor, but she still managed to stagger in there and onto the toilet.

Her head was spinning from the booze and the pills. Her body was heavy and leaden. Her muscles drooped. She was dizzy. As she stood up from the toilet and turned to flush, she lost her balance and fell backwards — crash! smash!

And somehow, she managed to break the toilet.

Water seeped out from the toilet tank onto the bathroom floor where she lay. She may have passed out, but the cold water wakened her at least partly. She came up on all fours. She forgot how she got there. She was woozy, but her heavy-lidded eyes saw the water pooling up on the floor.

"Heyyy!" her foggy brain thought. "There's a leak!"

She crawled to the telephone. Must . . . fix . . . leak.

In her stupor, she couldn't remember the apartment manager's phone number. But she knew she had to report the leak. The only phone number she could remember was "911."

So she dialed it. And, in her drugged-out, boozed-up state, slurring her words and making very little sense, she reported that there was a leak on her bathroom floor.

The 911 operator was sharp. She knew the call was about more than a leaky toilet. She knew what an O.D. sounded like. She got my friend's address and sent a rescue squad.

My friend passed out again, but they broke down the door and got her to the hospital.

She lived. With help, she got back her life, and it's sweeter now than ever. She's embarrassed by what she did, but amazed at the outcome. She thinks it's important to tell people.

"Tell them that God is real," she says. "That's all they need to know. They can take it from there."

She thought she was completely and terrifyingly alone, that night.

She wasn't.

She forgot that Someone had promised to always be with her.

He didn't.

She didn't think her life was worth living.

He did.

In her misery and confusion, she had forgotten that her best Friend is Almighty God – Who can do anything. ANYTHING! And Who can fix everything. EVERYTHING! He is always at our side, with perfect timing and endless solutions, waiting to help.

If God can use crazy things like a pillar of fire, a talking donkey and the belly of a whale to save people, get their attention and show them His love, why not a life-saving toilet?

My funny friend puts it this way: she was saved by the "throne" of grace. †

35. In the Bread Aisle

Give us this day our daily bread.

— Matthew 6:11

I have this funny, creative, loving friend who is truly the World's Best Grandmother. I know, I know, there are a lot of contestants in that category. But she'd be right up there.

One fine day in October, she ran to the drugstore to pick up some Halloween candy that she wanted to hide in little goodie bags for her grandchildren to find around the house. That's the kind of fun stuff she does all the time. On the afternoon of Halloween, she will show up, in her elaborate witch's costume, and make a candy "stew" with the kids.

She calls her iconic mixture of autumn candy "Wanda the Witch's Stew." There were specific types of candy that HAD to be in the mix. And darn it, she couldn't find all of them at the drugstore.

Then when she got home, she realized she was out of ziplock sandwich bags. She wanted to put the candy inside them, and THEN inside paper lunch bags, so that there would be no leaks. Therefore, she deemed it imperative to make one last "run" to the store. Maybe she'd find the candy she wanted, too.

She could've gone to the convenient mart around the corner, or to another store nearby, but she decided there might be a couple of other things she could pick up at her favorite grocery store, so she went there.

She made the rounds, picked up the zip-lock bags and a few other items, found the right candy, rejoiced, and even went back a second time to one aisle. On the way back up to the check-stand, she meandered along the racks of bread, which she did not need. She was just browsing and smelling those good, fresh-bread smells.

There was an older black gentleman with $2 in his hand. As she pushed her cart up the aisle, she could see that he was going back and forth in front of all the bread, leaning down to peer at the pricetags.

She knew immediately that he was trying to find what he could afford.

Suddenly, a still, small Voice said inwardly to her as she drove her cart past, "Give that man $20."

Hunhhh?

She pushed her cart a few steps further. The Voice said again, "Give that man $20."

There was nothing audible. The heavens didn't part. No choir of angels sang. She just heard that still, small Voice, and she knew what to do.

She backed up, opened her billfold, handed the man the $20, and said, "The Lord told me to give this to you."

He started to cry. Raising up his other hand, with the $2 in it, he said, "I was trying to figure out how I could buy bread. This is all the money I have."

Not now. Now he was set. He looked at her for a second, and then confessed, "I have goosebumps." He started trembling. "How did you know?"

"Well, I didn't, until the Lord told me to give you the money," she replied, a big smile spreading over her adorable grandma face. "I hope this blesses your day."

He gave her a wide, nearly toothless grin, and continued to cry softly as he rubbed the goosebumps on his arm, mumbling, "Thank you, Jesus."

The moment was priceless. She was soooooo glad she had obeyed. She could see what a huge difference it had made for him.

She didn't have to push her cart up to the checkstand. It practically floated . . . and she might have felt the brush of angel's wings.

You know, she's by no means rich. She's definitely in "the 99 percent." She lives on a fixed income. She's a little old lady in tennis shoes, splurging on candy for her grandkids. She could have ignored the Voice and gone on with her day.

NOT!!!

She starts every morning in prayer, and keeps it up all day, every day, 'til bedtime. She knows the Lord. She has "heard" His voice before. She knows what life is like with Him in the driver's seat, trusting Him to meet her every need – including the need to share whatever she can, just out of the joy of giving.

She leads the submitted life that characterizes Christianity, representing the Savior and doing His errands whenever asked, instantly and diligently.

That's why they call it "a relationship, not a religion." There's no greater thrill in life than representing the King of the Universe in directly blessing another human being.

The Christian lifestyle is kind of like bread: you can live without it every day. But why would you want to?

Of her trip to the store, she says with a smile: "I got not only what I needed, but apparently what I came for."

Next time you have a chance to serve the Bread of Life, don't loaf. Move your buns. And any way you slice it, you and those around you will be richly blessed. †

36. Down, FiFi

My flesh and my heart may fail,
but God is the strength of my heart and my portion forever.

— Psalm 73:26

So there I was in the dressing room at Dillard's in a death grip with a black strapless bra named "FiFi."

Let me explain.

Underwear is my nemesis. I hate buying it. I hate being "sized" for it, and haven't been since I was 13. Consequently, I still wear underwear that I've had since I WAS 13.

Now the DNA is breaking down in the elastic of these antique garments. The fabric is so worn, it's cheesecloth.

These undies are all so tattered, I'm close to doing the scandalous thing teenagers today are doing: wearing no underwear at all. They call it "GOING COMMANDO." Well, huh. Mine already looks like it's been through a war.

The bras are missing hooks. They have stretched-out straps. My husband forever destroyed the graceful mystique of breastfeeding by calling the flaps of my maternity bras "bomb bay doors."

The centerpiece of all this is a nuclear-strength panty girdle at least 20 years old, purchased, I believe, at a Strategic Air Command garage sale. This lethal weapon is so tight that, when I'm wearing it, I have to be hoisted by crane into a chair.

If I'm standing up, I can only balance by leaning on a wall, it has so much torque. When I'm ready to move, I stick my arm out for someone to pull me upright. When I pull on this powerful girdle, the national strategic defense underground command center near Omaha goes DEFCOM 4 because of the release of radioactive fusion molecules into the atmosphere.

Fortunately, my daughters are not so lingerie loony. They actually like buying it and having a lot in their undie inventory. When I take them shopping, though, the bras on the display racks remind me of hundreds of poodle noses pointing north, east, south and west. I get the willies. Once, a bra displayed down low scraped my shin. I turned, glared, and commanded, "Down, FiFi."

Ever since, we've called bras "FiFi's." It's a girl thing.

So, anyway, we got invited to a sweet, swank soiree. I'd known for months that I would need a black strapless bra for my black gown because it had sheer shoulders. The skin of my shoulders barely showed through the lovely fabric, but bra straps would definitely show and it would be a *Glamour* "Don't." But of course, I had put off buying a black strapless bra 'til the very last minute.

So the day of the ball, I raced to the mall, grabbed a FiFi I thought was about my size off the rack, and snuck into a dressing room. It was quickly apparent that the bra I had selected was my size, all right . . . four pregnancies and a few million Godivas ago.

But I was in a hurry. So I tried to make it work.

Beads of sweat dotted my brow. I bent over backwards, grimacing as if doing the limbo from hell.

Both hands fumbled to connect hooks and eyes I couldn't see, that stubbornly remained two inches apart.

My hands were greasy from a recent application of lotion, and my glasses were slipping down off my nose, when suddenly:

ZZZZZING!

. . . the bra shot out of my hands with the cups pointing forward like twin cannonballs, and smacked into the dressing room mirror. I heard a shocked gasp from next door.

I couldn't just do nothing.

So I said what came to mind:

"DOWN, FiFi!"

There was an eerie silence. I think she bought it, that a little poodle dog had made that noise. I hope she hasn't needed a prescription since.

I was so embarrassed I just grabbed a bigger size, paid for it, and high-tailed it out of there.

That night, I flossed with excellence and yanked my chin hair, rejoiced that FiFi was the right size . . . but couldn't find my favorite nuclear-strength panty girdle. Oh, well. I'll simply have to brag that I had had waist augmentation surgery.

My beauty routine included bag balm — that's right, the same smelly stuff that farmers put on pig udders — to try to tame my left eyebrow, which was trying to "Go Andy Rooney." At least that was better than "Going Commando."

But I never should have worried. Our daughter was the prettiest debutante, nobody even looked at the mothers anyway, my FiFi did its job without a bark, and best of all, nobody knew what I went through just to get decent underwear for such a swank event.

'Til now.

But let's keep these unmentionables unmentioned, shall we?

Or else I might have to sick FiFi on you. †

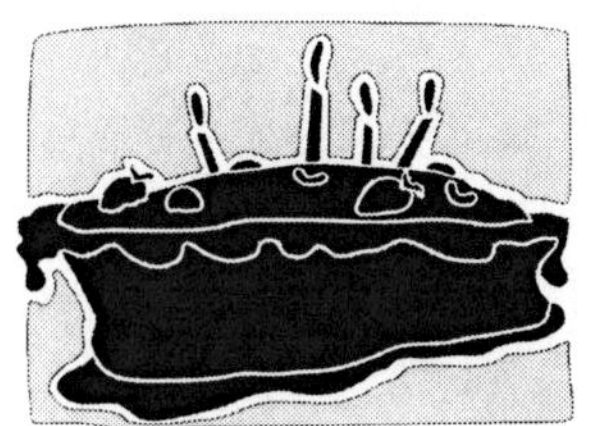

37. Madame Perfecto

Now unto him that is able to keep you from falling, and to present you faultless before the presence of his glory with exceeding joy. . . .

—Jude 24

I was late for the preschool carnival, and hadn't yet made the fluffy marshmallow frosting for the cake I'd promised to bring for the cake-walk.

The smart thing would have been to order a cake, or at least pick up some store-bought frosting to slap on a quickly-fixed homemade cake and go. But ohhh, nooo. Mine had to be the fanciest homemade cake on the planet.

I was . . . Madame Perfecto!

With one child attached to my left shin and the other child swinging from the chandelier, with dried juice on the floor collecting enough dirt to resemble the dots on a map of the United States, with the dog barking and the phone ringing and the potted plants gasping their last because they hadn't been watered since the Reagan years, I started to make the frosting.

For marshmallow frosting, you have to heat the ingredients in a pot on the stove and use a hand-held mixer to whip it into a froth. Heat and beat. You know?

Only I was the one whipped into a froth. Only after I got started did I remember that one of the beaters of my hand-held mixer was missing.

WHO LOSES ONE BEATER?!? Madame Perfecto could never admit that she might actually have made a (CROWD GASPS) (ORGAN MUSIC) mistake. So I kept on trying to make the frosting, anyway.

Have you ever tried to make fluffy frosting with just one beater? You can't, excuse the expression, beat it. What are you supposed to do, wiggle the pan or run circles around it while you're beating it with one lousy, ineffective beater?

I thought of the 20-horse fishing motor. That propeller goes around plenty fast! But it was clear out at the back of the garage. There just wasn't time.

Consequently, the frosting wasn't fluffy. It wasn't even frothy.

It was thin. It was runny. It was gloppy.

Glop would have to do. I spread the frosting out on the cake. It ran down the sides and pooled on the plate.

I scraped it back up onto the top again. It ran down the sides and pooled on the plate.

We had to go. I strapped the kids in the back seat, put the cake on the seat beside me, spatula in hand, and laid scratch.

At every red light, I scraped the frosting back up onto the top of the cake. By the next intersection, it had run down the sides and pooled on the plate.

When we arrived at the carnival, I thought of creating a diversion, like starting the clown's hair on fire, so nobody would see me walking in with my Pool of Cake. Somehow, I slipped it into the cake-walk lineup without being seen.

When the carnival ended, more than 200 lovely cakes had been joyously selected from the cakewalk. But there was one lonely, misshapen, sad little cake left over. It was no longer Pool of Cake. It was now Swamp of Cake. Nobody in six counties was willing to claim it. Least of all me.

I rejected it and abandoned it, and have never expressed so much as a tinge of remorse. This was nothing new: I have made some pretty strange and deranged cakes in my time. Lopsided. Cavernous. Crumb-bedecked frosting. You name it.

OK, so Martha Stewart, I ain't. The cake incident exposed Madame Perfecto for the sham I am. My pride, ego and over-confidence greatly outstrip my actual homemaking skills. God didn't make us all equally good in the domestic arts. AND THAT'S OK!!!

There are cobwebs over my rags and cleaners. Visitors think the dog-snot swirls and blotches on the sliding glass door are actually an expensive frosted-glass motif. They think my socks are hand-knit from fabulous yarns from South America, when it's really just the collected dog hair since the vacuum has been broken for I don't know how long.

My carpet looks like it has patterns, but when installed, it was a solid color. I wash my hair with dog shampoo and vice versa because the bottles look the same, I'm near-sighted, and what the heck.

I once had to jackhammer a frozen dessert out of the dish when I forgot to use cooking spray. Literally used a cordless power drill. (The drill bit was clean!!! Don't worry!!!)

My kids repair rips in their hems with masking tape. I am so lazy I only iron the FRONTS of blouses, figuring a jacket or sweater will hide the wrinkles on the backs and sleeves.

I once served ice-cold BBQ beef at a big party, mystified by why it hadn't heated up, and what was the "funny smell." After the party I discovered I'd put the rented serving piece together upside down. The sterno melted the plastic handle instead of warming the beef. So THAT was the funny smell, and that's why the beef was cold. Ohhhhh.

But back to cake. Another cake story proves I'm not the worst homemaker in the world. Nowhere near the most creative one, either!

See, one of the "other mothers" once confessed that she had gotten too busy to get ready for her son's birthday party adequately. The worst thing was, she forgot to bake the cake. Oh, no! But ding-dong! The hyperventilating party guests were here! She had the boxed mix, but no cake.

What's a mother to do? Improvise!

She made up the mix, sat the boys down on the floor in a circle, stuck candles in the batter, had them sing, and had her son make a wish and blow out the candles.

Then she let each boy lick one candle, something their own mothers NEVER let them do.

THEN, best of all, she told them that just this once, they were going to get a special treat. Instead of eating a piece of baked cake with a boring old fork, they were going to get to eat Birthday Batter – right out of the bowl – with their FINGERS!!!

Riotous fun ensued!

All agreed it was the best birthday party EV-er by the coolest mom EV-er.

I kneel and kiss the hem of greatness. †

38. Old Boyfriend Panic

Better is the sight of the eyes than the wandering of the desire: this is also vanity and vexation of spirit.

— Ecclesiastes 6:9

I was invited to a town a few hours away to give a speech. A long-lost boyfriend of mine was probably going to be there.

ALERT!

AA-OO-GAH!

EMERGENCY!

I admit it. I had fantasized about him over the years. We would meet again, and he would slap his forehead and wail, "How did I EVER let you get away?"

Listen: I am very happy in my longtime marriage. It's just that . . . when the stewpot boils over and the toddler bites your ankles and the hubby gives you a socket set for Valentine's Day, you sometimes play that "what if?" game in your head. You know?

But now I had a big problem: reality.

Back then, I at least had some semblance of babe-osity. Now, I kind of look like Boris Yeltsin in a dress. How could I re-hottify myself practically overnight?

That hair! Frump City! With a snazzy cut and some "cheat juice," I looked maybe a half-hour younger.

That middle-age pudge! For days, I did the stressed-out gerbil thing on the elliptical machine, and fervent underwater gyrations in the workout pool. Lost one pound. Big whoop.

That eyebrow! It has "gone Andy Rooney." My right eyebrow lays flat and sleek, like elegant sealskin. But my left eyebrow has gone *SPRRRRRONG!!!* It's as unruly as a class of third-graders on the last day of school. I've tried everything: Vaseline, hair gel, even udder balm. For this high-stress reunion, I might have to call NASA for some special sealant used in outer space.

That facial hair! My upper lip is starting to "go Gene Shalit." I'm pretty sure the old boyfriend didn't have a moustache, either, the last time he saw me. It's hard on middle-aged men to see others with more hair than they have, anywhere. Waxing? Youch! Laser hair removal was said to take weeks; if I tipped them well, could they zap me a quickie?

Eww, my stubby nails! The East German scrubwoman look! I was letting my nailbeds rest after years of having luxurious fake nails mortared on. I'd just have to keep my hands in my pockets, even if he wanted to shake hands.

Enough! The big day arrived. I picked out a doable outfit, maximized the makeup arsenal, and surveyed the ravages. Oh, well. Maybe he's nearsighted now.

The two-hour drive zoomed by. One mile to go.

Hmm. What if I'd married him, instead, and was living here in a darling farmhouse? With big, beautiful sunrises and sunsets? In glorious peace, with the silence broken only by the trill of a meadowlark? Would we picnic down by the old mill stream, toasting each other with wine from our own vineyard, munching on cheese from our own 4-H champion goats?

Poof! My daydream vanished as I rolled into the very small town.

It was like something out of a 1950s horror movie right before the aliens arrived, when everybody was hiding.

Where was the Panera?

Where was the library?

Museum? Stadium? Stores? Theaters?

For that matter, where was the traffic light?

What did they do for fun around here? Tour the SOD FARM?!?

Now, don't get mad. Rural living is fabulous for those who choose it.

But my spoiled, city-girl eyes were opened. I realized that I loved my life, and certainly my husband. I didn't need to daydream; my real life was a dream come true. I was one lucky little wacky-eyebrowed East German scrubwoman.

Of course I still sucked in my gut bigtime when I walked in.

But guess what? He never showed up. The chicken!

So now, in my fantasy scenario, I imagine that my handsome, beloved husband and I are frolicking through Borsheim's, the world's best jewelry store right here in Omaha, while up in Podunk the old boyfriend has an extreme combover, a '70s bowling shirt and outrageously prominent nosehair that makes my eyebrow look sleek and sophisticated.

That's the price you pay for chickening out on the gorgeous babe who got away. †

39. Floofed Up and Memo'ed Out

Whose adorning let it not be that outward adorning of plaiting the hair, and of wearing of gold, or of putting on of apparel; But let it be the hidden man of the heart, in that which is not corruptible, even the ornament of a meek and quiet spirit, which is in the sight of God of great price.

— I Peter 3:3-4

You know that scene in *The Wizard of Oz* where the characters all go to the beauty shop before they see The Wiz? The tin man gets polished, the scarecrow gets restuffed, the lion gets fancified, and Dorothy and Toto get the works "in the merry old land of Oz." Women need that, every now and then. It's in our genes.

We call that process "getting floofed." And recently, I got to do that. With a "floof, floof here," and a "floof, floof there," our daughters and I got ready for a swank event, the Symphony Debutante Ball. Daughter Eden curtsied in a beaded white ballgown with long white gloves, and the whole family got all gussied up and danced the night away for a very good cause.

The man of the house grumbled good-naturedly about having to wear fruit boots and fancy duds. I "got nails," dealt severely with my unwanted facial hair, and used my primeau double-wide dental floss. The sisters got beautiful evening gowns, mani-pedi's and beauty-shop do's, even Maddy, who, as usual, stole the show.

For a recent terrible, horrible, no good, very bad birthday, my Beloved had bought me a diamond bracelet at Omaha's world-famous jewelry store, Borsheim's. Unfortunately, the clasp had broken, and was off being fixed, unavailable to wear at this high-style occasion.

I called to see if maybe they could rush it through, but no dice. Then the customer service fairy kicked in: Borsheim's insisted that I "memo out" another bracelet. I had never heard of that concept. Translation: borrow it, for free, no strings attached. Wear it for your special event and then just bring it back.

The "replacement" cost was $14,000. *FOUR*-teen *THOU*-sand *DOL*-lars?!?!?!?!?!

All on my sturdily-built German wrist?!?

They could trust me with that? Based on my measly signature? That says a lot about that store, and our town.

However, it would be covered by our insurance. My Beloved said if a robber cut off my arm to steal the expensive bracelet, he would go after HIM, and ignore my bloody stump. Under the circumstances, I was OK with that.

The ball was wonderful. I fairly floated around. Soon enough, I'd be back to dryer lint and the sticky kitchen floor, and war news and worrying about dear friends with difficult diseases. In the meantime, I was living it up.

We each need to. We need a Camelot – one brief, shining moment when you feel like you're at your best, and time is standing still, and the world is a place of beauty and music and laughter. For some, it's a Prom. For others, it's a wedding, or a memorable dinner out, or a special vacation.

Our moment capped off our year with elegance, and I was grateful. Hours later, I waited up for Eden, still wearing the $14,000 bracelet – not because I was afraid I'd lose it, but because I was such a klutz, I couldn't undo the clasp. She came in. She helped me get it off and put it away safely. We reviewed the evening.

I told her what her sister Neely had said, that Eden had been so graceful onstage, and while dancing with her hunky escort.

"You really were a debutante tonight," I told her. "We're so proud of you."

She instantly grinned, lifted her left arm, cupped her right hand underneath her armpit, and slammed it down, pretending to make a rude noise.

We collapsed in helpless laughter. Reality check!

That's the thing about shining moments: they're brief for a reason. Burst the bubble . . . back to the salt mines . . . the fairy tale's over.

Or is it? Isn't life as a Christian BETTER than a fairy tale? Actually, storybook endings and happily-ever-afterings don't have anything to do with floofing up and memo'ing out fancy jewelry.

No, what's really valuable can't be broken, doesn't have to be borrowed, and doesn't cost a cent. It's ours to own forever, for the asking.

Love and joy and the other precious, free gifts from God are right here in everyday life, available to each of us. We can enjoy the gifts of the Spirit and look forward to the biggest debut of them all, when it's our turn to take a bow or make a curtsy, and join the dance in the ballroom of eternal light and love, just beyond the pearly gates. †

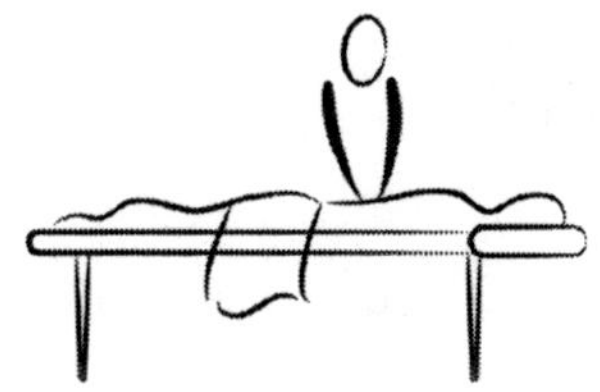

40. Reba and Me

(A)nd as many as He touched were made perfectly whole.

— Matthew 14:36b

My friend Jeannie and I were on our cell phones. She was off to a grocery store to get her granddaughter's favorite premade hamburger patties. I was going to the post office.

It's a thrill-a-minute celebrity lifestyle around here.

I whined about my dry eyes. Every morning, they hurt a lot. I stagger out of bed and grope stiff-legged to the bathroom like Frankenstein. I feel for the eyedrops, which I leave on the counter in the exact same place every day, like a blind person, so I can find them immediately.

I do a desperate backbend, eyes wide open, mouth gaping like a dead fish. I squeeze a few soothing, life-saving drops in, blinking and grunting in relief.

TOLD you it's a movie star lifestyle.

Well, Jeannie had just gotten back from an eye appointment. She was all excited about the new eye massage techniques the doctor had taught her.

"You get in the shower and hold a nice, warm washcloth over them, and hold it there for a while and just let the warm water wash over them. It feels awesome! Then, slowly, with gentle pressure, rub from the inside out, a gentle caress. . . ."

"SHHHH!" I interrupted. "What if Homeland Security or somebody is listening in?!? They might not have heard you say this is about our EYES! They'll think we're in some kind of a SEX RING!!!"

But next morning, I tried it. And she was right. It felt great.

There's just something about touch that beats everything else. It's always been that way. In fact, one of the greatest signs of Jesus' divinity and yet humanity is how He healed people with just a touch. His disciples could do it, too. Today, we hug and pat and high-five, and those actions have healing power, too.

Having a massage is the pinnacle of this. It's nice to be kneaded!

However . . . for stressed-out stiffs like me, the first time can be highly embarrassing.

Mine was during a sisters' trip to Scottsdale, Ariz. We left our husbands in charge of the thundering herds for some desperately-needed girls-only R&R.

We called it our "Take This Job and Shove It Victory Tour."

For the first two nights, we stayed in a cheapo hotel.

But for the grand finale, we checked in to a really ritzy resort. We made the most of it, swimming in its series of fabulous pools, walking its manicured grounds, dining alfresco . . . and capping it off with massages.

I didn't want to go. She made me. She said I would feel like a "noodle," the perfect ending for a relaxing, refreshing trip.

They said to disrobe to the point where I felt comfortable. "OK, then, I'm ready," I said instantly. I HATE exposing myself in any way, shape or form.

(They call customers like me "noncompliant.")

They told me to put my face in this round, padded capital "O" at the base of the massage bed.

A TOILET SEAT?!?!? I paid all this money to put my face in a TOILET SEAT?

Well . . . it was covered with the softest terrycloth, and it was well-padded. It was to relieve pressure on my neck as I lay on my tummy. It was supposed to help me relax. But it's hard to keep your face relaxed – as in, not howling with self-conscious laughter — when it's surrounded by a TOILET SEAT.

So I was laughing at my ridiculous posture. But the masseuse must've thought my shoulders were shaking because I was nervous. She asked if I wanted a massage that was "gentle" or "intense."

INTENSE?

My suspicious mind immediately began conjuring up what THAT would be like. My eyes darted to check if she had leather boots, fishnets and a whip. But the toilet seat blocked my view. Cringing, I said, "something kind of in the middle."

As she started bending, folding, spindling and mutilating my plentiful middle-class flesh, she tried to put me at ease with cheerful chitchat:

"I just 'did' (strrrrrrrrrretch) Reba McEntire!"

You know, the country and western singing star.

My shoulders started shaking again, wondering whether Reba put HER face in the toilet seat, too. Then I had to ask:

"Are you going to brag to the NEXT customer that you just 'did' aging matron Susan Williams of Omaha?"

Silence.

Then she laughed artificially, and completed the massage in stone, cold silence. I can imagine what she was thinking.

But what a massage! It was great. I emerged, just as promised, a complete "noodle." My hair was in a towel, and there was a . . . TOILET RING . . . around my face.

But for consolation, chances are, Reba had one, too.

It's a celebrity lifestyle. ✝

41. Accessories

And all these blessings shall come on thee, and overtake thee, if thou shalt hearken unto the voice of the Lord thy God. Blessed shalt thou be in the city, and blessed shalt thou be in the field.

— Deuteronomy 28:2-3

I thought he was into Internet pornography and carrying on a torrid affair. He'd be online for hours. But when I'd come near, he'd shield his computer screen from my sight, and divert my attention by saying something like: "Your hair's on fire!"

Then I'd overhear him on the phone, urgently asking, "Where can we go?" and "How long can you be out?"

He *IS* having an affair!!! WAHHH!!! And all these years, I thought I was married to a straight-shooting, G-rated guy.

Then I learned the truth: he's straight-shooting, all right. But he's H-rated . . . for "Hunting."

That's right: the midlife crisis of my Beloved has taken shape as an obsession with guns, ammo, fishing poles, the out-of-doors . . . and all the gear, boy toys and accessories that go with.

I guess I started it. He was invited to go out hunting with his best friend since kindergarten. He hadn't been hunting for decades. They had such a great time that he bought a shotgun on the way home. He was cleaning it on the porch when Maddy, 4, happened by, and frowned: "You'd better not shoot that in the HOUSE!"

But what a great, outdoorsy activity! Perfect for a Godly man who could be responsible around guns. He had worked very, very hard at his job, putting up with me, and rearing our four kids. It was time for him to get out some more, and have some guy fun.

So for his 50th birthday, to encourage him to get back into hunting as a hobby, I gave him a Rhino. Not the horned animal . . . the Yamaha all-terrain vehicle. It looks like a little camouflage Jeep with a cute back cargo hold and snazzy-looking roll bars.

The Rhino goes fast. Therefore, he loved it. He immediately went out and got a camo hunting cap to match his new camo hunting vehicle. Then an orange one. A friend gave him camo gloves, toe warmers, and some hunting-blind hors d'oeuvres. He got duck calls and ammo.

He went online and got a gun rack for the Rhino, a storage box and who knows what all else. Somehow, he had wound up with an old plastic windshield that fit a golf cart, and so he rigged that up on the Rhino, too.

Then he started going crazy. He got a 72-part hunting outfit, with layers, zippers and secret compartments enabling him to tough out the weather on six different planets. He got longjohns, liners and socks, mysterious clip-on dealies, and a hunting-dog kennel liner even though we don't have a hunting dog. (But ohhhhh, yes. That was next. Not one, but two!)

The girls got him hunting and fishing gear for Christmas, including cheesy videos with tantalizing titles like "Walleye Patterns" and "Crappie Wisdom." I got him a couple of hunting and fishing magazine subscriptions and even found myself wrapping his gifts in hunting-theme giftwrap.

He's just like a little girl with a Barbie doll. Accessories: it's alllllll in the accessories.

Actually, it's ruining our lives. We have one decent family picture: everybody's dressed up and smiling naturally, with no visible stains or bedhair. But now it's a worthless picture. We don't recognize Daddy without his camo hunting cap on anymore.

The accessorizing obsession deepens: now it's a duck boat, Global Positioning Satellite technology, trap and skeet ranges, sporting clays, steel targets for target practice, and endless phone calls arranging weekend jaunts with his old mutt friends.

He's addicted. They say the wife is the last one to know. But believe me, I know. And so do the timid woodland creatures. He clanks and rattles so much with all that gear, they know he's comin' miles before he gets there.

Recently, he went to his friend's acreage outside Kansas City to duck-hunt and goose-hunt with all his new glunk. They ATV'ed to a primeau spot, laid out all their decoys, and hunkered down in their super-secret blind with all their accessories at the ready.

Now, how many shots do you think they got off, in two days?

Not one.

All that equipment, and the critters still won. Why? Because THEY'VE got "accessories," too. Like instinct, fast getaway, and ways to protect and defend themselves. Nanny, nanny boo-boo.

But that's OK. The main thing was to be together, outside, relaxing and having fun. So, at day's end, my Beloved was loading back up his gear to come home, empty-handed, when one of his friend's pet geese waddled right up to him . . .

. . . and bit him, real high on the back of the thigh.

I mean REAL high. So high, it was right where he sits down.

Oh, the irony! The poetic justice! The mighty hunter gets a . . . goose!

At least he looked cool and well-dressed when it happened. It's alllllll in the accessories, you know. ✝

42. Mr. Dixie's Prized Black Colt

...Thou shalt love your neighbor as thyself.

— Matthew 22:39b

We have a red-headed neighbor man whom Maddy has loved since she was a baby. They are one in frecklehood. When he sees her, he grins and waves, "Hi, Maddy!" and she gets all excited that someone knows her name. He's the closest thing to a groupie she has.

She calls him "Mr. Dixie." His house is always on her list for May baskets and trick-or-treating. She loves to pet his horses' fuzzy muzzles every chance she gets.

She doesn't remember it, but he brought down the house at her first birthday party. We invited a few neighbors and friends to enjoy cake and ice cream with us in our basement, as the rest of the house was undergoing a major remodeling.

Maddy held court in her high chair, smearing birthday cake all over her face while the rest of us wished we could.

I unwisely decided to show off her new trick – pointing. She couldn't talk yet, but she could sure point. "Point to Grandma, Maddy!" I would say, and she would point with gusto at the adoring grandparent. "Point to Beamer!" and she would direct her chubby forefinger with glee toward her sister, Eden.

After several more people had been pointed out, I trotted out the grand finale. "OK, Maddy! Last one. Point to Daddy! Where's your Daddy? Point him out for us!"

Before my horrified eyes, she skipped her father, whirled to the right, beamed a great, big frosting grin . . . and pointed straight at Mr. Dixie!!!

Do you have any idea how bright the face of a red-headed man gets in a situation like that? Our air conditioning unit kicked in. Foreign satellite monitoring stations were going nuts wondering what all the radiation was above eastern Nebraska that day.

Guess Maddy knew that Mr. Dixie had three kids of his own, and was a daddy, too. That's our story, and we're sticking with it. I mean, as commanded, I love my neighbor . . . but . . . thankfully, the two people laughing the most after that episode were Mrs. Dixie and My Beloved. Whew!

Anyway . . . that was nothing compared to the Night of the Near Tornado!

See, Mr. Dixie raises Thoroughbred racehorses for a living. Just in case prospective clients read this, he is tremendously talented and discerning, and I believe these racehorses are each worth something like a squillion dollars. He purchases promising weanlings at the big sales down South and brings them to Nebraska to grow big, strong and fast. Many of them have won lots of races, and yet they grew up in the pasture across the street. We love watching the colts and fillies kick up their heels and run and play.

Well, one night, there was a terrible thunderstorm. It was practically a tornado. Mr. Dixie went out to check on his new colts. He saw that the black one had apparently been greatly distressed by the wind. The black colt was disoriented, down on the ground, trapped and struggling under the fence.

Oh, noooo! That's bad enough for what most people would see — a young horse in trouble. But remember, this was high-potential horseflesh, worth a squillion dollars. Or more!

He not only saw a struggling horse, he saw piles of currency with wings on them, about to fly away. If that horse injured his leg, a large investment would be . . . you guessed it . . . gone with the wind.

So, crouching down and creeping slowly, he moved toward the black colt, trying his best not to alarm him. He thought that if he crept up soothingly, and murmured reassuringly, he could keep the colt somewhat calm, and have a chance to untangle his expensive Thoroughbred legs from under that fence, before they broke.

This is a man with decades of experience in the horse business. He knew exactly what he was doing.

So he crept up, and crept up, gently murmuring "there, Boy" and "whoa, Boy," nearer and nearer to the struggling black colt in the dark and stormy night. . .

. . . and then he saw that it wasn't a struggling black colt at all.

IT WAS A BLACK PLASTIC TRAMPOLINE COVER!

It was OUR black plastic trampoline cover. It must have been ripped off by the wind in the Near Tornado. It had blown across the street, and got caught in Mr. Dixie's pasture fence. The edge of it was flapping furiously in the wind.

In the dark, I guess, it LOOKED like a squillion-dollar black colt's legs trapped dangerously under a fence.

Too late, he spotted his squillion-dollar black colt standing clear over on the other side of the pasture, safe and sound.

So now, when we are praising Mr. Dixie in front of his high-paying clients, we always mention his amazing knowledge of horseflesh . . . and trampoline covers, too.

The clients never get it. But that's OK. He's a redhead. We just like to make him blush. ✝

43. When I Hear 'Don't,' I Do

If they obey and serve him,
they shall spend their days in prosperity,
and their years in pleasures.

—Job 36:11

News flash: men and women are different!

This was brought home vividly one recent Fourth of July. One of my Beloved's most deranged and bizarre friends in another state managed to acquire several super-duper powerful boom-boom sticks. How big a boom-boom? Think of what they used to blow up Rocky Mountain granite to build the Eisenhower Tunnel. That big a boom-boom. Well, almost.

My Beloved was grinning from ear to ear because this so-called friend had given him one just for the occasion. And we had a houseful of guests, many of them of the male persuasion.

See, males think fireworks are . . . the bomb, I guess. ME MAKE POWER STICK GO BOOM! ME HAPPY! BELCH! NOW WHERE REMOTE? ME WATCH GOLF CHANNEL REST OF EVENING AND FALL ASLEEP IN CHAIR.

We females are significantly further evolved, emotionally. But you KNEW that.

Card-carrying mature, wise and prudent female that I am, I forbad him to set it off anywhere near anyone else, including our children, their spouses and friends and, of course, mature, wise and prudent moi. Especially not around moi because I had JUST spent over a hundred dollars on a new 'do and I'd be danged if I was going to have it go pure white and stick straight up in the air for the rest of my life, if he set that thing off.

This wifely instruction received the familiar Lead Balloon Response. As in, fuhgeddaboudit.

He marched out to the pasture, with several beaming male persons in lockstep beside him. Several mature, wise and prudent female persons reluctantly fluttered and muttered just behind.

"Are you sure this is safe?"

"Could we get arrested?"

"What will the neighbors think?"

I even used my most logical, compelling argument:

"You could get your hand blown off! THINK OF YOUR GOLF GAME!!!"

Not even that deterred his mission. He did some half-baked safety measures involving a spent Roman candle tube and an old plastic wastecan. The rest of us backed up into a quivering clump as he lit the fuse.

One second! Two! Three!

It didn't go off!

We're saved! Hallelujah!

Not so fast! Puzzled, my Beloved moved near the wastecan. I've known him long enough to know what he was going to do. He was going to bend over and put his face right over that lethal explosive, to see why it hadn't gone off.

I couldn't contain the decibel level of my warning shout, which no doubt is still echoing down the Missouri River Valley watershed:

"David! David! DOOOOOOOOON'T!!!!!!!"

Standing from the back of the clump of onlookers, I saw him swivel his face toward me – not remove his face from danger, mind you, but just slowly and purposefully swivel it toward me.

Then he uttered those priceless words of explanation which have been uttered by husbands since Cave Man days, which, come to think of it, this whole episode reminded me of.

He said, most cheerfully:

"When I hear 'don't,' I DO."

He instantly turned back to gazing downward at his explosive device. But something even more ominous appeared out of the corner of my eye.

A very bright, soft-spoken young man had been dating one of our daughters. He was standing in front of me. He evidently heard the comment, loved it, and from behind him I could see his cheek bulge out a good two inches, he was grinning so big.

Oh, no! NOW he's encouraging the YOUNG ones to become deranged, ignore prudent counsel, and take high-risk chances like HE does!!!

My kind of guy! the young'un was no doubt thinking about my Beloved's peacock-like dismissal of my wise and mature advice. No wonder he asked for our daughter's hand very soon after this. My Beloved was happy to grant it to a fellow pyromaniac.

Because, of COURSE, the dang thing went off a few seconds later. Of COURSE it went off AFTER my Beloved had indeed stepped back a few paces and his face was no longer just inches away from the explosive device.

Of COURSE it was tremendously loud, no one got hurt, the guys clapped their hands and laughed, and we girls rolled our eyes, sighed, and went back for seconds on chocolate cake.

I'm sure poor little dogs were cowering for miles around, and the oil companies scored many gallons of mysteriously unleashed "free" crude oil in four surrounding states. Free fracking! Free fracking, all right.

And what about our Lord? You know, the One Who is always reminding us that obedience and caution are key if you want to live a long, happy, prosperous, love-filled, unexploded, free-from-a-body-cast life?

Yeah, well, He's a guy, too. When voices say "don't," He decides to do, too. Think of the manna in the desert . . . David vs. Goliath . . . the certain death on the Cross that wasn't certain at all.

Sometimes, when the world says "don't," you SHOULD do. Maybe guys just know that better than us girls. We have millions of things on them. So they can have ONE special perk. I guess. Guys: you've got to love 'em.

I have a feeling when the big boom-boom stick went off, and those guys were clapping and laughing, the Big Boomer in the Sky was clapping and laughing, too. †

44. The Lamp Thief

And he said to me,
"This is the curse that is going out over the whole land;
for according to what it says on one side,
every thief will be banished,
and according to what it says on the other,
everyone who swears falsely will be banished. . . ."

— Zechariah 5:3 (NIV)

Dishonesty has been in the limelight lately, as never before. Illegal immigration. Corporate cronies rooting around in the public trough. Entire union memberships faking sick to get time off work. Trusted journalists caught lying. Teachers having sex with their students. A doctor who falsely told patients they had cancer so he could cash in on their treatments, expensive but unnecessary.

I'm glad the deceit is being brought to light. Expose it, punish it, and you might put a stop to it. But it seems as though widespread suspicion about dishonesty is hurting us all, even those for whom integrity is still everything. We're all getting painted with the same broad brush. No trust! Nobody expects truth and honesty any more.

But I'm prepared to fight back with humor, like a friend of our family did.

It was winter in Nebraska. But he got invited to stay for a few nights for free at a new development in the swank and ritzy Palm Springs, Calif., area. It was a condominium model unit. Besides the free room, he got to play a free round of golf. It was a promotional visit, and he was a prospective buyer. All he had to do was purchase his round-trip air fare, pay for his meals, and submit to a boring tour and sales pitch, which he did.

He had a great time, and even thought about purchasing one of the condos in the future.

A few days after he returned to his home in cold, snowy Omaha, though, he got a cold, nasty, accusatory email from the condo manager.

It stated that he owed them $750 because he stole the bedside table lamp from the condo unit.

If he didn't pay within 10 days, they would unleash their legal hounds, haul him into court, slash his tires, short-sheet his bed, etc. etc. etc.

Our friend laughed. The bedside table lamp was immense. It must've weighed 200 pounds.

Suuuuure – he snuck out of the condo with it hidden up his shirt, and then carried it on his lap on the plane all the way home.

Suuuuure – he stashed it between his legs and wore a kilt to get away with the theft.

Suuuuuure – he dressed it up as a baby and held it in his airplane seat all the way home.

He wrote back a polite letter of denial, and thought that would be the end of it.

But noooooo! They wrote back again, in even more insulting verbiage, calling him a "thief" and threatening all kinds of retribution if he didn't send that lamp back immediately, or the $750 in cash.

Whaaaaat? Must have been the cleaning crew. Or maybe the demand for cash was some kind of a scam.

They must have stuff get stolen all the time, to jump on him like that. He felt sorry for them, but also pretty mad at being falsely accused. As a Christian, he knew he was still a sinner. But he really was an honest and truthful person. He did not take that lamp. How to make them see that?

A man's "rep" is his most precious possession, after all. He wanted to defend it in an effective way.

I believe that only a guy would think of this. I applaud him for it! Here's what he did:

He went to the well-known and gigantic Nebraska Furniture Mart. He went to the lamp department, where there are hundreds of lamps on display.

He had someone take his picture in the lamp department, with hundreds of lamps all around him. Big ones, little ones, tall ones, short ones, in every color and all kinds of materials. Overhead light fixtures, lamps on chains, reading lamps, and numerous, numerous bedside table lamps.

Then he emailed the picture to the California condo manager, with this message:

"You caught me. I'm a lamp kleptomaniac. If you can identify your lamp among all these other ones I've stolen, I'll gladly send it back to you."

What was their response?

They laughed, withdrew their accusation, and wished him well.

If you read the Bible, you know that eventually, truth will reign. Everything that is false will be revealed and overturned. No sense lying, stealing and cheating. In the long run, you'll get caught, and you'll be sorry.

The good guys – the honest guys – the ones who seek to find the truth, who stand up for it, and who share it with others – shouldn't really be too upset about the public dishonesty going on. Each breach of morality and ethics is an opening for us to plug with the truth of the gospel. With more bad things going on, we can help people develop and exercise their God-given sense of right and wrong. We can bring more people to saving grace and start them on the Christian walk toward holiness and Christlikeness.

Believers are going to live eternally in the warm and gentle Light of the World. In the meantime, we keep living in honesty and truth the best way we know how.

The darker things get, the brighter His light shines. †

45. El Magnifico

But if any provide not for his own,
and specially for those of his own house,
he hath denied the faith, and is worse than an infidel.

— I Timothy 5:8

My mild-mannered husband once morphed into a powerful, courageous matador. Oddly enough, it was due to the Sapp Brothers Coffee Pot on Interstate 80 just west of Omaha. That's a landmark for a fairly famous truck stop and headquarters of a large vehicle leasing operation in the Midwest.

You'll see how a matador connects with a gigantic coffee pot in just a second. I hope.

Actually, my Beloved wears golf caps and would never dream of donning one of those little black Napoleon jobbies that matadors wear. Jeweled suits with capri-length pants are not his look. The closest he comes to a Toro is our snowblower.

But I digress. We were on vacation in Cancun, Mexico, with our daughters. Things were going a little bit wrong. Murphy's Law Goes South. *Ay, carumba.*

First, we planned to go hang-gliding. But a fat bird had recently been killed when it slammed into our picture window at home, and we saw the hang-gliders swooping awfully close to the high-rise hotels along the windy beach. NO WAY!!!

Next idea.

We went snorkeling. Wearing my thick eyeglasses under my mask in Full Nerd Mode, and knowing my girls were embarrassed by the mere sight of me, I swam out ahead. Suddenly, I heard screams:

"SOMETHING'S EATING ME!!!!"

Between me and my daughters, a snorkeler lady was thrashing about. Instantly, the Mother's Book of Emergency Factoids opened in my head. Pages turned:

"Noooooo, it's not a shark; I don't see a fin."

"Noooooo, it's not a piranha; that's a fresh-water fish."

"Noooooo, it's not my husband tickling her; he's over there."

But there were my babies, on the other side of the thrashing woman. If I swam straight over to protect and comfort them, I would get eaten, too. So much for all those hours locating a not-too-horrible swimsuit for the trip.

I bet you thought this was when my husband morphed into a courageous matador and saved everybody's life with derring-do.

Naw. The snorkeling guide did. Turns out the lady had snorkeled where she shouldn't have, into a clearly-marked no-go area, and accidentally startled a jellyfish with a terrible case of PMS. It had let her have it. They jet-skied her to the hospital for mild burns. Later, we learned that she had been released, just fine, shortly thereafter.

But we were still shaken by the near-miss. We resolved not to get slammed into the side of a building, or eaten alive, or sprayed with noxious chemicals for the rest of the "relaxing" trip.

On the last day, we pre-paid for an all-day bus excursion down the coast to the Xcaret resort to see the Mayan relics. To be cool, one must pronounce it correctly. No, not "Ex Carrot." Raise one eyebrow mysteriously, and say: "EEEEESH-cah-rette." *Bueno.*

We were going to go cave snorkeling in an underground river, and pose Mom next to other ancient ruins for hilarious souvenir pictures. "Which One's the Ruin?" (EEEEEESH!).

My husband had thought to bring a zip-lock bag to stash our money for meals during the 12-hour adventure. He put the bag in the pocket of his swimsuit. Lockers cost 50 cents, you know. Hey! Why not save four bits? (When men are on vacation, why is it that they go stark, raving mad?)

Well, of course his bag of money floated out of his swimsuit pocket during the snorkeling, and went *adios.*

Penniless on the Yucatan Peninsula, with 10 hours to go 'til the next meal back at the hotel!

The girls and I were OK with this. My not-too-horrible swimsuit's brand name was "Orca From Majorca" and I could have lived on my blubber for many *mananas.*

But the husband and father, the family provider, couldn't stand the thought of his family not eating.

It was noon. The crowd filled the beach. Everybody had plates but us. Aromas wafted. We ignored them. He was tortured. Suddenly, he stalked off.

A while later, the crowd parted to make way for the triumphant return of . . .

EL MAGNIFICO!!!

He strutted like a matador before an adoring crowd, even though no one paid attention to him but us. Instead of a sword and red flag, El Magnifico wielded a huge tray with five plates of hamburgers and fries, and five tall Cokes.

"Daddy! Daddy! Daddy!" the girls shouted, in the same decibel as the crowds in Madrid shouting "Toro!"

He grinned, his jelly belly blobbing out over those traitorous swim trunks, his stark white feet and lower legs worn curiously hairless by golf socks. Magnifico!

"How?" was all I could ask.

"I hocked my watch," El Magnifico said.

It was a freebie he got somehow that depicted the Sapp Brothers Coffee Pot, that I-80 truck stock landmark west of Omaha. He wore it instead of his good watch in case we got rolled on our trip. (Matadors know all the moves.)

Fortunately, a Mexican waiter thought the Sapp Brothers Coffee Pot watch was a radically stunning designer watch from America, worth the cost of lunch for five. So they swapped.

With courage and cunning, grace, ingenuity, and just a little bit of old-fashioned fast talking, our provider provided.

Burgers never tasted so magnifico.

Ole! †

46. Trust and . . . TIMBER!

Wives, submit yourselves unto your own husbands, as unto the Lord.

— Ephesians 5:22

There I was, Paula Bunyan, playing tug of war with a tree.

I held one end of the rope. The other was tied to a magnificent 50-foot Austrian pine in our back yard.

The neighbors peeked out their windows and tsk-tsk'ed: "We already knew she was crazy. But now she thinks she can pull down a tree with her bare hands."

What they couldn't see was PAUL Bunyan, my husband, crouched down low, doing a Nebraska Chain Saw Massacre on the trunk of that same tree.

The tree had blight, beetles, borers, fungus, sad sap and bad bark.

It had to . . . leaf. So he was cutting it down, and I was called in to help.

I was wondering whether I could trust my husband to cut it down without killing us, whether he was mad at me that day and just how mad, whether it was wise to make slanted cuts on not one but both sides of the trunk, and whether it was a good idea for me to be standing out there like an idiot, pulling a tree down on myself on purpose.

Was I out of my tree, to trust him this way?

Yes. We were a team. I came. He sawed. Together, we would conquer.

He said my job was to pull on the rope and try to influence the direction of the tree's fall. Therefore, I found myself standing in the middle of our back yard, pulling on that tree for all I was worth, as if trying to pull it down on myself.

Why, you ask? Because of Paul Bunyan's many concerns. He didn't want it to fall on our other trees. He didn't want it to smash the neighbor's house. He didn't want it to fall on the power lines and send a fireball into any of our houses.

Oh. Fine. So he wanted it to fall . . . on ME?!?

Well . . . at least he was saving big bucks by taking the tree down himself. Plus he got to play with his loudest toy. A Boy and His Chain Saw.

So I went along with it. I try to be a supportive wife, as long as the request is timely, legal and non-fattening. Yes, I submit to my husband, all day, every day. No big deal.

Some say it's retro and foolish and, cruelest cut of all, just like Donna Reed.

I say phooey. Read Ephesians 5:22, and onward. See? THEY submit to US, too. It's not some nasty male dominance thing. People who say that haven't read the Book.

The divine design for marriage is not a hierarchy; it's an exchange. The power is reciprocal, zigzagging back and forth.

The lines of command are a circle. That's not demeaning. It's balanced. It's strong.

Trust is the trunk that marriage is built around. Without this give-and-take, marriage is as futile as . . . well, trying to pull down a 50-foot pine tree with your bare hands.

Which reminds me:

The chain saw whined. There was a crack. Paul Bunyan shouted, "TIMBERRRR!"

It was falling! Right toward me! Tons of solid wood, about to part my hair in a big way!

You know how in an emergency, cartoon characters run in place for a few seconds, getting up traction, and you hear bongo drums, and then they take off running in a cartoon skedaddle? That was about to be me.

But then Paul Bunyan, this feller who is a feller of trees, had the arrogance and audacity to shout:

"RUN!"

Run??? Run!!! Hmmph!!! It made me really mad, to think he thought I was that stupid.

Run?!?

No! Duhhh!!!!!

I glared at him, hands on hips, highly irritated:

"WHY would you FEEL you HAVE to TELL me to do THAT?"

(It's hard to be, excuse the pun, sappily submissive ALL the time.)

But after my "power moment," yes, I ran. I ran fast! Fast! Fast! Fast! Bongo drums aplenty!

The tree fell — WHAM! — right where he'd planned for it to fall, missing all the obstacles . . . including me.

I had to hand it to him: he did a good job. It fell right where he planned it to fall. Nothing and no one got hurt. Now we had firewood for centuries. I should've trusted him more.

Trust makes marriage fun. A marriage deeply rooted in trust stands tall.

So, couples, pull together. Trust each other. Give each other enough rope so that, if things come crashing down around you, you'll both be left standing, together. Love, honor, obey.

It's an old saw . . . but it cuts true. †

47. Love in the Fridge

Husbands, love your wives, and be not bitter against them.

— Colossians 3:19

They had been married for a couple of years. The honeymoon was over. They were really, really, really, really busy.

She was teaching. She had to go to bed early because she had to get up early.

He was in medical school. He had to stay up late because he had to study for exams.

Days would go by and they wouldn't see each other, at least not in a waking state. He would hole up at the library every night. She would spend the evening alone with the TV and a book. She would go to bed by 10 p.m. so that she could be up by 6 a.m. He would arrive home after midnight, and often study for a few hours longer, falling into bed not long before she had to get up.

While she was getting ready for work, he would lay there sound asleep, his tousled head on the pillow so recently filled with new scientific knowledge. She didn't have the heart to interrupt his precious sleep just to talk to him . . . hear his voice . . . see his sky-blue eyes.

Of course, that meant that he didn't get to talk to her . . . hear her lovely voice . . . see her sparkling brown eyes. . . .

So it was a problem. They were like two ships that passed in the night, one snoring, the other just about to, or one getting ready for the new day, the other still recovering from the one before.

It's hard to work on your relationship when you're barely ever together. Oh, their marriage was fine. There was no threat. They were solid, united, OK.

But she missed the contact, the interaction, the romance. She wondered if he did.

She knew his long hours were for both of them, for their future. She wasn't going to squawk about being emotionally impoverished. It was only temporary.

She thought this is what marriage is: you show your love for your spouse by not demanding that your spouse show love to you, if he was too busy at the moment.

And that's how things went, for quite a while: sort of lukewarm, but OK.

Then one morning, she got up, got dressed, and tiptoed into the kitchen to fix herself some breakfast.

And she saw "The Moron Eggernacle Choir."

That's what the sign said on the open carton of eggs which took center stage on the refrigerator's top rack.

In the middle, with "his" back turned to the audience, was an egg. It had been transformed into a conductor in a black top hat and tails, his arm out to the side with a baton in his hand. Facing him were eight or 10 "singers," each with a different hairdo and clothes, their mouths open in song. Aha! The "choir."

Of course, they were only eggs. Their arms were pieces of paper, taped on. Their faces and hair were drawn on with markers. The conductor's top hat was made out of scratch paper. His baton was a toothpick.

She laughed and laughed.

He was letting her know that he was thinking of her when he came home so late after spending so many tough hours hitting the books.

He was letting her know that making her laugh was as important to him as becoming a doctor.

He was letting her know that he loved her and still pursued her, wanted to entertain her, wanted to woo her.

She got choked up, and needed a tissue . . . which she kept right next to their bed . . . and there he was, sound asleep and looking angelic . . . just this once, it would be OK to wake him up and see his sky-blue eyes dance when she told him how much she'd loved his little egg choir in the fridge.

Her students never knew exactly why she was late to school that morning.

Or eggs-actly why she was smiling so big. †

48. Boy! I . . . I Say . . . Boy!

I am my beloved's, and my beloved is mine:
he feedeth among the lilies.

— Song of Solomon 6:3

It was our 10th wedding anniversary. It was coooooold out. It was early January. Our children were 4, 3 and 1 month. Our floors were a seven-layer salad: Christmas gifts, newspapers, toys, laundry, mail, new diapers, old diapers . . . utter chaos.

My husband was so frazzled and sleep-deprived, he looked like Humphrey Bogart pulling the African Queen through the leech-infested swamp.

I was a housecoat-wrapped, zombie-like, breastfeeding Dairy Queen, since, speaking of leeches, our latest baby whopper seemed to want to top off her tank 24/7.

It was coooooold out, too. So no, even though it was our anniversary, and a big one at that, I didn't FEEL like going out to dinner and anyway . . . AA-OO-GAH!!! Lash me to the mast! Here comes another postpartum hormone hurricane!

I got a little teary-eyed. I was worn out – not feeling at all like the strong, energetic, blushing bride of 10 years before.

Tell you what, he suggested. I'll take the two older kids to Burger King and feed them and let them play in there 'til they're tuckered out. Then I'll get some takeout from that good Italian restaurant and pick up a video. We can put them all to bed, and have a peaceful dinner and movie together at home. How's that?

What a man! What a plan!

The baby fell asleep shortly after they left. I ran the Zamboni through the house, folded last month's laundry, and read an entire week's newspapers in a bubble bath. Heavenly!

When they got home, I was a noodle of bliss, with toys and unmatched socks completely removed from my hair, smiling serenely as we put the children to bed.

It was time for our private party.

I was famished. What culinary delights had my stalwart provider brought in that big takeout sack from our favorite Italian restaurant? What romantic movie had he selected to kindle the flames of matrimonial desire?

But noooooo.

The restaurant had forgotten everything in that sack EXCEPT the hors d'oeuvres: six little itty bitty toasted ravioli. They forgot the salads, breadsticks and entrees. At least there were mass quantities of dipping sauce for the ravioli. But that was it. Whaaaaaat? How could this have happened?

Meanwhile, the movie he'd gotten was . . . not Kevin Costner . . . not Tom Cruise . . . not Clark Gable . . . but FOGHORN LEGHORN CARTOONS.

Sixty minutes of cartoons featuring a blathering, rednecked, Southern-fried rooster. You know, the one who yells, "Boy! I . . . I say . . . Boy!"

He thought I'd think they were funny.

I looked at him. He looked at me. He could go back for the rest of the food. But it was sooooo cold out.

We sighed. This is marriage. Most of the time, everything's great. Other times, you make do.

We cut those six itty bitty toasted ravioli into itty bittier pieces, and put them on plates. They looked lonesome. We sighed. But oh, well. We carried them to the TV, turned on Foghorn Leghorn, speared each little ravioli molecule with a single fork tine, and took turns dipping them in the sauce. At least there was plenty of sauce.

No waltzes, no sparkling diamonds, no moonlit walk on a Caribbean beach. Just ravioli molecules and rooster jokes.

You can see why it was another dozen years before our next child was born. Just kidding.

But fast-forward now to a much later anniversary. By now he had distinguished silver streaks in his hair, and my figure was beginning to look a lot like Foghorn Leghorn.

But we were excited. We were going to a swank soiree. We had to get really dressed up. He would be in white tie and tails. I got a smashing black dress with elegantly-named "caviar" beading. Posh!

He was standing at the foot of the stairs when I started down. He turned.

Our eyes locked.

Dang! He looked GOOOOOOOD!

I forgot all about the hassles and headaches of all those years of marriage. I saw the silver hair I'd caused, the broad shoulders I'd cried on, and the hand that had held mine tight when necessary, and guided it forward lots of times, too.

My heart went plippety-plop, just like when we were teens, and just like at our wedding. I thought back to that meager 10th anniversary deal, and realized that, overall, I'd gotten far more than just hors d'oeuvres in my marriage sack. I got the whole meal deal.

With a rooster like this, I was one lucky hen.

Boy! I . . . I say . . . Boy!

How 'bout we slip out after the dance, go to our favorite make-out place, and split a toasted ravioli? ✝

49. Windfalls and Ice Cream Cones

Riches and honour are with me;
yea, durable riches and righteousness.

— Proverbs 8:18

I don't know what it is with my husband and Automatic Teller Machines. When they first came out, we were teenage sweethearts. We went to a brand-new ATM near his college campus.

He put his card in and requested his bank balance. It came back: "$2,500."

WHOA! He thought he had, maybe, $25 in there, consistent with a perpetually-broke college freshman. Obviously, that bank still had some bugs to work out with their new technology. This was supposed to be user-friendly, but don't think they meant it THAT user-friendly.

He's an honest guy. Plus, he knew the machine wouldn't dispense any more than $200. So we went inside and requested the balance again from the teller.

This time, it came back: "$25,000."

WOW!!!

Vice presidents' heads popped out of offices. They gathered, consulted, and had the teller do it one more time.

It came back: "$25,000,000."

Now you're talking. My husband asked casually, "May I have a withdrawal slip?" Everybody smiled, and then frowned.

Eventually, they straightened it out. He really only had $25 in there. I think he took out $20 for gas, a movie and dinner. Those were the days!

He says now that it was all just a trick, to impress me with his dazzling resources.

But I got him back on a hot summer night years later.

We were longtime marrieds by then. We had loaded up the kids to go get ice cream cones after a typical burger dinner in the back yard. But neither of us had any cash. So we went to the ATM. By then, they had worked out that $25 million bug. Sigh.

So we drive up . . . and what to our wondering eyes should appear in the slot but a $20 bill!

The person before us must have left it by mistake. There was no one in sight. The bank was closed.

Poof! A little bitty white angel popped out on my husband's right shoulder. "That's not yours. Turn in the money to the bank tomorrow morning."

I'm just kidding about the angel. But you KNOW what was going through his mind.

Immediately thereafter, another poof! A little bitty red devil popped out on his LEFT shoulder. "To ____ with THAT brown-nosing idea! That money was left out in the open. Finders keepers! Not your fault the person ahead of you left it. You snooze, you lose! Take the money and run!"

He reached for it, gleefully, and started putting it in his pocket.

"HEY!!!!!!" I protested, Sunday School perfect attendance award winner that I am. "Let's wait a minute and see if they come back."

We did. They didn't.

I still protested: "You can't take that money! That's probably some poor single mother's grocery money for the week! Maybe it's for her dying grandma's medication!"

Naughtily giggling, he stuffed the $20 into his wallet. "Naw, whoever left it there must be so loaded they didn't even miss it. They're probably on their way to the casino boats or something."

He zoomed off, whistling, "We're In the Money."

I kept whining, all the way, cajoling him to put it back. "They're probably back there right now, in tears, searching the bushes and the median! That could be all the money they have in the world! This could be the last straw! They could go to a bridge and jump off, and it'll be all your fault!"

He kept grinning. "Naw. I just taught 'em a LESSON. They'll be more CAREFUL next time."

Ooooh. I did the slow boil of a woman scorned.

We got to the ice cream shop. He went in. I sat in the car with the kids and stewed. I watched him through the glass, all jolly because he was going to get five "free" cones on his unexpected windfall. Hmmph.

An older lady pulled up in the next stall. She looked like a sport. I hopped out of our car and whispered. We conspired.

She went in and stalked right up to him. He turned toward her, smiling pleasantly, as the girls and I watched through the glass.

She said something.

We watched his jaw drop as he reeled back. His eyebrows rose, and then his shoulders leaned back toward her, his face in shock and disbelief.

It was exquisite. Here's what she said:

"I SAW YOU TAKE THAT MONEY FROM THAT ATM! IT WAS FOR FOOD FOR MY BABY! NOW HOW AM I SUPPOSED TO FEED MY BABY?!?!?"

It took him a few seconds of high-speed brain processing to realize that she was 70 years old, with no baby in sight, and she was by now laughing hysterically.

GOTCHA!!!

He turned around to see us through the ice cream store window, in helpless hysterics, too. He pointed, and grinned. His red face nearly melted all our cones.

He paid for the lady's cone, too, and left the change as a huge tip for the counter person. So everybody was happy.

That ice cream tasted like a million bucks. No, $25 million!

Now, I suppose a spiritual perfectionist would have left the money there. But he was an honest, hardworking husband and father. Who's to say HE didn't need that $20 boost more?

You never know, with God's economy.

Maybe it was meant to be. Maybe it was a little reward, a double-dip of fun for a guy who could've been elsewhere, spending money on questionable things, but he chose to be with his wife and kids that night, getting ice cream cones.

That's why the ATM camera always shows me smiling when I drive up. I'm ready for anything.

You just never know when it's your turn to get . . . pennies from heaven. ✝

50. Talk Little

A soft answer turneth away wrath:
but grievous words stir up anger.

— Proverbs 15:1

My husband and I were having a discussion. A very lively one. OK, we were yelling at each other. Loudly. With gusto. With our neck veins bulging out, in fact. It was a loud argument.

It was late at night, the kids were in bed, we were very tired, and we were in those maximum-stress years of parenthood. We were juggling jobs and sitters and bills and chores and children ages 4 and 2, with a third on the way.

Now, marriage is like music: you've got your melody, you've got your harmony, and by golly, you've got your percussion. Big-time.

That night, instead of making beautiful music together, we were making *"The 1812 Overture."* It was pretty out of character for us. We were hurling angry words at each other like cannonballs:

Kaboom!

"Oh, YEAH?"

"And ANOTHER thing. . . .

Kaboom!

"I did NOT!"

"You ALWAYS do!"

Kaboom!

"That's STUPID!"

"Well, so are YOU!"

Who started this war of words? I'm sure I did. In our marriage, I tend to be the gas, and he tends to be the brakes. Together, we ride. But sometimes, we crash.

All I know is, when you're tired and stressed out, stepping on crayons and Legos, changing diapers, giving baths, trying to figure out what to make for dinner when all you have on hand are some roofing tiles and pimiento because you haven't had time to go to the store, with an extra 30 pounds strapped to your gut and straining your back because of the pregnancy — with all that going on, one can become rather irritable and easily provoked.

So thaaaaaar she blows! In my case, sky high.

I'm sure the big fight started when he said something hugely provocative such as, "It's a nice night out, isn't it?"

And I took it wrong, and retorted, "Yeah, but I got gum on my shoe, and the kids dumped flour all over the kitchen floor, and the dog has bad breath, and YOU still haven't fixed the closet door!"

"The CLOSET door? How'd we get from 'nice night' to the stupid CLOSET door?"

And it was off to the races. You know:

Kaboom!

"It hangs CROOKED."

"No one's going to SEE it."

Kaboom!

"*I* see it, all day, every day!"

"So?"

Kaboom!

"You PROMISED to fix it. You didn't. You don't CARE about me."

"Well, why don't YOU fix the closet door yourSELF, if it's such a big deal?"

I had morphed into Brunhilda the Warrior Woman. Red face, bulging neck veins, fists clenched: a terrifying sight in my frumpy mint green robe with the brown plaid fuzzy slippers. (Warrior women only look hot in the comics.)

He was Thor the Terrible: pulled to his full height, intimidating in his striped boxer shorts, head down like a bull, eyebrows forming that ominous black "V."

Just then, our sweet and beautiful daughter Jordan materialized at our door.

She was 4, a vision in beribboned jammies, squinting, her blonde hair squashed funny into a bedhair bouquet. Obviously, our loud argument had awakened her. She had clambered out of her little bed to come stand in our doorway.

"Mommy! Daddy!" she said, rubbing her eyes in the light.

"TALK LITTLE!"

We stared at her. She smiled. Our anger icebergs immediately melted. We smiled back.

"Talk little," eh?

Great advice. Out of the mouths of babes. . . .

Chastened, we kissed her and carried her back to bed, leaning over to embrace her and tuck her in. "Sorry," we whispered. "We love you. We love each other. We will work this out. See you in the morning light. Night-night."

From that day, we resolved to "talk little" in working out the inevitable marital conflicts. We have to remind each other from time to time, but we've found that the mantra works.

When you speak in a small voice, disagreements seem smaller, too.

When you're big enough to "talk little," problems may still "snap, crackle, pop" . . . but they no longer go "kaboom." †

51. Hormy

They that sow in tears shall reap in joy.
He that goeth forth and weepeth, bearing precious seed,
shall doubtless come again with rejoicing,
bringing his sheaves with him.

— Psalm 126:5,6

It is not until a man has to live with a pregnant wife that the full ramifications and permutations of raging female hormones can be fully perceived. It is a marital challenge beyond compare.

One night, my Beloved came home to find me slumped at the kitchen table in despair, my tears wetting my maternity blouse.

He flew to my side. "What's the matter? Is there something wrong with the baby?"

I blinked at him stupidly. "No! Of course not. I had to get gas and didn't have my gloves so my hands got really cold. Plus, there was snow on the paper so the pages are wet and I can't read it. And I got ink on my favorite dish towel and it won't come out."

He blinked back. "And THAT'S why you're crying?"

Sobbing, I retorted: "David, David . . . these are AWFUL things!!!"

You should have seen his face. In the ensuing silence, I felt the points of the compass whirl and the tectonic plates shift. I was no longer a mature, rational human being. I was now transformed to the molecular level by pregnancy hormones.

I had become . . . Hormy!

That's what he called me, through all four pregnancies. When I got emotional, he would say that I was playing my "hormone-ica."

While seated, if I would drop a piece of paper on the floor, it would take five minutes to gingerly bend sideways and pick it back up. It was frustrating and I would cry.

While standing, if I wanted to plug in the vacuum cleaner, I would have to stand with my feet as wide apart as they would go in order to bend down to get the plug into the outlet. I looked so ridiculous, I would laugh.

While getting the nursery ready for the new baby and organizing all the soft and tiny little sleepers, blankets, towels, washcloths and other darling baby gear, I would feel such a surge of cuteness-sparked estrogen that I would burst into tears.

While chatting with the elderly neighbor man, bless his heart, who got a little mixed up on his terminology and asked me if I had become "diluted" yet, instead of "dilated," I looked down at my swollen ankles and feet, quipped that "You BET I have become diluted!" and laughed and laughed, until I cried, and then laughed again because I had cried.

Through it all, my Beloved did not make fun of me, criticize me, roll his eyes or pull his hair out. He remained respectful. Better word: wary.

Even after childbirth, the hormone storms raged. One nurse carried the baby back to the nursery after an attempted late-night feeding, and in the dim light I could see her genuine smile. "Jordan!" she exclaimed. "What a cool name! That sounds like an AUTHOR!" The surge of pride and pleasure about knocked me out of bed.

But later, another nurse came for Jordan after another unsuccessful breastfeeding try. The baby had been crying a lot in the nursery that first night, because the Dairies hadn't yet kicked in. This nurse was carrying the baby out of the room, and again, in the dim light, I could see the nurse's face. She was frowning and irritated. Apparently our baby's crying was interfering with her ability to concentrate on her book or play cards in the nursery. "Poor little thing," she said histrionically to the baby, obviously within my earshot. "You're so hungry! So . . . HOLLOW!!!"

That really hurt. My shame and dismay were made even worse by the flood of hormones.

See, our daughter had weighed well over 10 pounds at birth and had been three weeks overdue. She was used to a constant feedbag in utero, but breastfeeding was taking a while to "work" because of my labor trauma. As pudgy as she was, there wasn't any danger of starvation, I didn't think.

Because of her size, the jokes from our friends and family were flying fast and furious. If she was sleeping when visitors came, we would shuffle down to the nursery to see her through the glass. Naturally, she was the only girl baby in the nursery. All the rest were baby boys, and they must all have been born prematurely. They were only half her size or thereabouts.

One relative exclaimed, "Little bitty blue blanket! Little bitty blue blanket! GREAT BIG PINK BLANKET! Little bitty blue blanket!"

I chuckled, but only to hide my feelings of dismay. I was jolted by emotion, picturing her at age 17 as 6'5", 350 pounds, getting inquiries from the NFL but without a Prom date. The teasing was getting me choked up.

Just then, another visitor arrived, elbowed her husband, and pointed toward our baby daughter – pink, precious, and huge. "Hey, Marv! GET A LOAD OF THAT ONE!"

Get a LOAD? Fighting back tears, I shuffled back to our room.

There, the guys in my family kept joking about the baby's 3-week overdue delivery and spectacular birthweight. "She'll be palming a basketball any day now!" one quipped. "She'll be able to drive the car home from the hospital – her feet should reach the pedals," quipped another.

Tears of hurt filled my eyes.

Just then, my dear Aunt Nancy interrupted the raucous joking. "Say, Susan," she said, authoritatively. "At the preschool where I work, there's this adorable, precious, delicate, tiny little girl that everybody calls 'Tweety Bird.' And do you know what? SHE was a 10-pound baby, too!"

Our eyes met. Hers twinkled. Mine radiated back extreme gratitude. The jokers shut up. We smiled in contentment. Hormy had an ally, and everything was going to be OK. God put wise, loving people in our lives to help us surf through all kinds of storms, including hormonal.

Aunt Nancy was right. Jordan is grown up now, 5'7" and about a size 4. Totally gorgeous. No NFL bids in sight. And yes, she had Prom dates all through school. She now has a wonderful, handsome husband who has adored her since he first "got a load" of her.

And on that note, I will play a triumphant chord on my "hormone-ica" – which, for mothers of any age, is always perfectly in tune. †

52. Pregopotamus

(F)reely ye have received, freely give.

— Matthew 10:8b

The Omaha steakhouse Gorat's has been the scene of at least one good time for almost every Omahan for three-quarters of a century. Its melt-in-the-mouth beef, kitschy décor and salt-of-the-earth waitresses make it "the" place to take out of town guests who want that Omaha steakhouse experience.

One unforgettable night at Gorat's, some Omahans proved that our international reputation for being "Nebraska Nice" is absolutely true.

It was many years ago. I was working as a reporter for the local newspaper, and my Beloved was a junior captain of industry. Between our two paychecks, we were doing OK. In fact, we had just purchased a house and were fixing it up. And we were starting our family. I was, as they used to say, "in the family way."

Bigtime! I mean, literally bigtime. I was nearly 11 months pregnant. My nicknames included "Pregopotamus" and "Hugette." My belly would come into a room several minutes before the rest of me. I could balance a glass of water on the shelf of that big belly. For party entertainment, people would poke my swollen lower legs and lay bets on how long it took for the dent to disappear.

See, my legs and feet had swollen up like Macy's Parade balloons. I had outgrown my regular shoes, and had bought a pair at a dollar store just to tide me over. These cheap shoes had already started to split, and the foam was coming out. They looked terrible, but oh, well. It was June, and I had one lightweight maternity dress that I wore over and over in the heat and humidity. I was really sick of it. It was no doubt beginning to fray and I think there was a rip in the seam, but I didn't care because as soon as I had that baby, I WAS GOING TO BURN THAT SUCKER!!!!!

Well, one evening after both of us had worked late, we decided on the phone to meet at Gorat's for a special Friday night dinner. By the time we got there, the dining room was packed.

I don't remember people gasping as my big belly came into the room, followed gradually by the rest of me. But I probably was fairly conspicuous. The fraying dress and cheap shoes were out of place. I think we sat right in the middle of the restaurant, with my chair a good two feet from the table's edge because of my mountainous baby bump. I don't remember what we ordered or anything about the meal.

Except that, when we were finished and had the bill in front of us, we realized that WE DIDN'T HAVE ENOUGH MONEY ON US TO PAY THE CHECK!

I thought he would have his wallet with cash and credit cards, as he does 99.9999% of the time. He was thinking the same thing about me. I had my purse, with 102 important essentials for my day, but for some reason, not my billfold.

We had plenty of money to pay the check . . . just not right there, that night.

Whoops! With my belly, there was no way we could sneak out and stiff 'em on the check. We would never do that, anyway. But how to get out of this? My feet hurt too much for me to have to wash dishes. And my Beloved was 'way too proud to try to talk his way into a free meal.

So, we began a fervent campaign to find enough money.

Eureka! He found a few dollar bills folded in his pocket!

Voila! I found some more in the "emergency" compartment of my purse!

I ever-so-gingerly bent over to the side and picked up my briefcase from the floor. Ah ha! At the bottom, here was a bunch of change. I counted it all out. Hooray! We covered the dinner bill, with about 42 cents to spare for the tip. Not enough. But ohhh, wellll, We resolved to leave a huge tip next time we came in.

The waitress returned. We counted out our change and dollar bills for the total. It filled up her hands. She smiled at us with the most caring, beneficent smile I have ever seen. She left to deposit it with the cashier.

She came right back with seven or eight plastic sacks in her arms. She put them down on the table in front of me.

"The other diners wanted to give you their doggie bags. There's a lot of good steak here. You can eat for a week!"

HUNHHHH?

We looked around. All of the other diners were smiling and waving at us. Oh, no! They thought we were POOR because of my cheap get-up, and because we had been searching our pockets for change to pay the dinner bill. They thought we were STARVING! Little did they know that the poor, malnourished baby would be born a few days later weighing over 10 pounds. Amply nourished, if you ask me.

Out of concern for our well-being, as we were searching for coins to pay the bill, the waitress had gone around and begged everybody's doggie bag for us. It was an outpouring of "flash charity" for the poor Pregopotamus and the soon-to-be first-time father.

Isn't that sweet?

It would've been wrong to insist on returning all the bags. By then, how could they tell whose was whose? And we wanted that waitress to think that she had done a special good deed for two people in need. Which, in a way, she had. No wonder she misunderstood our financial state: one look at my $1 shoes, and anybody would think the wolf was at our door.

So we went along with the gag. We smiled and waved back at the diners, blowing them kisses, letting them pat my belly (people ALWAYS want to pat a Pregopotamus's belly!), and saying we might name the baby Gorat (thank goodness we thought better on that one!).

We left the restaurant with our arms heavy-laden with fantastic, corn-fed Nebraska beef, and our spirits uplifted, encouraged and reassured.

This is, indeed, a wonderful world into which to bring a child. People do care about one another – even strangers they'll never see again. If there's a way that people can find to help, they will. We're all "in a family way" together.

There are many other cities and many other restaurants around the world that have more "sizzle." But here in Omaha, at good old Gorat's, we've got "steak." †

53. The Sounds of Canvas Ripping

There is no fear in love;
but perfect love casteth out fear....

— I John 4:18a

If you want to perpetuate the human race, never, no never, let mothers tell their Terrible, Horrible, No Good, Very Bad labor stories to downy-cheeked teenage and young adult females.

Or we're toast. No one will ever want to have babies again. It's just too scary.

We definitely need censors in the childbirth classes. Somebody needs to muzzle those truth-tellers who laugh hysterically when the instructor insists those aren't labor "pains," but "contractions." They lie, I tell you! They lie!

In our class was a darling rural Iowa couple. They were dairy farmers. Jesse, the father-to-be, shared with the group that he had already participated in over 100 births. But they were all calves. For this first human birth, he drawled, "I hope I don't have to take a hold of this one and YANK."

The way he said "YANK" put a chill in my bones which resides there yet today. I pictured a massive set of cold steel forceps yanking my baby out by the head and reshaping it into a Hershey's kiss. Try getting a football helmet or a bridal veil on.

Turns out Jesse's wife went into premature labor in the middle of the night. But he wouldn't leave 'til he had milked all the dairy cows. First things first! They broke all speed records trying to get to the midtown Omaha hospital where our classes had been held. They had to divert to an inner-city hospital when the baby crowned on the Interstate while they were still in western Iowa.

The baby was born in the hospital parking lot. At least it wasn't in a dairy barn stall. Mother and baby were doing fine, Jesse reported to our instructor for the next week's class . . . and no, he didn't have to YANK . . . but the vicarious stress was mooooo-ving to the rest of us. (Note to self: line up pet sitters in advance to feed Buford and Budge, come what may.)

Another class member then shared that this was her second pregnancy, which was also miraculous, since the first labor was very difficult and went on for a lot of hours. But she wanted a second child and was hoping this labor wouldn't be as hard. She had had to push for over an hour, she said, and in the effort burst every blood vessel in her eyes and face. They were bright red, and her hair was matted and sticking straight up.

Her helpful, helpful husband said she looked like that scary MEDUSA from Greek mythology. You know, with the writhing snake hair and all.

(Note to self: pack hair care stuff in the overnight bag to make a nice, neat bun during labor, and put in some concealer and eyedrops as well. Second note: also pack a stun gun should my Beloved dare to say something like that.)

One by one, the other couples in our childbirth class had their babies. Each had a different story and each story had its scary elements that made me wince. Beads of sweat!

I quit my job as of the last of May, knowing that my insurance would cover my maternity costs through the following month. With a due date of June 7, I was set.

But the due date came and went. My preggie belly got larger and larger and LARGER. My ankles swelled up to redwood size. My getaway bag, complete with a whole array of hair-care products, had been sitting at the ready so long I literally had to dust it.

This was in the day when they didn't get too worried if you went past your due date. Mine might have been the case that changed their thinking on that.

Through the hot and humid days of June, as my preggie belly got bigger and bigger and BIGGER, I did all the rituals prescribed by the ancient scholars to bring on labor: cleaned the stove's drip pans, alphabetized the spice drawer, cleaned the fireplace andirons. My doctor winked, "You know, a due date is only an approximation." I hate doctors with a sense of humor. Don't you?

Finally, three weeks and a day past the projected partum date, it happened in the early morning hours. Labor had begun! By the time we got settled in the labor room at the hospital, my cervix was already dilated to four centimeters. At 10 centimeters, the baby would come. Yay! Forty percent done! We're going to make that insurance deadline, with a day to spare!

They had this big blackboard out in the hall with the last names of each laboring mother-to-be and data such as time of arrival and centimeters dilated. There were quite a few. I was the furthest dilated. My husband, ever the golfer, crowed, "Hey! You're the leader in the clubhouse!"

Even though the – ha! ha! – "contractions" did hurt, the pain was purposeful and positive. But then, though the pains continued, the progress stopped. I quit dilating. The other mothers eclipsed me.

We could hear other babies being born, one after the other. UNHHH! SLAP! WAHHH!!! UNHHH! SLAP! WAHHH!!!!! We heard drama: "I can't! I can't! I can't!" "Yes, you can, and you WILL!" UNHHH! SLAP! WAHHH!!! "Doctor, Doctor, is it a boy?" "No, it's a girl. Shall we throw her back?" UNHHH! SLAP! WAHHH!!!

The other labor rooms emptied out. Day fell into night. I remained the leader in the clubhouse only because all the other "players" were already celebrating in the 19th hole.

When was I going to get MY turn at UNHHH! SLAP! WAHHH?!?!

Seventeen hours after arrival, I heard Dad, who had been in the waiting room for hours, call down the hall: "Hurry up, Sus, Dairy Queen closes at 10:30!!!"

Oooh! The nerve!

Suddenly, my cervix responded with a mighty move of self-righteous indignation. It creaked open from 4 centimeters to 10 in mere seconds. Three pushes. Double-triple UNHHH! SLAP! WAHHH!!! And out popped our firstborn, Jordan Jennifer.

She weighed 10 pounds, 2 1/2 ounces. Go pick up a sack of potatoes at the grocery store and see for yourself how much that is.

My husband later helpfully explained that "she threw a big block being born," and unfortunately her clavicle had snapped. It was not uncommon with big babies. We just had to pin her little cuff to her opposite shoulder for a week or two and it would heal all by itself. SHE WAS NOT EVEN A SECOND OLD AND I'D ALREADY HURT HER!!! AAAIIIEEE!!!

My doctor, the funny one, supplied one of the only things I remember about the whole ordeal as he tended to the minor post-partum tear that had occurred because of that big birth. Did he compliment me on my stamina and fortitude? Say I did a great job delivering a beautiful baby? Nooooo. "Great news!" he remarked. "Your sphincter's intact!" Heyyy! There's one to needlepoint for the nursery and brag to Bridge Club!!!

My older brother, contemplating the feat of my fast-acting cervix accommodating that super-sized baby, helpfully supplied the caption I can never get out of my head: "The sounds of canvas ripping!!!"

My Beloved, eyes like saucers, added, "Wow! What a whopper!"

I looked terrible, like I had just been through a 17-hour ordeal.

I had pictured myself with a ribbon in my hair, smiling for the camera with lipstick on, cradling a precious little baby. Instead, I was Medusa with an intact sphincter but ripped canvas because of my new whopper, who had gotten her first broken bone at age one second.

That's the bad news.

The good news is, I never really got scared the whole time, because I knew my Savior was with me every step of the way. So it was all good. Shocking, but good.

Best of all, this new baby was perfect. And no one had to YANK! ✝

54. Dairy Queen

I have fed you with milk, and not with meat: for hitherto ye were not able to bear it, neither yet now are ye able.

— I Corinthians 3:2

I visited recently with three young mothers who are breastfeeding for the first time. It reminded me of my four reigns as Dairy Queen.

It started off badly. Our oldest was a 10-pounder, and hungry. But early on, breastfeeding is far from fast food. It takes time to get production going.

Plus, I was clueless. I had scrupulously avoided reading up on lactation throughout my pregnancy because I am the global procrastination champion. The "deadline" wasn't here yet because the hungry baby hadn't yet popped out. But dealing with a crying newborn whose tiny lips can't get any nourishment from big, beautiful breasts, even though they were obviously bursting with milk, was no time to – excuse the expression – cram.

I just couldn't get those dairies jump-started. I was pretty much saucer-eyed, confused and dismayed those several days before my dairies got up to speed. The baby cried and cried, and disrupted the nursery. I cried and cried, too.

It was so ironic. I had these huge, hot, hard dirigibles on my chest. But when I put the baby there, nothing happened. We were both newbies and inept. It didn't help that the nurses trying to coach me used odd terminology, like "latching on" – sounded like those big buckles on a steamer trunk – and "colostrum," or foremilk, which was kind of like eCreamery ice cream compared to the grocery store kind. I couldn't keep it all straight in either memory or mammary.

The nurses tried weird devices to train my dairies, including a plastic doughnut that reminded me of a petri dish out of the weird '60s movie *Barbarella*. They cast aspersions on the shape of my nipples, accusing them of being too flat.

Hey! Dissing my nipples? Them's fighting words! My breasts would – excuse the expression – stack up to anyone's in the country! And I would prove it!

Next morning, I told the nurses that I was determined to get 'r done. Two! Four! Six! Eight! Come on, dairies, let's lactate!

Time for one last tactic. They brought in The Mean Machine, a large, bedside electric breast pump. They hooked up my dairies to two suction cups with long, clear hoses, and turned it on. There was an ominous whirring noise – a build-up. To what?

Suddenly, the machinery started pulling my dairies what felt like three feet in front of me, rhythmically, first the left, then the right. It kind of hurt. I didn't know whether to say "Ow!" or "Moo!"

At least they pulled the curtains so no one would see this oddball taffy pull. But was I hallucinating, or was that "Seventy-Six Trombones" on the hospital Muzak?

Suddenly, I noticed white liquid filling the tubes and running along into a receptacle. It quickly built up to two or three ounces.

Brilliant scholar that I am, I asked, "What's that?!?"

No one answered. I realized that I was alone. Ah ha! That was the ticket! Having those nervous nurses around peering at my dairies, trying to induce them to lactate, was real inhibiting. But they hadn't left to give me privacy. Hoping to improve the decibel level at last, the instant they saw milk coming out of my dairies, they fled to the nursery to bring my squalling, starving baby to me.

We got latch! Ohhhh, yeahhhh! Latch! Finally, success! Once I knew it was really milk in there — nooooo! what'd you think? Jim Beam? — I could relax, get a (excuse the expression) grip, and go with the flow. Soon, I was a pro.

Oh, it was rough at times. You know how they say babies sleep 20 hours a day, and eat for four? Try the opposite.

I got up to speed fast on the soap operas; there's not much else to do while your baby's strapped to your feedbags almost all day. I memorized the all-night song lineup on the radio. I stomped my feet in time to the music to get over the pain of those first few seconds of latch, which are the most intense. It seemed like the radio played a lot of funny, relevant songs like, "Baby, Baby, Don't Get Hooked On Me."

After we'd been home for a while, with all that nursing, I got what my husband delicately termed "sore spouts." Remedy: udder balm. It's like stinky, medicinal Vaseline for mama cows and pigs. Smelly! But boy, did it work, along with tincture of benzoin, an old-fashioned remedy you'd paint on your "spouts," smelled like root beer and caused the baby to make the funniest faces.

I had to wear weird bras with what my husband called "bomb bay doors." I got wet spots on my blouses when the dairies "jumped the gun." That fall, I shocked a restroom full of Cornhusker football fans at an away game. They were staring at the breast pump in my hand. I told them it was my "sex toy." They gasped! They would have called the cops if I hadn't come back out of the stall with five ounces of the purest, most precious stuff in the world.

Because that's what it is.

Straight from heaven. Proof of heaven, actually.

Breastfeeding is so miraculously complex and intricately interactive, it proves God's purposeful, specific design and provision better than anything else you can name.

It gave my children perfectly-balanced nutrition, vitamins and priceless immunities. It helped me lose weight, save money, and bond with my four girls.

Most of all, it made me into a mother. There are other ways to get there, all good. But this was mine. Exactly as God planned.

I loved being a Dairy Queen. And for that, I thank God my King — with a "moo, moo" here, and an "ow, ow" there. †

55. Whoopsie Daisy

And Sarah said, God hath made me to laugh, so that all that hear will laugh with me.

— Genesis 21:6

The morning before I was supposed to have laser surgery to fix my nearsightedness, I woke up with a sty on my eye the size of Argentina. I had to cancel the long-awaited surgery.

I whined about it to a very dear friend. She lent me her couch for my temper tantrum. She hotpacked my eye and listened to me tell about the pre-op phone call from the eye doctor's office. It was weird:

Had I ever had heart disease? High blood pressure? Those were OK questions. But the next one: could I possibly be . . . PREGNANT?

I was nearly 45, with middle-aged spread and three teenage daughters. We laughed uproariously.

'Course, I told my friend, it's true that I hadn't had my monthly visitor for a while. But I was probably just starting the change of life.

And true, my chest had felt like watermelons encased in the skins of grapes lately. But I must've just pulled some muscles, power-walking.

She trained those X-ray eyes on me.

"Susan! Go get a pregnancy test."

Hunhhh?

Nawwww.

HUNHHH???

NAWWW!!!

"Humor me," she said.

AWWW . . . OK.

I snuck to a store off the beaten track, in sunglasses, flipping up the collar of my trenchcoat, skulking in a circuitous route to the "female aisle." Naturally, the biggest blabbermouth in town was lurking there, antennae erect. She'd think the pregnancy test was for one of our teenage daughters! That'd be all over town by dinnertime! I beat it to another part of the store before she saw me.

When the coast was clear, I bought the test, went home and set it up, smirking at how silly my friend would feel, when what to my wondering eyes should appear but a miniature "X" in the "positive" position.

"AAAIIIEEE!" is echoing to this day down the Missouri River Valley.

I ran up to my room. I flopped to the floor in the place where I pray when I pray big.

You know the "Magnificat" in Luke 1:46-55, where Mary responds to news of her unexpected motherhood with beauty, acceptance and grace? THAT was her. THIS was me:

"Oh, God," I sobbed, "You're all-powerful. I'm not. You're all-knowing. I'm not.

"But I'm PREGNANT!" I shouted, shaking my fist skyward, "and YOU'RE NOT!"

I belched fires of anger. How could You do this to me? You're messing everything up! I've got these teenagers about launched! Now this! There goes my freedom! My snooze time! My relaxing lunches out with girlfriends!

I'm back to 2 o'clock feedings! Sneezed peas! Stinky diapers! And eww! Maternity clothes again! Trying to read the itty bitty instructions on medicines with bifocals? Diapers and baby vitamin on the same grocery list as Maalox and prunes?

I started to laugh.

I'm so old, the baby and I will have matching walkers.

We'll both be gumming our food.

What are we going to name this one, Whoopsie Daisy Williams?

I laughed some more. I knew God was humoring me. He always does, to get me over the bumps of life.

I thought back. My husband had said that as our daughters were getting so busy with school and sports, doing stuff with their girlfriends, and starting to date, he felt sad to be moving out of the center of their lives. So I had prayed to God to help me be a blessing to him. I thought that meant I would make him some nice steaks and listen to his golf game blow-by-blow.

But God thinks big. A baby is a chance to be a hero to a child again, to influence the future in a way that only a good father can.

Ohhhh. I get it. This baby is no accident. This baby is for him. For us.

A wave of peace washed over me. No, I didn't have eye surgery. But I got my nearsightedness fixed after all.

Sniffling, but somewhat stabilized, I thought some fresh air would help. I staggered out to the mailbox. In it, I swear, was an invitation to join the American Association of Retired Persons.

Oh, God: You and Your perfect timing! That's one for Whoopsie's baby book.

No more tears. No more anger. Just joy.

New life, old mother, new twist on an old story:

Babies are a gift from God. And ohhh, baby! Does God have a sense of humor. †

56. The Changing Table

But we all, with open face beholding
as in a glass the glory of the Lord,
are changed into the same image from glory to glory,
even as by the Spirit of the Lord.

— 2 Corinthians 3:18

A few years ago, a little girl I didn't know came up to me at our neighborhood school. "My mommy went to college with you!" she said. She told her mother's maiden name. I remembered her, fondly.

"She said she didn't even recognize you when we moved here," the little girl continued.

"Oh, yes, well, I've changed," I replied.

"That's WHAT she SAID!" the little girl answered.

AAAIIIEEE!!! But here's the crazy thing: I'm glad I've changed. I needed to. Rearing children changes you. They grow you up, once and for all.

I used to care about all kinds of things in this world that didn't really matter, until that first week at home with our first baby. All I could see was her face and its every changing expression. All I cared about was getting "the dairies" to work, and feeding and cuddling this wondrous little being, night and day, experiencing those first few jolts of pure, fierce mother love, in it to the hilt.

Everything else melted away – the headlines, the weather and especially the laundry pile. Everything! Vanished! She was that captivating. It has been the same way with her three sisters, each in turn. I wouldn't be "me" without them now. And vice versa.

Children turn you inside out and "toast" your inner side, so that by the time they're grown up, you're "done."

That's because while they are growing up, you are, too.

You and your children grow and change, together. There's no going back. Who would want to?

When they get an owie and you hug them, it doesn't take long to realize that two arms are encircling you and hugging you back, making you feel better because you've been able to make that child feel better. Motherhood: the original two-fer.

Once you know what that's like, you're changed forever. You're no longer self-contained. Your heart has multiplied. Your eyes see on new levels.

Their hurts are your hurts. Their laughter is your favorite thing. Their tears cut you to the quick. Your dreams have them in starring roles. If you're lucky, you'll adopt their simple, innocent faith, the one you used to have. They help you remember: "Jethuth loveth me, thith I know. . . ." It's all you really need to know.

You see yourself, and their father, and the people of generations past, right there in those chubby, new faces. It makes you love all your relatives all the more. It's as if a drawstring of love pulls you all in, snug and tight. Completed. Connected.

And changed.

I finally figured it out: this is how God feels about each of us. Only more so. The funny thing is, He never changes . . . and we should. We become more like Him, through rearing children. Mainly, we grow in love. You don't think you could ever love your child one bit more, and then the next day dawns . . . and you do.

A few years ago, there was someone very special who was going to become a mother for the first time. My niece, Theresa, was going to make me a great-aunt. I was going to get to act dotty, pinch those soft little chubby cheeks, and marvel, jowls swinging, "My, how you've grown," while they roll their eyes but secretly love it.

I was going to get to watch Theresa grow and change, the way I did, and discover the profound, private and enduring joys that only mothers know.

I was honored to give her something very special, to mark the moment:

A changing table. Our changing table. That's where I stood while a lot of the changing was going on, in more ways than one. Now she could, too.

It was for morning greetings and evening partings. Lots of diapers, lots of giggling. "Itsy Bitsy Spider." Nuzzling. Deep conversations. Silly jokes. Lots of kissing of the bottoms of little feet. Tender, lingering caresses of baby skin, certainly the most beautiful feeling in the world.

Standing at that table over the years with our four daughters, I did a lot of changing, hopefully for the better.

Oh, the changing table has a few miles on it, some dings and some dents . . . like me. But it has held up: sturdy, strong and ready for action. Just as we mothers are supposed to be. Just as I knew Theresa would be. I looked forward to the privilege of journeying alongside her, and watching her change as I continue to, too.

Theresa, I told her, you can't begin to guess what the resident of that "hump" you've got going on in front is going to do to your heart and your life. You will never, ever be the same.

You are blessed beyond measure.

God is giving you such a gift.

Welcome to the sisterhood of motherhood. You're going to be great at it. You're going to love it.

And my, oh my. How you are going to change. †

57. Thunder and Birdsong

Now therefore hearken unto me, O ye children: for blessed are they that keep my ways.

— Proverbs 8:32

We took our kids to golf camp in the Ozarks so they could fine-tune their swings and yuk it up with teenage golfing mutants from all over the country. While they were at camp, we stayed at an adjoining golf condo for a mini-vacation.

My husband got to play lots of golf, far from his office in downtown Stressopolis.

When they weren't at camp, the girls joined him swimming and boating and jet-skiing and Putt-Putting.

But I was stuck in the condo . . . with our new baby.

She was just a few weeks old, pretty fussy, and up a lot at night. Not exactly a prescription for a restful, carefree vacation.

The best thing for her was to stay quiet in the condo, take little naps in the porta-crib, and be a baby.

That meant I had to stay quiet in the condo, take little naps on the pull-out couch, and be a mommy.

This baby was a big surprise. We referred to her as "Whoopsie Daisy." We were in our mid-40s. Our other kids were 17, 15, and 12. Was a late-in-life baby inconvenient? Physically, emotionally and financially challenging?

Let's put it this way: Whistler's Mother wasn't smiling, and neither was Whoopsie's.

Some people "go postal." I was "going post-partum."

By the third day of the trip, I was cranky, lonely, sleep-deprived, and feeling terribly sorry for myself. Hmmmph! While everybody ELSE was out PLAYING, here I was . . . STUCK, STUCK, STUCK.

At mid-morning, I finally went out to sit on the deck of our rented room and give the baby her bottle. Big whoop. Sitting outside: the big thrill of the day.

I hunched over like Poor Pitiful Pearl, tears trickling down my nose and chin, as she sucked. My life sucked, too. I couldn't even breast-feed this one; she had been born several weeks prematurely, I had gotten toxemia and nearly died in childbirth, and my "dairies" didn't kick in very well in the aftermath of all that stress. I felt like a real loser as a mother, settling for bottle-feeding. WAH!

A year ago, it would have been ME out on that golf course, ME racing that jet-ski, ME hiking up that mountain trail, ME power-shopping, ME having a peaceful dinner out. . . .

ME! ME! ME! ME! ME! That's not singing. That's whining.

I just felt so left out, so pointless, so worthless. It was a horrible pity party.

How many other new mothers, throughout time, have had these thoughts? I bet most of us.

Suddenly, I looked down, and noticed a teentsy hand gripping my finger, pressing that bottle closer. The baby's tiny fingertips were white, she was so intense about getting that feeding.

I stared at her, as if for the first time.

A little light dawned. Heyyyyyyy! At least I count with HER! At least I matter to HER!!!

And what a cutie! I'd almost forgotten! I had been too busy pouting to enjoy her baby face, lately.

Then I looked up, and realized that my view onto the golf course was breathtaking. It was the first fairway, emerald green and tree-lined, majestic, like a golf poster. Wow! Why hadn't I noticed before?

It was one of those mysteriously wonderful Ozark mornings: still and foggy, then a rumble of thunder over those hills. RUMBLE RUMBLE RUMBLE BOOM CRACK BOOM. All still again. Then thunder. Then silence. Then a blaze of sunshine and a riot of birdsong:

"Tweeeeet! Zip diddle zip diddle tweeeeet! Doodly doodly doodly doodly tweeeeet!"

I love birdsong. Birds are quite the musicians! You so rarely get a chance to just sit and listen.

Suddenly, across the fairway walked a graceful doe with adorable twin fawns. They grazed. The babies frolicked. They stayed for a long time. I drank in the sight with my eyes. Then the deer mom turned, whisked her tail, and the little ones tumbled obediently after her into the woods.

How about that? She's handling motherhood just fine. She looks like she's having fun. And SHE'S got TWO! Why can't I suck it up and do my job with just the one baby? What a wuss I've been!

I love deer. I always wear a gold deer necklace that my dad gave me years ago. It reminds me of our Minnesota wilderness cabin, and him. It's precious. Like this time in my life . . . like this new baby.

People say thunder is the voice of God. But I say birdsong is, too. The captivating sounds were literally music to my heart.

How did it happen, on such a beautiful summer morning, that no golfers came by during this whole time? Because it was a private show, that's why.

Whoa! God!?! Can He do that?!?! Of course He can, and He did. Power and authority mixed with the music and beauty of nature are guaranteed to get your attention, every time.

I knew He was speaking to me in that moment. God wants us to be blessed, and His favorite way to do it is to give new life.

Susan, Susan, He was saying, don't miss this blessing. Don't miss the big picture. Don't mistake motherhood as a burden. It's a joy! Embrace it! Enjoy it! I sent it for YOU! A precious little baby is the very, very best I have to give. You can be a good mother and still have fun, just like that doe. I'll be with you, every step of the way.

I lowered my head. Tears plopped down onto the baby: tears of humility and acceptance.

If I HADN'T been "stuck" there that morning, I would never have seen and heard the beauty and the majesty and the message of the thunder and birdsong . . . and the God-sent model of another mother gracefully doing her job.

And that's worth more than just a little tweet: zip diddle zip diddle RUMBLE CRACK BOOM! †

58. Fogie Mama

But unto every one of us is given grace according to the measure of the gift of Christ.

— Ephesians 4:7

I really blew my chance in the hospital.

Word had spread about the really, really old lady who had given birth in Room 702. Volunteers bringing bouquets would look me over, look away, roll their eyes and smirk.

The other new mothers, considerably younger than I was, eyeballed me in horror as we all staggered stiffly down the halls in our bathrobes: "Oh, my God! Do I look that bad?"

Nurses were peeking their heads into my room to get a load of this phenomenon, this fossil in her mid-40s who'd delivered a baby in between Lawrence Welk re-runs and bingo.

But darn. I blew my chance. What I should have done was coax my grandmother, who was 93 at the time, to get into the bed and pretend to be me. She could've put her teeth in a glass right next to the baby's first binky on the hospital bedside table. Shock the pants off those rubber-neckers! Ha! It would have been fun.

And fun is what this late-in-life, bonus baby has been. For whatever the reason, we got a double dose of grace to handle this situation, and turn it to gold.

It's fun for the rest of our family, too. Having a new grand-baby has knocked off at least 10 years from the apparent ages of the two grandmothers. They love it and they flaunt it. They're both Numero Uno in their bridge groups again, bringing cute baby pictures while everybody else comes empty-handed because their grandchildren are in those terrible spiked hair and nose ring years, or long since grown and gone.

It's been fun for my husband. When he comes in the door, he flings his briefcase one way, his trenchcoat the other, grabs the baby, who by this time is hysterical with anticipation, and decades literally drain off his face as he transforms from a graying captain of industry, a dignified company president, into . . . Captain DaDa!

"Maddy FWYYYYYYYY!"

"Oh, Bouncy Girl! Bouncy! Bouncy, bouncy, bounce! Boocha, boocha, booch!"

"Biggie go wump-pum! Googlia, googlia, goo."

What if his employees witnessed this? Then again, he probably sounds the same in those technical engineering meetings. The thing is, with younger dads, they can blame youthful exuberance when they act weird. Old ones are just weird.

Then there's me. During pregnancy, I enjoyed alternating between the two prestige parking places at the grocery store: the one for "Expectant Mothers" and the one for "Senior Citizens." Now I enjoy having Grecian Formula and baby formula in the same cart, just for the irony of it all.

But there's a down side. I can't tell if it's a hot flash or embarrassment when my cheeks fire up after someone exclaims, "Oh! Look at your cute GRANDbaby!"

Then there's the fear of accidentally poisoning Maddy when she wakes up crying with teething pain at 3 a.m. and I have to slide my glasses down my nose and zoom in on the medicine bottle with one aging naked eyeball to try to stabilize my fogie focal point enough to read the proper dosage.

Then there's the tendinitis from carrying that heavy carseat with my aging right arm . . . the humiliation of sneezing in front of unsuspecting grownups and saying, inexplicably, "Muh-SKOOZ me!" . . . the worry that I'm skimping on my attention for our three teens.

The new baby is their joy, too. But they're jealous of her. They say she'll have a lot more freedom as a teenager than they have now.

They say it'll be easy for her to blow off her curfew and sneak out of the house late at night, since their dad and I will be so old by then, we'll be COMATOSE by 9:30 p.m. every night.

Shhh. Nobody tell 'em. WE ALREADY ARE! †

59. The Bess Mom

But covet earnestly the best gifts:
and yet shew I unto you a more excellent way.

— I Cor. 12:31

We had three daughters in under five years. Life was fun, but the pace was sometimes overwhelming.

You could say I avoided the perfectionism trap. The floor of our home was like a giant Seven-Layer Salad. You know the recipe: old newspapers, diapers, toys, IRS forms, banana peels, grocery receipts, last week's laundry. Repeat. Why spend precious moments away from the bambinos doing something boring, like cleaning house?

Lots of dinners were mac 'n' cheese out of a box. Mount Laundry had sprung up near our washing machine, with Ivory Snow at the pinnacle. The older girls amused themselves by broad-jumping off the coffee table while I nursed the baby sister.

The worst came the day I vacuumed (did, TOO, vacuum, on occasion) and found a yellow plastic ducky barrette. With no pockets, I clipped it into my hair, intending to put it away in the girls' room first chance I got. Hours passed. The doorbell rang. It was a meter reader. I'll never forget his eyes darting up to that yellow plastic ducky barrette in my hair, his face contorting in pity, his feet edging away. "I'll come back some other time, when your caretaker returns and your straitjacket's back on."

Well! Whoever said motherhood was DIGNIFIED?

Our eldest was in kindergarten that spring. She got invited to a birthday party. I knew the "other mother" was the Martha Stewart type. But nothing prepared me for the elaborate spectacle of that kiddie birthday party:

- Crepe paper, signs and balloons on the front porch.
- Mother-daughter matching outfits.
- Pony rides.
- Carnival games.
- A clown making balloon animals.
- Cupcakes that were a miniature of the Disneyland castle.
- An ice sculpture of Barney.

I can't even remember the rest. But it was fantastic! Amazing! Incredible!

I felt totally out-mom'ed.

When I brought Jordan home, she went upstairs. I pushed several layers of glop off a chair, slumped, and started complaining to my Beloved about what a lousy housekeeper, cook and entertainer I was, compared to Mrs. Perfect.

I told him about the decorations. I told him how Jordan bubbled all the way home. I told him I felt completely, totally helpless and inadequate. There is no way I could ever pull off such a complicated social event without a three-alarm fire or breaking one or more limbs! I can't even find my GLASSES, most days!

As a mother, I was a LOSER! Wah, wah, wah, wah, wah!

He belched, scratched, and went back to his paper. Men! They just don't get it about SuperMom vs. MomLite. I sulked.

A little while later, here came Little Lady Jordan. She was holding out a piece of scrap paper. She must have overheard my rant. She gave the note to me with a shy smile.

In crooked letters, laboriously crafted by 5-year-old fingers, in purple crayon, it read:

How R U dog?

U R the BESS mom.

Love, JORDAN

I'm a "dog," huh? But I'm the "BESS" mother?

What more could you want?

From that moment on, I was "dog" just fine, thank you! Martha Stewart, eat your heart out. †

60. Disappoint Mints

Why art thou cast down, O my soul?
and why art thou disquieted within me?
Hope thou in God: for I shall yet praise him,
who is the health of my countenance, and my God.

— Psalm 42:11

She's an executive culinary expediter and nutritional accounting executive. OK, she's a grocery-store cashier. My favorite. She's always smiling, always pleasant. So I get in her line, even if there's a wait. It's worth it.

She's easy-going and tactful. She doesn't even blink as she rings up my purchases, usually in a logical order such as this: Weight Watchers yogurt, Oreos, celery, ice cream, zero calorie salad dressing, and a sack of Snickers (hey! at least they're mini's).

We solve the problems of the day: the Middle East, the price of gas, post-nasal drip. Along the way, we've figured out that we're both mothers. But that hasn't really been our common ground. Until the other day.

I was musing that she probably was a really cool mom. So I decided to ask her a personal question:

"What was the best Mother's Day present you ever got?"

That was easy! You could just tell. Her face just glowed.

The story poured out:

"Well, last year, I had been having some really bad problems with my son. I mean, I can't even tell you how bad it got."

I figured he must be in his 20s. Based on her tone, I imagined some serious stuff had gone down, like drugs or arguments or problems with law enforcement.

She continued, "There were days where I really didn't know how it was going to turn out – whether I'd ever see him again. I was just so worried, and driving myself crazy wondering what I could have done differently – how I could have kept him from getting in to some of the things that were causing such problems."

I could tell it had been an enormous burden. Evidently she had sunk into rebukes, accusations, bitterness and disappointment, all the things we mothers try so hard to avoid, but sometimes, just can't.

Her sunny smile popped back, bigger than ever. "Then it was Mother's Day, and he showed up at my door at 8:30 in the morning. Eight thirty! When was the last time I had seen the whites of his eyes before noon? But there he was. And not only that – he was dressed for church."

For church! This "bad boy" was going to take his mama to church!

There was hope for him yet.

Turns out he had planned a whole day with her. He took her to church and out to brunch, and then over to a historic house that she had always wanted to tour. She loved the pampering.

And then out of his pocket came a letter – a long, hand-written, heartfelt letter of love.

What did it say?

She looked up, as if picturing the words; I could tell she'd read that letter a lot. "Oh, just that he was sorry for all the trouble that he had put me through, but that he loved me very much, and he was so glad that I never gave up on him, and he would try to do better and make me proud of him."

Our eyes locked across the fudge sauce and sack of carrots.

Twenty years had fallen off her face. She was beaming. My heart soared. I beamed back.

"It was just so refreshing," she said. "I can go a long time on that."

That's God. That's how He encourages us. Another refreshing mint from the Breath of Life, at just the right time. He knows when things are starting to go sour. He steps in, makes something happen, and makes everything right again.

One day, I'm going to be rung up by the Great Cashier. I'll recognize Him, all right. I've already seen His smile. I saw it on the face of a mom I know from the grocery store — a mom who loves her child enough to never, ever give up. ✝

61. Daddy Games

***And He answered and said unto them,
Have ye not read,
that He which made them at the beginning
made them male and female. . . .***

— Matthew 19:4

There's velvet in my voice when I put Maddy to sleep. We cuddle "doing story." She gets cozy as I softly drop to my knees bedside. We say a prayer. I tell her a quiet story about her Care Bears or a brave little mouse or kitten.

Then I sing her a song. It has HAD to be "Silent Night" since Christmas, but for variety, I've been trying those same lyrics to the melodies of "Tiptoe Through the Tulips" and "April Showers." She protests, smiling sleepily. I sing "Silent Night" the right way.

We hug. I tuck her in, kissing her rosebud mouth and soft cheeks. "Sleep tight! Don't let the bedbugs bite!" She watches me silently back out of the room, blowing kisses. Her eyelids flutter closed. She says drowsily, "Tell Daddy to come."

I congratulate myself on my skillful mothering, TLC and well-honed nurturance, pass my husband in the hall coming as I am going, and then . . . BOOM!!!!!

IT'S TIME FOR DADDY GAMES!!!!!

SHOUTS AND SHRIEKS ERUPT FROM THE ONCE-TRANQUIL BEDROOM!!!!!

EYES THAT WERE DROWSY ARE BUGGED WIDE OPEN AGAIN!

ADRENALIN LEVELS ARE SKY-HIGH!

A HEART RATE THAT WAS AT REST IS NOW IN ABJECT HYSTERIA!!!!!

They do Tickle Monster.

They do Ceiling Walk.

They do The Up Game.

They do Pillow Ride.

They do Shoulder Ride.

They do Get Your Neck.

They do Timber!!!!!

They do Head in Bed, making Maddy into a cross between a human tamale and a giggling mini-mummy.

They do Hot Dog, with lots of imaginary ketchup and mustard.

They do Tick Tock, featuring an upside-down, laughing human pendulum.

So much for my soothing bedtime routine. It takes another half-hour to settle her back down after Daddy Games.

The female brain just does not conceive games like these. I whined about it to friends the other night, hoping for sympathy about this rowdy wildhair mayhem instigator I married.

But noooooo. The OTHER husbands ALSO do Daddy Games, and the other WIVES don't get it, either.

They do Bucky the Wild Squirrel.

They do Horsie the Buckin' Bronco.

They do Coldy Roldy, tickling the lower legs 'til the kid gets the shivers.

They do The Chase Game.

They do Boogie Man.

They do Monster.

They do Couch Potato: the dad pretends to be asleep, kids walk by in faux nonchalance, and he JUMPS UP AND GRABS THEM!!!

They do Roly Poly: giant group hug off the bed onto the floor.

They do Tornado: everybody gets under the covers and starts whipping them around and up and down until the kids are hyperventilating, the sheets are ripped, or both.

It takes THEM a while to get THEIR kids settled back down, too.

We wives don't understand this. But you know what? *Vive le difference*. This is how it's supposed to be. This is legitimate "diversity." Men show love to children differently than women do. Both are creative. Both are good.

That's why I don't buy same-sex "marriage." It rips off kids. They miss out on half of what they need to be whole persons. Their parenting is all male style, or all female style. We all know 50% is an F. Halfway is never good enough. Kids in those settings are getting distortions of the other sex role, or at best a pale imitation.

There are a lot of legal, political, financial and religious reasons to oppose same-sex households, too. But what cinches it for me is that they deny kids what they need most — the complementarity of having BOTH a mom and a dad — distinctly different, and delightfully so. There's a reason we were made this way. An important reason.

How do you understand what a mountain is, if you've never seen a valley?

What good is music all in the treble clef, but no bass?

How do you define sweet if you've never tasted sour?

Maleness and femininity are both good, just different. And you can't fully experience one without the other.

That precious, consistent complementarity of true marriage — one man, one woman — is the only way to model how to be and how to love, to make the next generation of people complete.

Preserving marriage really is a matter of life and death, for our society.

Let's don't play games with it. OK?

Or Bucky the Wild Squirrel will make you a Head in Bed and Get Your Neck! †

62. In a Hockey Dad's Pocket

Only take heed to thyself, and keep thy soul diligently, lest thou forget the things which thine eyes have seen, and lest they depart from thy heart all the days of thy life: but teach them thy sons, and thy sons' sons.

— Deuteronomy 4:9

It figures that our daughter would have a friend she loves like a brother, and he plays hockey. If she'd had a brother, he would doubtlessly have been a hockey jock. Eden's dad played hockey. We follow the local college and semipro teams. One nephew is so hockey-crazy, he has collected enough broken hockey sticks to make a chair.

Eden's friend Chris attended all of her big softball games and was her No. 1 fan. Naturally, she has tried to go to his big hockey matches in return. They're both seniors, winding down their high-school careers.

Well, last week was the last regular-season game of his elite traveling team. Eden couldn't go, so I represented her, joining the sizeable cheering section for Chris' last game.

When Chris skates, he's smooth and fluid and oh! so fast. His eyes scan the ice constantly. He knows where that puck is every instant.

He's in such good control that he never gets in fights, rarely has penalties called on him, and rarely has to check anyone or make physical contact. His movements are surgically precise and analytical.

The team was playing their rivals from a nearby city, ahead 3-1 late in the game.

They were going to win. But Chris hadn't scored. He'd had a long series of "almosts." Meanwhile, his mother's hilarious commentary was "almost" making my sides split:

"Oh, nutsola!"

"Get out of the way, you big boob!"

"Cheese and rice! Cheese . . . and . . . rice!" (That, she explained, was how her father cussed when he didn't want to take the Lord's name in vain.)

We did the wave, we stomped our feet, we took group pictures. But time was running out.

Suddenly, players bunched up around the front of the goal. Here came Chris, rocketing by with the puck. He seemed to be levitating horizontally.

He was patiently seeking a way to the net in between all those legs, skates and sticks. He juked a couple of times, faking the goalie out of position.

Then as he rocketed by the net's far corner, he artfully popped it in . . . like a sugar cube into His Lordship's cup of tea.

GOAL!!!!!!!!

Everybody went crazy. It was unassisted, and they were playing short-handed, which made it all the sweeter.

The game ended soon thereafter. We fans in Chris' entourage greeted his dad, who spends every game across the ice, helping the team with stats and so forth.

Gentle and sweet just like his son, he was beaming as he walked up to us with his hand in his pocket.

"You know," he said, "I got the puck that Chris shot as his first goal as a PeeWee, many years ago. I got the winning shot Chris made, a rocket from the blue line, against a real hotshot goalie in a big tournament in Minnesota."

He took his hand out of his pocket. "And now, I've got a third puck: his last goal from his last game."

He showed us. We squealed "Ahhhh!" and got tingles.

His eyes glittered. Tears? Or just the reflection from the ice that had framed so much of his life for all these years of youth hockey?

For all the hours you gave . . . for all the money you paid . . . for all the miles you drove . . . for all the slumps you helped him through . . . for all the moves you taught him . . . for all the joy you shared in teaching this great sport to your son, and in the process teaching both of you so much more . . .

. . . this puck's for you, Dad.

He and Chris' mom exchanged a glance that said it all.

He slipped the puck back in his pocket, gave his pocket a pat, and turned to go find his son. †

63. The Daddy Drawer

As ye know how we exhorted and comforted and charged every one of you, as a father doth his children.

— I Thessalonians 2:11

My father had a very special ballpoint pen in the top drawer of his bureau. That drawer is where he kept all his treasures. The pen was one of his World War II souvenirs. We kids knew it was there and peeked at it from time to time. It was right there next to the hideous woodworking projects and fat clay ashtrays we'd given him over the years, amid old tie clips and golf balls and forgotten receipts and Rotary pins.

It had a pretty lady in a black one-piece swimming suit. All well and good. But the trick was, if you held it upside down, the black ink all drained away and there she was . . .

NAKED!!!

In a totally G-rated way, of course. My dad was a totally G-rated guy and the pen was just kitschy, for fun.

But why did he keep it in his top drawer for all those decades?

I think I know why. It was a reminder of the time in his life when he left his father and mother, and went out on his own into the cold, cruel world. He was only 17, and skipped his senior year to lie about his age and get in on the tail end of the war. Well into his life, when he stood there at his dresser and saw that pen, I bet he remembered his great war adventure, and how he went away as a boy and came back as a man.

He survived, all on his own. He flourished. He gained his independence.

And he did a terrific job of making sure that his four children all knew how to do it, too.

So even though that crazy pen looked like something silly, it was actually a symbol of significance to a loving father who did his job, and did it well.

What better place for such a thing, than in your top drawer where you can give yourself a daily reminder of what really counts?

We mothers have coffee klatsches and how-to books, long telephone calls and thoughtful walks with faithful friends, to help us shape our mothering. That's how we focus on what we should be doing in that most important endeavor of our lives, rearing our children.

But fathers? I think they all have a special drawer.

At least, every dad I've ever known has one – a drawer where they keep special "stuff" for reasons known only to them.

They keep reminders of the best things about their own fathers. They keep souvenirs of special times. They keep mementoes of their glory days. All these things, as individual as each man's fathering style, help them rev themselves up to be the best husbands, fathers and men they possibly can.

One of my friends has a special compass in his top drawer that his father gave him long ago. He has only rarely used it, but he always knew he had it if he needed it. He could always know where he was, and where he wanted to go. That gift is a symbol of good fathering if there ever was one.

Another has World War II medals earned by both his parents, his father as a doctor and his mother with the Red Cross.

Although he doesn't say so, I think they symbolize an ethic of service in his family. Based on the cool things his two children are now doing for others, following his example, I see the living proof.

What's so fascinating is how these men don't store away this otherwise pretty useless stuff, out of sight, out of mind. They keep it where they've likely to see it all the time even though you'd think it was just wasting space.

Now, every week, I lug a basket of clean undershirts, socks and, as one of our daughters dubbed them, "box panties," from the chaotic room we lovingly call "Mount Laundry" up to my husband's closet. They go in his second, third and bottom drawers.

One day, not long ago, I peeked into his sacred top drawer. Yep! It's a Daddy Drawer! Here's what he had:

- Seven hockey pucks – a man always needs hockey pucks at the ready;
- A golf prize from a 1990 tournament;
- Not one but two zip-lock bags of golf tees and ballmarks;
- A Bushnell Yardage Pro;
- A green rubber squeezy egg to make your hands stronger for golf;
- Four old watches;
- Three plastic home-movie reels from his childhood, although the exact location of the projector has been rather iffy for years;
- A lint brush;
- Three 25-cent stamps;
- Three little black film canisters, each containing the baby teeth of one of our older three daughters, evidence of the many years of faithful duty he put in as the resident Tooth Fairy Par Excellence.

Most striking of all, there was a thick pile of old Father's Day cards from years past. These were hand-drawn by our girls with cartoons of us boating and skiing and playing golf and softball and going to Nebraska football games and jumping on the trampoline he finally let them have.

All of these were things they never would have done if not for him.

The cards expressed precious sentiments in their careful little girls' handwriting: "To the Best Dad in the World" and "Thank you soooo much for dedicating your time and love to us."

My throat tightened.

Ohhhhhhh.

Now I see why he keeps these crazy things in his top drawer, where he can see them every day if he wants to. Or needs to.

I held the cards in my hands, bowed my head, and gave thanks for having a father for my children who put so much stock into his parenting portfolio.

A salute today to him, and to daddies everywhere.

Hey, you guys: thank you for caring so much, and doing so much for your children and the world they populate. Know what, guys? You're top drawer. †

64. Father of the Bride

So then he that giveth her in marriage doeth well. . . .

— I Corinthians 7:38a

It was exactly one week after our eldest daughter's wedding. We were attending the youngest daughter's piano recital. Maddy, 9, sat with back erect, frowning in concentration, dwarfed by the piano, long ponytail swinging. She was banging out the cartoon theme from "Looney Tunes" as her recital piece.

I glanced over to see that her father was sitting there next to me BLUBBERING!!!!

Geez! She wasn't playing THAT badly!

Geez! What's to cry about in "Looney Tunes"?!?

Then I finally got it: his paternal emotional dam had finally given way, after his first-born daughter's wedding the weekend before.

I had been wondering how he got through the whole wedding weekend without tears. Those strong fatherly feelings were on display, all right. Everybody could tell he was joyous and proud. But he kept a stiff upper lip, and was a genial host and joyous FOB (that's Father of the Bride, to the uninitiated).

But ahhh! Delayed reaction! Seeing the littlest Williams daughter at the recital going through that familiar rite of childhood reminded the FOB of his first little daughter at the same age so many years ago. They looked alike, swinging ponytail and all. Suddenly, all his joy in witnessing the little puckered baby face we named Jordan transform into a magnificent, beautiful, radiant bride just came spilling out.

So the FOB just had to SOB, a week later, during "Looney Tunes."

The other parents shot him puzzled glances, thinking, "My, what a SENSITIVE dad!!!"

They got that right.

And oh, how this father – like most fathers – maybe ALL fathers – wanted so much to get his job right. He wanted to be the kind of a father that his child deserved, so when he married her off, he could feel that he had done everything he possibly could for her. I'd say he did all that, bigtime.

It all happened so fast. The whole thing is surreal. Married?!? So soon?!? Wasn't she JUST born? Wasn't that just yesterday that she came barreling down the hill on her Big Wheel, beaming at her new-found independence? Wasn't it just last night that she got her first bra, and drove a car for the first time?

It all happened in a snap. The years whizzed by. All the countless things my Beloved did for her, as the responsible and loving father he was, are mostly forgotten.

But each and every act of paternal love and duty are very much still there, invested wisely and permanently in her heart. Reflected in her eyes.

So when he turned her over to her bridegroom on her wedding day, he was turning over a big part of himself, too. And he was elated to do it.

I wish everybody would focus on fathers like these – the quiet ones, the good ones, the ones who go by the rules, and are man enough to say "no" enough.

I mean the responsible ones, who keep their promises, stay out of trouble, who go without so the kids can have, who teach them everything they know and a lot of things they didn't think they knew, who are humble enough to learn from their kids, who listen, who rassle with them, and make funny faces with them, and go out in the back yard and play catch even though they're drained, go to their parent-teacher conferences and sit on those little bitty chairs looking ridiculous, and stretch out on the cool grass on a summer's evening with them and just talk and dream and look up at the stars.

Dads like these are the ones who point us where we should be looking: up. A good dad is the God model every child deserves.

We need to do everything we can to encourage fathers like these, and develop as many of them as we can. The more like the Father in heaven that our earthly dads can be, the easier it is for each of us to understand who our real Father is.

A good father gives us a picture of how our Heavenly Father has been there with each of us, through our journeys from childhood and beyond, every step of the way.

It's beyond a blessing to be the maternal partner in a pairing like this. It's better than anything. Anything! I'm the gabby one in the family, but I can't even begin to explain how it felt to see my two beloveds, father and daughter, dancing together at the wedding reception. It was a night of transformation for them both, knowing that she is who she is largely because of him, and vice versa. They kind of grew each other up. Now they move on. And I couldn't love either of them any more.

Luckily, my mother found this poem, clipped from a magazine decades ago around the time we four kids were getting married. It sums things up perfectly:

WEDDING WORDS

By Maureen Cannon

The day is hers and, oh, it is
As clearly jubilantly his!
But, Dear, it's ours as well in ways
She cannot know, not yet. The phrase
"Who gives this woman?" echoes deep
In both our hearts. We do – who keep
Some special part of her as one
By one her steps match his, this son
We've – gladly – gained.
The day is his,
The day is hers. What marriage is
Is ours, though. We have lived it and
We know, as they will. Take my hand
And hold it, Dear, with joy, with pride. . . .
I love you, Father of the Bride. ✝

65. Love and Lallersloos

For I will pour water upon him that is thirsty,
and floods upon the dry ground:
I will pour my spirit upon thy seed,
and my blessing upon thine offspring.

— Isaiah 44:3

Every Fourth of July when I was young, a whole bunch of families we knew would get together and have a big breakfast. The moms had all been in the same sorority in college. Everybody looked forward to a get-together once a year. It was really fun to interact with the other kids, and kind of compare and contrast our families as we all moved through life together. Hmm, maybe my old man is all right, despite wearing white tube socks and black shoes with his Bermuda shorts. Sigh!

The host family would scrub the garage, set up card tables, and put up streamers and flags. They'd mow the lawn within an inch of its life. They'd dig out the croquet set, put up the volleyball net, set out the sprinklers to be run through, and brace themselves.

The rest of us would haul in eggs and bacon, sausage and pancake batter, orange juice and extra lawn chairs, plus cap pistols, water weenies, squirt guns, Slip 'n' Slides and those colored pellets you'd throw on the driveway and they'd go "pop."

I loved the Fourth of July. I loved the bright colors and bold flags, the music and the banners. Most of all, I loved the spirit of joy and friendship among all ages.

How blessed we are to live in freedom, able to do the important things in life, like maintaining longtime friendships in peace and happiness, and blessing our friends and their families just by getting to know them and enjoy their company.

I loved it at those breakfasts when my parents' friends would know what school I went to and what sports I did. They would ask me about my freckles, chuck my chubby double chin and say, "My, how you've grown since last year."

I soaked it up like a Nebraska cornfield in a July thunderstorm. Kids need encouragement so much, to be known and appreciated.

My dad had his own way of doing that. He made home movies of all of us kids at those breakfasts. He called himself "Cecil B. deMille," with typical goofiness pronouncing it "CEE-cil."

He would line us up by height. I was always next to a skinny boy in a great, big baseball cap.

We would have to walk across the yard, turn, and stand in line for Dad to pan the camera. It made us all feel special. One kid, a big ham, would always throw a croquet mallet in his path first, and then "accidentally" trip on it to get more "screen time." He grew up to be an attorney, naturally.

One year, I was in my powder-blue eyeglasses and wide headband, making funny faces for the camera, when the skinny boy in the great, big baseball cap next to me frowned, turned his head the other way, and blew out air:

"Girls! Bleah!"

Another year, a little, bitty girl with curly red hair confronted my father, pointed to her feet and demanded, "Lookit my laller-sloos."

"Lallersloos"?

He looked down. Her brand-new sneakers were bright yellow. And was she proud of them!

Ohhh. "Yellow shoes." He loved words, and loved making up new ones, too.

Dad made her grin by raving about her "lallersloos," and featuring them on that year's movie.

For years later, at those breakfasts, he would rave about her "lallersloos." She loved it.

When she became a bride, Mom found the perfect wedding gift: a figurine with a little girl . . . in yellow shoes. Dad wrote a tender note to go with it. It made everybody cry.

Dad has been dead for some years now. But the grown-up Lallersloos still talks about those Fourth of July breakfasts, the figurine and Dad's note. He connected with her, decades ago, and it blesses her still.

We watch those old movies from time to time, knowing we were loved, seeing each other grow up all over again.

Look! There's me! I remember that pixie haircut! I was cute! What happened?

Look! There's Lallersloos!

There are my brothers, with big grins and happenin' buzz cuts.

There's Lisa, who grew up to be such a beauty.

There's my sister, ever stylish in red, white and blue.

There's that skinny boy in the great, big baseball cap.

By the way, I've been married to him for over 35 years now.

Told you those Fourth of July breakfasts served up something special. †

66. Tyler's Firetrucks

Blessed are the pure in heart:
for they shall see God.

— Matthew 5:8

Our good friends were living in Sheridan, Wyo., with their three small sons. One day, adorable Tyler, age 2, starting walking at a slant and falling over, like a drunken sailor.

"Tyler! What are you doing, Buddy?" his mother laughed, thinking he was being silly. "Why do you keep losing your balance?"

"I can't stand up, Mom," was his reply.

Her smile vanished. He wasn't kidding. She took him to the doctor. At first they thought he'd been poisoned, but the tox screens were clear.

Then the nightmare began in earnest: the CAT scan showed there was a mass on Tyler's brainstem.

A mass!

A tumor!

Oh, my God!

But that's all they knew without more extensive medical testing.

It was 3 p.m. on the day before the Christmas weekend, and most of the clinic staff had already left. The nearest facility with an MRI machine and spinal tap capability was in a hospital in Billings, Mont. It was two hours away. And they closed in two hours.

It was a total blur: she sped home and packed up bottles for Tyler's baby brother, just three weeks old. She slogged his baby clothes from the washing machine into a plastic sack because there was no time to dry them. She tried to keep the baby happy, and Tyler and his older brother somewhat calm. Her husband picked them up with screeching tires, and they literally set sail for Billings. At the time, Montana didn't have a speed limit. You can imagine.

All the way, every moment of that drive, they prayed. They got on their cell phones and called all their loved ones, everyone they knew, and got them to pray, too. It may be the only time in recorded history in which "prayers per minute" exceeded "miles per hour."

They got there in time. Tyler went through all the tests, and spent the night in the hospital, where everybody fell in love with him. What's not to love about a 2-year-old boy who was crazy about firetrucks, and chattered about his firetruck toys, and the firetrucks he'd crawled all over during his visit to the fire station, and how his grown-up cousin had let him try on his firefighter gear, and it was really, really cool.

Finally, Tyler dozed off, innocent and rosy-cheeked. They slept the fitful sleep of parents out of their minds with worry.

Next morning, the neurologist came in with the test results. He had a funny look on his face.

"Whatever was there, is gone," he told the parents. "To be honest, I don't know what happened. Maybe he had a virus."

Joy erupted all over everybody's faces. They had no doubt it was the power of prayer.

They hugged their boys, and kissed them, and gathered up their stuff and started for home. They got the seats wet in the car with their tears. A couple of days later, they had the happiest Christmas ever, and then some.

Now fast-forward a few months. They were having supper. The older brother had some spiritual questions, as children do. He asked what heaven looks like, and whether his mom or dad had ever seen God, or talked to Him.

Before they could answer, little Tyler piped up from his high chair:

"I've seen God! I talked to Him, too!"

His parents exchanged glances, and smiled.

"Remember when I lost my balance and the doctors put me in that long machine?"

Hunh? They listened intently.

"I talked to Him then. He was really nice, Mom. He told me it was going to be OK and I should go on and ride some more firetrucks."

Firetrucks?

Ride some more. . . .

They were so flabbergasted, they forgot to ask what God looked like. But that's OK: they'll see Him soon enough.

And something tells me He'll have Tyler next to Him, and they'll be riding in the biggest, shiniest firetruck you ever saw. I mean, it'll be really, really cool. †

67. Is God Furry?

***And this is the will of him that sent me,
that every one which seeth the Son, and believeth on him,
may have everlasting life: and I will raise him up at the last day.***

— John 6:40

I'm grateful for books and movies about Jesus Christ that are true to the Biblical accounts. They help clear up a whole lot of misconceptions that can really help parents in their quest to rear spiritually mature and well-informed children.

No, He wasn't a liar. No, He wasn't a lunatic. No, He isn't dead.

And no, He isn't furry. At least, I don't think so.

The thing is, you can't begin to anticipate all the questions that kids are going to ask. No way can you specifically prepare. So you just have to be ready to improvise.

See, I was driving with Maddy, age 3. Moms know all about Distraction 101. You have to keep up the sparkling conversation and fascinating improv while in the car, or bored and hemmed-in kids will chew through their carseat straps, bounce around like a pop bottle rocket in a barrel, and watusi on your head.

So, at a red light, I was showing her how, when you turn the knob on the car radio 'way down, you can't hear the music any-more — but it's still there. Turn the knob back around, and you can hear it again. Voila!

Suddenly, I realized it was a "teachable moment" that I could use to explain God to her a little better.

"Hey, Maddy," I said, "God is like music on the radio. We can't see Him. We can't always hear Him or understand Him. Sometimes we tune Him out on purpose, like turning this knob on the car radio. But He's still there. He'll never go away. He wants us to know Him and listen to Him. And when you trust Him, you can be sure that He's alive, right here in your heart."

SCORE! At least, I thought so.

But noooooo. You NEVER score on a 3-year-old. She came back with a barrage of questions:

"What does God look like?"

"Does He have a wife?"

"Is God furry?"

I opened my mouth to try to answer, but then turned to my time-tested strategy:

"I don't know. Ask your Dad."

How do you explain God to a small child? In the same way, how do you explain water or air? I'd die without them, just as I'd die without my personal relationship with Jesus Christ – my all-day, every-day, death-defying, awe-inspiring, ever-humbling, ever-encouraging walk with the living God.

But how do you explain Jesus to somebody who doesn't know Him and doesn't have that big of a vocabulary? Who doesn't have enough life experience to make distinctions and understand spiritual truths correctly? It's hard enough for the old graybeards, after all. How do you accurately explain to a young child the same religious concepts that have stumped philosophers for centuries?

You have to find "teachable moments." And brace yourself for what could happen.

Yes, another "moment" came just a while later.

We were worshipping with our oldest daughter in the beautiful, historic University Presbyterian Church in Chapel Hill,

N.C. She was a student at the University of North Carolina there, and we were visiting. We took Maddy up to the balcony to try to minimize the impact of her mushroom cloud of sometimes loud, disruptive behavior.

A young couple brought a beautiful baby boy up front to be baptized. Golden sunlight pierced through the tall windows onto his tiny face. The light made his long christening gown glow bright white.

In the hush, Maddy asked loudly, so that, of course, with the great acoustics in that historic sanctuary, the whole congregation could hear:

"IS THAT JESUS?!?!?!?"

A titter ran throughout the pews. The shoulders of the other worshippers shook with mirth. I got sweet tears in my eyes and hugged her close.

"No, Maddy. But He's right here. We can't see Him. But we can feel him. He's here."

He's not "fur" at all. He's very near. As near as the bottom of your heart. †

68. The Stranger and Maggie McGuire

Be not forgetful to entertain strangers: for thereby some have entertained angels unawares.

— Hebrews 13:2

Maggie McGuire was a little cherub with red-gold curls, a Cupid's-bow mouth and dimpled knees. The dear daughter of dear friends, we've watched her grow up into a beautiful young lady, one you'd really like to know.

But if it weren't for a total stranger, Maggie wouldn't be here today.

When she was eight months old, her mother and grandmother took her shopping and stopped for dinner at a busy restaurant. Maggie had only a few teeth, so her mother cut up a few pieces of soft banana on her highchair tray.

The two women ate their dinners and visited. All of a sudden, they looked at the baby. Her face was paralyzed, her eyes staring straight ahead.

They knew right away that she was choking. A piece of banana was stuck in her throat, blocking her air. Her mother rose from the table and firmly patted Maggie's back, hoping to help it down. But Maggie's face just went from pink to white.

She couldn't take a breath.

"Everybody pray!" her mother shouted. "My baby's choking!"

The restaurant fell silent. Then people gathered. Several tried to help.

"Stick your finger down her throat and try to get it."

"Does anybody know the Heimlich maneuver?"

"Hold her upside down and shake her."

"Rub her throat."

"Call an ambulance!"

Nothing worked. Maggie's face was turning blue.

A waitress came forward. She said with confidence, "Let me see if I can do it." She tried a few techniques, but failed, too. The waitress saw the fear and panic on the young mother's face. She kept her hands on the baby and said loudly:

"In Jesus' name, let it dislodge."

Out of the crowd came a man. He grabbed Maggie, laid her face-down over his forearm, and struck her between the shoulder blades with the heel of his hand. The banana piece shot out.

In the confusion and commotion, the crowd closed around Maggie and her mother. The baby gasped, wailed, and gasped again, changing colors back to normal.

Meanwhile, the stranger disappeared.

Who was he? An angel? An answer to prayer? Jesus Christ Himself?

Naw. Just a guy. Maggie's grandfather tracked him down through restaurant patrons who recognized him as a fellow who worked in the neighborhood and walked by every day at about that time. The family offered him a reward. He wouldn't hear of it. "I was just happy to have been able to help," he said.

Maggie's dad wrote us a letter about the incident: "I just believe very strongly that we're here on Earth for a purpose, and God acts directly in our lives if we ask Him to."

I cried, and then cried again because of something that came in the same day's mail. A catalog fell open to some Irish prints based on old Gaelic poems. This one caught my eye:

RUNE OF HOSPITALITY

I saw a stranger yestreen:
I put food in the eating place;
Drink in the drinking place;
Music in the listening place;
And in the blessed name of the Triune
He blessed myself and my house,
My cattle and my dear ones.
And the lark sang in her song:
Often, often, often
Goes the Christ in the stranger's guise;
Often, often, often
Goes the Christ in the stranger's guise.

I ordered one. It's framed by our door.

Ever since, I've felt differently about strangers. I used to be a little afraid of them, kind of ignore them, avoid them, not let them get close. But now I look them in the eye, and smile, and wonder:

Maybe this is the one who saved our darling Maggie McGuire. †

69. Jordan's Wish

And He said unto them, Take heed,
and beware of covetousness:
for a man's life consisteth
not in the abundance of the things which he possesseth.

— Luke 12:15

It was the climax of our daughter's birthday party, many years ago. Jordan stood before the candles on her cake, about to make her wish.

Martha Stewart, I ain't. But I do try to eke out decent birthdays for my children. So we had kiddie games. We had party favors and streamers. We had hot dogs and chips. We had a cake, pink and sweet, just like the birthday girl. And we had a colorful pile of presents, waiting for her to open.

But first, she had to make her birthday wish and blow out the candles.

Jordan studied the candles.

I studied Jordan.

She's one of those children who never asks for anything, so you want to give her everything, from the moon on down. She's thoughtful and kind, sensitive and sweet.

The light from the candles shone in her eyes as she paused delicately before the cake. Her friends hushed. She seemed to be taking longer than usual, thinking of her wish.

As her mother, brimming with love, I tried to see into her heart:

What did she REALLY want for her birthday? What goodie? What gizmo? What cool "thing"?

What was she thinking about? What was she wishing for?

Was it a new bike? Darn! We should have gotten her a bike.

Was it a game she saw on TV? Sports equipment? Some computer program? Something one of her friends has? A fancy outfit? Art stuff? Electronics?

Too late. She shut her eyes, and blew, "WWWWWHH-HHH!"

Everybody had cake. She opened presents. Her guests went home on sugar highs with chocolate milk moustaches. In the excitement, I forgot to ask whether Jordan got her wish in the colorful pile of presents that day.

Weeks passed.

Then one afternoon, we were at our family's summer cabin on a northern Minnesota lake. It was one of those "Seven Dwarfs" rainy days: you feel sleepy, dopey and grumpy, cooped up, reading books, playing cards and pinging off the walls.

When we were kids, my father used to try to give us hope on days like that by saying, "Aw, it's just a 'clearing-up shower.'"

Well, it had been "clearing up" all day. It was nearly dinnertime, and I was stressed out. When Mom's cabin fever gets rough, the kids get going. Outside with you! It was still a little rainy, but clearing up after all.

I packed them off in old yellow rainjackets and hats, with orange life preservers, looking like three rubber ducklings. They waddled down through the mist and patches of sunlight to the lakeshore.

After a few minutes, Jordan's urgent shout yanked me out of the kitchen:

"MOM! MOM! COME QUICK!!!"

I sucked air. Had somebody fallen in? Was there a bear? I raced down the slippery granite rocks to the water's edge.

Jordan stood, barefoot in the shallows, pointing joyously to the east as her sisters looked on. Pine trees blocked my view. I waded in next to her so I could see what they saw.

It was a huge double rainbow. Awesome. Glowing. Resplendent. Radiant colors set off by dark purple clouds. Wow!

"On my birthday, I wished that I could see a rainbow," Jordan whispered. "Look! Here it is. And it's a DOUBLE!"

She squeezed my hand, radiant with joy. We held hands, stood and looked, for a good, long time. I was humbled, and properly so. And here I thought she'd wanted some toy or other "thing." This is so much better! I bowed my head. I had been so wrong about her birthday wish, so shallow, so short-sighted.

She was so young, but she already knew that "things" aren't what you wish for, once a year, when you have a chance to wish big.

Moms should know better.

Luckily for Jordan, she has a Father in heaven Who heard her silent wish, when I didn't, and granted it, when I never could have.

He put a piece of His heart in the sky, big and bold, just for her.

Jordan got her wish . . . and it was a DOUBLE. †

70. The Great One-Up

Dearly beloved, avenge not yourselves,
but rather give place unto wrath:
for it is written,
Vengeance is mine; I will repay, saith the Lord.

— Romans 12:19

A year and a half in advance, some parents bought tickets to take their preteen daughter and two of her "besties" to a concert in another city. A worldwide sensation "boy band" was coming. This was to be the girl's birthday extravaganza. It was a hot ticket, but they managed to get seats on the floor, in Row 24. The daughter was in heaven.

The parents reserved a room at a swank downtown hotel blocks away from the venue, and arranged to take the girls to a nearby amusement park the day after the concert, too. A dream weekend! The two "besties" enthusiastically accepted. But remember: this was a year and a half before the fact.

Drama intervened. Near the date of the concert, the inevitable middle school "stuff" happened. All of a sudden, the daughter was forced into a different lunch group. She was "out." Her two "friends" were still "in." Then the two "besties" did a "worstie":

They backed out on the weekend trip.

They told the daughter they didn't want to go with her, were too sophisticated for such babyish material, and "nobody" liked that singing group any more.

The "cut" hurt, because the daughter really loved those girls and felt totally rejected. It was a dark couple of weeks for the ordinarily bright and happy girl.

Her parents coached her about giving grace and forgiveness to others, no matter what. They encouraged her to view this as a challenge in her Christian character development, that will help her in the long run. You can get past this without hurting them back! No matter what, show love.

She gulped, dried her tears, and moved on. By then, the concert was a sellout. Tickets on the floor were selling for $700 apiece. The parents had paid $75, which, for them, was still huge.

They urged her to let them sell the tickets for enough money to have the back-to-school wardrobe of her dreams plus take TEN friends to the next concert!

No way. She was determined to go and have fun despite the drama.

Just a few days before the concert, she finally felt up to asking two other girlfriends to come with her. They were thrilled to bits. All seemed well.

Until 10:15 the night before.

One of the original invitees text-messaged one of the new invitees to brag that SHE had been invited first, and therefore the other two girls were low-status afterthoughts. The ex-bestie revealed that she and the other original invitee were going to the concert after all, only not with the girl who had originally invited them. They were traveling together, exclusively. They were going to stay at the same hotel, but they had better tickets. Apparently, they had convinced their parents to cough up the $700 a seat.

AAAIIIEEE!!! It was news to the other two girls that they had been "second choice." The treachery! It was devastating.

Tears were spurting out of the daughter's eyes on a night that they should have been sparkling with anticipation. The girls were text-messaging each other, rapid-fire. The birthday girl just sobbed.

Again, her parents coached her: you have to forgive them. Jesus commands it, for your own good. Be able to say, honestly, that you are happy that they will get to see the concert after all. Make peace. Let it go.

It took a lot of tears and some sighs, some drinks of water and some pats on the back, but the daughter forgave, put it behind her, felt better and went to bed. Next morning, she awoke refreshed and rarin' to go.

She and her two friends got to the concert, and found their 24th row seats on the floor of the massive auditorium. There was a small center platform amid the chairs on the floor. The girls were in the back row of the front floor section. They feared that maybe their seats weren't so great. Everybody stands up at a concert. They might not be able to see.

Then they spotted the two ex-besties in their $700 seats. They were up off the floor, several rows up, on the side, much nearer the front. They were still about 100 feet away from the stage, and their view would be only from the side. But they would have a bird's-eye view.

Sigh. Let it go. Again.

The concert began. It was fantastic! The daughter and her friends jumped and raised their hands high in the air, singing along, alternately crying, beaming and screaming. They couldn't see that well, but that was OK. It was exciting just to be there.

All of a sudden, the five singers clambered onto a platform onstage. Slowly, it raised up and moved over the crowd, toward them.

Several feet overhead, the platform glided over the front section of floor seats until it was right over the girls' heads. The singers were practically close enough to touch. The birthday girl was sure that her favorite singer looked her right in the eye and waved. She sobbed for joy. It was the same for her two guests.

The platform sank down to the center stage area right behind them. They turned around. All of a sudden, they weren't in the back row any more. They were, as Bob Uecker used to say in those funny old Miller Lite ads:

IN THE FRONT ROOOOOOOOOW!!!!!!!

They could see every nuance of the singers' expressions, every detail of every dance move. They were practically in reach of high-fiving them. Ecstasy! After a few minutes, the platform lifted the singers back up and over to the stage to finish the show. The thousands in the audience envied those girls who got to be so close to the singers.

It was the greatest one-up of all time in the preteen set.

The daughter had not retaliated or gossiped. She had not yelled at the two double-crossers. She had not sought vengeance. Yet, miraculously, she had one-upped them anyway – extravagantly so, and right before their eyes.

In the cacophony, amid the laser lights, confetti cannons and bolts of sudden flame, a still, small Voice spoke to her heart:

When you forgive, I bless you.

Wow! That made her feel even more special! It was the biggest Star of the universe speaking, directly to her. You know what? He puts on a HECK of a show.

With grace and mercy, forgiveness and love, come what may, He puts on the concert of your dreams using the melody of your life in rhythm with His. ✝

71. How're We Gonna DOOOOOOO This?

(A)ll things are possible to them that believeth.

— Mark 9:23

So what's it like to be a fogie couple in your mid-40s, unexpectedly expecting a baby?

His eyes were all bugged out. And my hair stood on end, like Kramer on "Seinfeld."

How're we gonna DOOOOOOO this?

"I'll be 62 years old when this one graduates from high school," mathhead Dave proclaimed seconds after I broke the news. "This sets back my retirement plan 7.3 years."

We had three daughters, 16, 15 and 12. I gave away all the baby stuff eons ago.

How're we gonna DOOOOOOO this?

He said by the time this one is done eating baby food, our teeth will be shot and WE are going to need it.

I said they won't know at the hospital whether to send me to Maternity or Geriatrics.

How're we gonna DOOOOOOO this?

He said his knees were too far gone to teach this new kid any sports.

I said my brain was too far gone to focus on which Tele-Tubby was which, much less to survive listening to another 14,000 hours of songs like "It's a Small World After All."

How're we gonna DOOOOOOO this?

One minute, we were fat, dumb, happy middle-agers with a degree of our sanity back. We were babysitter-free. You could walk through our house and not gouge your bare feet on scattered Legos or squish them on unidentified globs of goo.

The next minute, I was a fogie preggie. Everybody at my doctor's office snickered as I sat in the waiting room next to other pregnant women 20 years my junior.

Meanwhile, the expectant fogie father went ballistic: "We're too old for this! 'Way too old! We have UNDERWEAR older than most children in this world!"

How're we gonna DOOOOOOO this?

Our friends didn't help. Kyle, king of tact, cupped his hands at about his waistline, and warned me, "Watch out you don't smother the poor little thing when you nurse!"

Jeannie, my combination neighbor and unpaid psychiatrist, advised, "You'd better start sneaking 'Grecian Formula' into Dave's hair now, or everybody will think he's the grandpa."

Our family didn't help. My mom, far from feeling compassion for me or whipping out her well-worn worry beads, burst out laughing: "That's the funniest thing I ever heard!"

My sister asked, "HOW did this HAPPEN?" (She's a blonde. Can you tell?)

Our own kids? No help. The oldest will wear a bag over her head for the rest of her life.

No. 2 insisted on a fancy name for the new baby that might be great for Scrabble, but I was too old to remember how to spell it for the birth certificate: "Schuyler Mackenzie."

No. 3, who at 12 is still a kid and not real sympathetic, grinned from ear to ear and put a hand on my belly. "So, like, Mom," she goes, you know, and stuff. "When are you gonna get, like, you know . . . MONDO?!?"

We thought it was going to be awful, terrible, constricting, exhausting . . . everybody was making fun of us . . . we would never live this down . . . our lives were ruined. . . .

And then one day, a darling infant seat was left on our porch anonymously.

People started saying, "This baby will keep you young and be the light of your lives."

Women in their 40s and 50s admitted how jealous they were of me. Baby Lust!

They said, "Older parents have children who are independent, pick up after themselves, cook, clean and do laundry . . . because their parents are too tired to do it FOR them."

We finally started the see the bright side of things. Maybe this wasn't such a horrible thing to happen. We love babies, after all! We were good parents! As long as we didn't mix up the Diaperene with the Dentucreme, maybe we could make it.

The one-liner from a friend that really convinced me that we could handle old-age parenthood put it this way:

"The last pancakes are always the best of the batch!"

Our loved ones and friends made it sound do-able. Fun, even.

That's how we're gonna doooooo this: by believing that we can. †

72. Four of a Kind

A word fitly spoken is like
apples of gold in pictures of silver.

— Proverbs 25:11

We didn't care if our first child was a boy or a girl. We prepared a gender-neutral nursery and layette with kelly green carpet. We chose the name "Jordan," an equal opportunity name, m/f.

Jordan Jennifer it was. And what a girl! We've never looked back.

Same thing with No. 2. Again we picked out a unisex name — Neely — which can be short for Cornelius or Cornelia, and is a grandma's maiden name to boot. We chose the shorter form because it really wasn't safe to name a baby "Corny" in the Cornhusker State, regardless of whether it was a girl or boy.

Neely Susan it was. Again, what a girl! Again, we've never looked back.

Then came the third pregnancy. My husband honestly didn't care what flavor we got. But I was boy-crazy this time, dreaming about frogs in pockets and stuff.

But Eden Elizabeth it was.

Today, I can't imagine life without "Beamer." She was nicknamed for the way she smiles like a sunbeam. She is the prettiest, funniest, smartest, most creative, most athletic, most talented girl in the world.

However, in the hospital, it's embarrassing, but I cried myself to sleep. I admit it. I wanted a boy, for my Beloved. Ohhhhh, wellllllll.

At about 5 a.m., I was awakened by the phlebotomist. He needed a post-partum blood sample. He was tall, dark and handsome in a white lab coat, mysterious in the dim light.

He greeted me, quietly and gently. "How are you feeling?"

He didn't mean emotionally. But I answered, anyway: "I'm sad. I just had our third daughter, but I had really wanted a son."

He was silent as he finished his work, then looked at me kindly and said:

"Well, I think we just have to play the hand we're dealt."

And he was gone.

Wow! What words of wisdom! It was a message from heaven. How could I have ignored the fact that all three of these precious daughters had perfect health? He gave me some much-needed perspective.

I cheered up. Thanks. I needed that.

Now fast-forward 12 years. We had just found out we were going to have a fourth child. Surprise! But we were thrilled. Naturally, I thought it would be poetic justice if this "tail-ender" were a boy. At long last!

But on the way to break the news to my husband, I saw a car with this license plate:

"JST A GRL."

Hmm. "Just" a girl, eh? As in, it's a "gift" baby late in life, but it's not as good a gift as a baby boy would be? Some feminist I was!

Tests confirmed it: a fourth daughter.

OK. Play the hand you're dealt. That's the line I took.

I figured we could find a set of cute boy quadruplets named Williams for our four girls to marry in a quadruple-ring ceremony. Then I'd only have to get El Magnifico into a tux for one wedding. And this way, we could keep the Williams name going, as if there aren't already five million Williamses running around anyway.

Since my husband's dad would now have six granddaughters and no grandsons, I'd just have to be his spin doctor and teach him to say he is not "0 for 6," but "6 for 6."

We'd put up a sign at our house: "Welcome to Estrogen Acres."

We'll post a "Beware of Raging Female Hormones" sign at the front door.

We'll boast that the streetlights around our house are lit by estrogen gas.

So yes, I joked. But secretly, I was still sad. I still wished we were having a boy.

Then we went out to Las Vegas, of all places, considering our G-rated Christian family. My husband was giving a business speech on "planning," of all topics, considering we had a "midlife surprise" baby on the way. He got in a lot of cheap jokes about his qualifications to speak about "planning." Hardy har har.

Anyway, while waddling through the casino to get to a restaurant, trying to look inconspicuous with my jumbo belly out front and my shoes in my hand since my feet had swollen to the size of the nearby Hoover Dam, I waddled past a poker table.

Someone was just then exclaiming:

"Four of a kind? Wow! That's a *GOOD HAND*!"

I stopped in mid-waddle.

Four of a kind . . . in my case, four daughters.

I grinned.

Wow! I've been dealt a *GOOD HAND*!

Wise words, spoken with the perfect timing of the Master Dealer.

Thanks. I needed that. Thank You for four beautiful, precious, wonderful daughters. I will do my best with them. Truly, Lord: I'm playing this hand with everything I've got. †

73. The Chicken Dance

Love never fails....

— I Corinthians 13:8a

My good friend Linda has a son, Adam, who has autism. When he was younger, every day of her life was like a hurricane. There were humoungus meltdowns, screaming fits and lots of dull stares. I admire how she held it together for Adam and for her two older sons, who are healthy, and her patient husband, a former college football standout who is strong in every way in life.

With grace and a heaping helping of humor, Linda threw herself in to her life as the mother of a severely handicapped child.

She also helps other families with autistic children, both informally as she meets them, and formally, in her work to establish that thimerosol, a preservative that contains mercury in children's vaccinations, is what has caused the explosion in autism over the past few years.

Recent statistics show a 700 percent increase in the nation, and a 10,275 percent increase in Nebraska alone. Estimated overall cost, long-term: $2 trillion.

In Linda's case, the thimerosol was in the shot she received to compensate for her Rh negative blood during pregnancy. She didn't have that shot with her older two boys. Her research indicates that more than 80 percent of autistic children are boys; possibly, estrogen in little girls protects them from developing it.

There may be a link between these substances in immunizations, and other conditions that are on the increase, ranging from ADHD to Alzheimer's.

Linda appears on radio talk shows. She writes op-eds. She speaks. She lobbies. She shares information with anyone who'll listen.

When I first met Adam, I began to see why she is so passionate about supporting families affected by autism. Adam, you see, was perched on top of their refrigerator in a Batman costume. He wouldn't look at me. He wouldn't come down. I reached my arms out to him; he didn't acknowledge me. He was speaking rapidly and staring off into space.

Here's how Linda describes what it's like to mother an autistic child:

"When you hold them, they arch their back. They wriggle to get themselves out of your arms. When you talk to them, they avert their eyes.

"When he gets on a schoolbus, I'm waving like crazy, but he doesn't wave back.

"If somebody is angry, and coming toward them with hands on hips and a big frown, they don't get it. They neither use gestures nor 'read' gestures."

For many years, they could barely go anywhere as a family because of Adam's erratic behavior. She has had to do countless hours of special therapies with Adam, and has had respite helpers for a few hours a week to give her a break.

Her husband and two older sons "have given up everything," she said. The two older sons "don't like having friends over because of Adam. They're terribly embarrassed by his actions, but of course, they love him, so it's confusing. The stares when we go out and he tantrums. He gets in people's way. He stands too close. He doesn't know things other people know. He says exactly what's on his mind: 'Eww, your breath stinks.' It would almost be easier if he were terribly deformed."

Linda is lucky: half of autistic children don't speak, but Adam does. He'll even parrot back her "I love you" at bedtime, which thrills her.

But like most autistic children, he can be overly aggressive. Linda tells of driving 20 miles a day to take her older son to school, and all the way down the Interstate, Adam, who kept wriggling out of his carseat like a mini Houdini, was pummeling her and pounding her, throwing things at her, nearly making her crash.

"They're just aggressive and they don't know why," Linda said. "He'll throw anything: videotapes, shoes, glasses. . . . If anything is ever different from the way he left it, like his chair pulled away from the table, he goes nuts."

So there's a lot of pain. But sometimes, life with Adam is funny and sweet, too. Once, at the neighborhood swimming pool, Adam was running on the wet pavement. The lifeguard shouted at him: "Adam! Don't run!"

Silence. Everyone stared. Everyone knew Adam was a special-needs child. How would he react? Adam then shouted back a line from the movie, "Heavyweights":

"YOU ARE A STUPID LOSER WITH A USELESS, SKINNY WEINER!"

Whaaaaat? At first, everyone at the pool was shocked. Then, they all laughed. The lifeguard still gets teased about it. Adam was the hero of the day.

That same day, Linda next went to the grocery store, and was telling the clerk the story, when she noticed that the man behind her in line was sobbing.

His anguish came spilling out. "My little boy was just diagnosed as autistic and I don't know what to do," he said.

Still stressed out from Adam's outburst, Linda could have just said, "That's too bad," and rushed off, avoiding the effort and the pain. But oh, no. Not Linda.

She took him aside, put her arm around him, comforted him, and started writing down names, phone numbers and websites.

"I felt for him because I know what a devastating blow that is," she said. "These kids will never be able to live on their own. It's only a dream that they can do something. You really get tested because it just keeps going – problem after problem after problem."

How about her faith? How has this affected that?

Tears roll. "It makes you think," Linda said. "Why, God? Why give this to me? I want to have fun in my life. How can You let these kids suffer in such pain?"

She said that, although she plans to "have words" with the Lord when she gets to heaven, she understands why she's in the place she is.

"It's because I'll fight," she said.

Most parents of autistic children are so beat down, they aren't politically active or able to do research. So Linda's there, doing it for them. She knows what they're going through, and what they need.

"I just keep thinking that someday, Adam will be in a better place and we'll all understand."

Until then, she'll keep on going. Keep fighting. Keep making life as enjoyable as she can. For example, Adam loves it when she gives him "puppy and kitty licks," even in public. So she does.

"Every day, he does this thing to me," she says, demonstrating a one-two punch that Adam thrusts in her direction. "It means I'd better get my chicken act ready."

The two of them run outside, and Linda staggers around the yard flapping her arms and dancing around . . . like a chicken. Bawk! Bawk! Bawk!

The neighbors are used to it. They know they're witnessing the most powerful force in the universe, even in the form of a silly-looking chicken dance.

It's love. Mother love. Fearless, borderless, bottomless mother love.

Love in action, love under stress, love that never gives up, love that keeps going even when life isn't understood, love that is admirable, love that is inspiring. Love that never fails. †

74. Duodenum Desperado

And I heard a loud voice saying in heaven,
Now is come salvation, and strength,
and the kingdom of our God, and the power of his Christ:
for the accuser of our brethren is cast down,
which accused them before our God day and night.

— Revelation 12:10

We know this young couple who just had a scare with their precious baby boy. The mama laid him in the middle of their big bed on the main floor of their house one day, sound asleep, with pillows on either side. His crib was upstairs and she just wanted to tend to a few chores while he took a nap. He hadn't rolled over yet so she never dreamed there'd be a problem.

You guessed it: the little fellow woke up, rolled over for the first time, crossed over the pillow, and fell to the hardwood floor, conking his head.

Oh, the guilt! Oh, the self-torture! There's nothing more miserable than hurting the ones you love, and little ones most of all.

I'm happy to say that the young'un has just a hairline skull fracture, which the doctors believe will heal by itself faster than you can say "splitting headache." No long-term consequences, no brain damage, nothing like that in the least.

But in the aftermath, this neat young couple felt very sad, and were beating themselves up over the incident.

We've all been there, haven't we? Anybody who has ever taken care of kids has at least one story like that to tell. To young first-timers, us confident veterans must make it seem like NOTHING has EVER gone wrong on our watch.

AS IF!!!!!

It happens to everybody. But ironically, being overly cautious can make things even worse. I'm thinking of the time I had my sewing basket out in the living room, reattaching the stubby stuffed arm of Tony the Teddy Bear. His mistress, Jordan, not quite 2, "attended" the surgery at my side, while her baby sister, Neely, about five months old, lay on a blanket on the floor, cooing and content.

I had completed the "surgery" and put the sewing basket up high on a shelf, intending to put it away upstairs later, when my Beloved came home. His Laser Eyeballs of Eternal Vigilance immediately zeroed in on the sewing kit. "What's THAT doing down here, around the kids?" he accused.

"I had to repair Tony. I was very careful. Nothing sharp got anywhere near them," I protested.

Then a miracle happened: he got down on the floor and bent over Neely to change her diaper. (Just kidding; he is and was a great dad, and changed them all the time.)

But suddenly, he stiffened.

"THERE'S A NEEDLE IN HER THROAT!!!!!"

Whaaaaaa?

She was laying there, smiling and wriggling happily. How could there be a NEEDLE in her throat?!?

But he was frantic. "I SAW IT! I SAW THE GLINT OF A NEEDLE! WE'VE GOT TO RUSH HER TO THE EMERGENCY ROOM RIGHT AWAY!"

My guts immediately descended 14 stories below ground level. My baby! My darling! Was the needle shredding her internal organs? Had I killed her? Would she have to have a trache? A feeding tube? Would it pierce her windpipe? Would she spend the rest of her life in a full body cast, in traction, and it would be ALL MY FAULT?!?!?!?!

We quickly packed both children into the car and sped to the E.R. My Beloved, who is the prudent, careful type, withheld mean comments. But his frown was blacker than black, and I'm sure he was wondering why he hadn't given me a prenuptial I.Q. test or put a nanny cam on me all day.

The medical team shot into action and took x-rays. Please, God, let them come back negative. Ha ha! Just a false alarm! Go home, folks!

But noooooo. Here came the nurse, one of those officious, efficient types, with a frown on her face, holding out the x-rays. "Here it is, right in the duodenum," she spat out disdainfully, making me feel like an abject child abuser. "What time did this happen?"

Her cold, contemptuous tone of voice knifed my guts. Though they (my guts) were still deep below ground-level out of fear and shame, the rest of my body was now floating high above the E.R. in out-of-body shock and amazement.

This can't be happening!

Mentally, I paged through my memory banks trying to remember what the heck the duodenum was and where exactly it was located. How could they get the needle out of there? THIS WAS BAD!!! I imagined the needle poking holes in all her vital organs. Tears gushed from my eyes. My baby: the human sprinkler!!!

But the whole time, cradled in my guilt-ridden arms, Neely was cooing and smiling — the cutest, happiest baby ever.

Hunhhhhh?

The nurse pointed to the spot on the x-ray. Heyyyy! THAT doesn't look like a skinny sewing needle. THAT looks like a THUMBTACK!

More like an upholstery tack!

But there was nothing like THAT in my sewing kit, or anywhere in our child-proofed home.

Maybe she didn't swallow a sewing needle after all. MAYBE IT WAS SOMETHING BIGGER! MAYBE IT REALLY WAS AN UPHOLSTERY TACK! OR A ROOFING NAIL!! AN AXE!!! A MACHETE!!!! A CHAIN SAW!!!!! AAAIIIEEE!!!!!

But the baby was gurgling and laughing, in my arms.

Hunhhhhhh?

In my devastation and confusion, I didn't even notice the radiologist walk up to look at the x-rays.

"That's not a needle," the doctor said firmly to the nurse. "That's just an artifact."

An artifact? Like, something from archaeology? Did she swallow THAT, too?

Noooooo. The doctor explained that an "artifact" is just a marking on the x-ray. It's like a crosshair. It just happened to print out over the duodenum on the x-ray. And it just happened to be a short, straight line, sort of, kind of, like a tack or a needle with a skinny head on it.

But there was nothing actually in our baby's innards that shouldn't be there. She was as clean as a whistle!

He proclaimed that the nurse was mistaken. No needle! No tack! No machete! No nothing! She was clear! Ha ha! False alarm! Go home, folks!

Our nurse-accuser slunk away. No apology. But we were so happy, we didn't even care.

Neely just kept on being a happy, healthy, un-skewered baby.

My Beloved got that rueful smile that he gets when he knows he's wrong, in deepest marital doo-doo, and going to have to pay in the form of incessant reminders, pep talks and debriefings by me over the next 50 years. But we were both so relieved, nothing more was ever said.

We drove home, a happy marital duo, glad our baby's duodenum was A-OK. I praised him for being such a protective dad, and for resisting the temptation to, well, NEEDLE me about the suspected injury before we knew there was none.

Nothing hurts as much as false accusation. Which reminded me of Someone.

Someone we know was falsely accused. He was pierced with nails, not needles. He died a horrible death. But it had a beautiful purpose, as He rose again: to make sure that we can join Him in heaven, where no one will ever hurt us again.

Hallelujah! He is risen! The evil, accusing Needler is defeated!

Take that, Satan. And STICK IT!!! †

75. Do Maddy

. . . (A)nd a little child shall lead them.

— Isaiah 11:6d

We were gathered around our youngest daughter's crib. She had on her favorite lallow jammies, hugging Blanky, Binky and her elephant, "Fop."

Because she is highly skilled at delaying bedtime beyond human endurance, we were finishing up a long conversation about kings, queens, princes and princesses.

"Is Daddy a king?" we asked her.

"Daddy's a king," she whispered.

"Is Neely a princess?"

"NeeNee's a pwinceth."

"Is Beamer a princess?"

"Beamo'th a pwinceth."

Then it was my turn. I decided to razz my husband:

"Is Mommy the BOSS?"

Maddy looked left. She looked right. She looked left again. And then she chortled:

"*MADDY'S* the boss!"

We all roared. But you know something? She's right.

Our family's "boss" has a Pebbles Flintstone vertical ponytail. She insists on wearing her ducky rubber boots with her Fourth of July skirt and University of Nebraska football jersey, size 2T. Hers is a fashion style that can only be described as "schizophrenic interdenominational."

She sits at the lunch table talking to her roast beef sandwich:

"Are you the meat?"

"Yeah!"

"Hi, meat. I'm Maddy."

"Who's eating me?"

"Maddy."

"OK!"

And she's our family's boss. I mean, does YOUR boss talk to meat? Don't answer that; I probably have stock in your company.

Actually, she has excellent executive skills. She has mastered the art of exaggerated nonverbal communication. She has an intimidating unibrow scowl if anyone should dare to give her any bad news, like we're out of Froot Loops.

She is very pro-active, as a boss should be. She is a do-er. She says she "do's the puzzles" and she loves to "do the piano." Her favorite thing is to go out on the driveway in her ducky boots after a rain, and "do the puddles."

The trouble is, there are things Mommy likes to "do," too. And it's hard, with a little one always there, tugging at a sleeve and hugging your shins.

One day, I was trying to do a little work at the computer. It was a bad-hair day and I was struggling. For a while, Maddy was busy with her toys. But then she started clamoring for attention. She pulled open my desk drawer and knocked over the cup of paper clips. She pulled on the arm of the chair to swivel me around. She tried to grab the keyboard.

I confess that I literally turned my back on her, blocking her, and kept writing, because I was hoping to get SOMETHING done that day. Something "important."

OK, guilty. I tried to blow off my own daughter.

But like a good boss, she didn't yell. She didn't whine. She didn't cry.

She just said:

"Mommy, don't do 'puter. Do Maddy."

I swiveled around.

She beamed at me, and tilted her head.

I melted.

In the long run, what would matter most, getting a few words together on paper for people I don't even know who may not even read them? Or investing my time and my self in this child's heart? No contest.

So I clocked out of "important" things and clocked in to motherhood once again.

We put on the ducky boots and the winter gear and went out into the season's first snowfall. She sat on the sled and I pulled it a jillion times around the back yard. We followed bunny tracks and had a snowball fight and made a snowman, or at least a snow blob, with grapes for eyes, a carrot for a nose and a little slice of red pepper for a smile.

We laughed and fell down and afterwards we threw our wet stuff into the washer and she got to "do the buttons" to make it go, and then we had cocoa and story, and she took such a long nap that I had ample time to "do the 'puter" as I had wanted to. It was a very good hair day after all.

I did something "important." For both of us.

Little ones will do that: grab your attention, make you see what counts, and lead you to spend your time doing things that may seem mundane at the moment, but have eternal significance. Really do.

We've all got to listen more to the little ones in our lives. Focus on them. Hear them. See them.

So don't "do" your grown-up stuff so much. If you're lucky enough to have children in your life, "do" THEM.

Let them be the boss and choose what to do. You'll both gain.

Even if it doesn't involve pulling on ducky boots and talking to sandwiches, where children lead, you'll love to go . †

76. Easter: The Napkin

And the napkin,
that was about his head,
not lying with the linen clothes,
but wrapped together in a place by itself.

— John 20:7

The more years that are piled into my Easter basket, the more I come to love and appreciate our amazing Lord Jesus Christ. Also the Bible, the most fantastic piece of literature in world history, bar none.

Take the story of Easter morning. We're all familiar with how Jesus' dead body was wrapped in cloth and laid in a tomb, with a heavy stone placed in front of it and guards set up to prevent His followers from stealing away the body.

When His followers came and discovered that the stone had been rolled away, and the tomb was empty, that's amazing enough by itself. But wait: there's more.

All these years, I've read and re-read that passage. 'Til now, I've never noticed the part about the linen clothes being set in one place inside the sepulchre, and the napkin that was around His head wrapped up and lying separately.

Come to find out, that was God's way of debunking the future claim of the Jewish leaders – a claim that persists today among nonbelievers – that the disciples took the body in order to perpetrate a hoax.

The fact that the graveclothes were still there, in the tomb, while Jesus was not, is some of the strongest proof that He did, indeed, get resurrected.

I mean, think about it: if His followers or some robbers had somehow overpowered the guards, rolled that stone away, and grabbed His body, wouldn't they have left the expensive linen graveclothes on the body? I mean, would YOU take graveclothes off a corpse and carry it, naked, through the streets? Ew, ew, ewwww.

And even if the body was stripped and carried away, how come the napkin – the head wrap, used to keep a dead person's jaw from slacking open – how come it was wrapped up neatly and set separately from the other cloth inside that tomb?

If the disciples had snuck in there, had to hurry so they wouldn't get caught, and hastily stripped off the laboriously-wrapped cloths, would they really have taken time to be neat and tidy with the napkin? Or would they have dumped it unceremoniously with the other cloths, and split?

You don't have to be a Sherlock Holmes or Columbo to see that there wasn't any haste in that process, the way that napkin was wrapped and lying separately. It debunks the whole "stolen body" assault against the truth of the Resurrection in one fell swoop.

But, typical of the Bible, there's even more depth of meaning in this one little sliver of the Easter story. Of course we know that Easter always falls around Passover, the high Jewish holiday, because that's when the Crucifixion occurred, and there are many links and parallels between the two stories.

The Exodus from Egypt, which is what Passover commemorates, is all about deliverance – just like the Easter story. God led the Jews out of Egypt miraculously, and He will lead us out of our earthly lives into heaven, miraculously, because of Jesus' work on the Cross.

Passover is associated with The Feast of Unleavened Bread. They call it that because the ancient Jews had no time for yeast to rise in their bread before they vamoosed it from Egypt. The "leaven," or yeast, came to symbolize corruption or sin. Ancient Jews were supposed to remove all yeast, or leaven, from their kitchens before Passover begins. The whole idea of unleavened bread is to remind us to be special, set apart, sanctified for service to God. The flat, crisp unleavened bread called *matzah* is still a big part of a Jewish family's Seder meal on Passover.

Did you ever notice that *matzah* is basically what Christians have during communion? And that Bethlehem, the place where Jesus was born, means "House of Bread" in Hebrew? And that Jesus called himself "the bread of life" (John 6:35)? And that Christians agree with Jews that "a little leaven" in our lives – a little sin, a little corruption, a little compromise – will quickly spread to infect our lives totally, just as yeast spreads throughout a lump of bread (Gal. 5:9)? And so, as the only sinless man who ever lived, Jesus is just like that unleavened bread that symbolizes what God has done for us?!?

Now, here's the amazing part: a highlight of Passover is when *matzah* is hidden in a napkin for the children of the family to search for and find. It's called *afikomen*, and it symbolizes the Messiah, who will come to restore all things.

Hidden in a napkin, the unleavened bread symbolizing the Messiah . . . just as the resurrected Jesus, the unleavened Bread of Life, took time to wrap the napkin that used to be wrapped around Him, and placed it, folded neatly, in a place set apart, where people would be sure to see it.

Do today's Jews know about this, when they celebrate the Seder meal at Passover? I don't know.

But, as always with the incredible, supernatural Bible, there are still two more levels of meaning to this tiny little piece of the story involving, of all things, a napkin.

First, in ancient times, when carpenters would finish a job, they were illiterate, and they couldn't write out a bill for their customer. But they all had a cloth to wipe sweat while they worked. So when they were done, they would fold that little cloth neatly and put it on what they had just made, to signify that they were finished. Jesus was a carpenter. He finished His work on the Cross. The folded napkin was just part of His routine.

And last, but certainly not least, think about that napkin lying there in that tomb. Jesus was bodily missing, but the folded napkin remained. It brings up another ancient custom which persists today:

In those days, the master of a household would crumple up his napkin and leave it on the dinner plate when he was finished. That was the sign to the servant that it was time to clear the table.

But if the master folded the napkin neatly by the side of the plate, that meant that he was coming back.

Don't you do that, too, in a restaurant, if you leave the table momentarily? We all do.

Folded napkin: the master is coming back.

Could it be that Jesus left the folded napkin in the tomb because He was going to come back? Who can doubt it?

Our Messiah, the perfect man, the unleavened Bread of Life, who was hidden in the napkin, and sacrificed for us, will one day come back.

That's what we celebrate on Easter. That's what we celebrate every day.

Come, Lord Jesus. Come back to us, Master. We want to feast with You and our loved ones, together for all time. Then the meaning and truth that we can only glimpse now in the Bible, will be revealed to us completely. And we can worship You and everything that You are to us, always and forever.

HAPPY EASTER!!! †

77. Memorial Day: Smoke Signals

For as in Adam all die,
even so in Christ shall all be made alive.

— I Corinthians 15:22

They used to call it "Decoration Day." Americans would go to cemeteries and decorate the graves of those who'd fought and died for our country, as well as their other loved ones, to honor and remember them.

On the surface, Memorial Day doesn't seem logical. Cemeteries were decked out with flowers and banners, bands played, speeches were made, and a lot of hoopla was being made around all those names solemnly etched in stone. But none of those being honored could see it or hear it. What good's a party for the dead?

Rejoicing doesn't seem to fit this holiday very well. When you lose someone, there's nothing fun or exciting about it. I'm thinking of the longtime friend whose wife died of cancer this past year, and he sobbed through the funeral. I'm thinking of the family and friends of the popular teenage girl who was killed in a freak car crash. I'm thinking of all those who gave their lives in military service to our country, and of so many others, young and old, who passed away in the last year. It must be hard for their loved ones to go to the cemeteries and have reality thrust upon them.

Now, I knew from reading the Bible that believers in Jesus will never die, but have eternal life in heaven. I knew it, but didn't "get it" in my gut. So, like a lot of people, I was a little freaked out by cemeteries. What's the point, if nobody is even there, after death? You can't connect. A graveyard is a cold, sterile place.

And then I heard this crazy story, from a friend who, like me, had lost her dad. They were both in their 60s and had heart problems.

This friend had been almost in a trance during the funeral and for a few months thereafter. She was going through the motions, receiving people's condolences, helping her mother dispose of his things and so forth.

It was as if she was in shock. She hadn't really dealt with the fact that he was dead. She knew he wasn't around any more, and wasn't coming back. He was a believer, so she knew he wasn't in hell. But this heaven thing perplexed her. What, did he float up there like a ghost? How could she be sure? Overwhelmed and still grieving, she back-burnered her questions and worries.

Then came Memorial Day weekend. She thought she'd go visit his grave by herself. She was whizzing along in her car with the air conditioning on, on the Interstate, almost there, when suddenly . . .

. . . she was overpowered by the aroma of cigar smoke.

Whaaa? She didn't smoke. No other adult had sat in her car for weeks, much less smoked in it. She cracked her windows open. But the aroma remained. If it seeped in from a passing car, it would have seeped right out again. But it didn't. Where on earth did that come from? Nobody smoked cigars any more.

And then it dawned on her:

Her father had smoked cigars.

As soon as that thought crossed her mind, the aroma was gone.

The incident lasted only a moment. But it was enough for her to perceive that it wasn't just a coincidence. It was a message.

Tears rolled down her cheeks. She was laughing and sobbing and gasping.

Dad! Dad! You're *alive!* You're still *with* me!

She pulled off the Interstate, parked at the cemetery, ran over to the headstone, threw her arms around it, and laughed and cried and prayed for a good, long while.

Today, she tells the story, shakes her head, and smiles a big, beautiful Decoration Day smile. That smile of assurance and peace was all I needed, to help me understand. I could finally do what I needed to do, which was to leave grief and numbness behind me about my own dad's death, and finally, rejoice out of the blessed assurance that I'll see him again.

So now, when I go out to those cemeteries and see those names solemnly etched in stone on those graves, I put an imaginary cigar between my lips. I take a luxurious imaginary puff on it. And breathe in deeply the priceless joy of knowing that none of these Christians are really dead after all! Nyahh nyahh nyahh to you, Death!

Now, THAT'S something to party about.

You came close, Death. But no cigar.

And one day, oh, yes, no doubt, thank You, Jesus, one day my loved ones will transform again from just memories into reality before my eyes. Because, thanks to Jesus, praises forevermore to my Lord and King, one day, I *will* see them again. †

78. Fiasco of July

The thoughts of the diligent tend only to plenteousness; but of every one that is hasty only to want.

— Proverbs 21:5

We went over to a nearby country club to see the spectacular Fourth of July fireworks show. We sat there in the car in the dark, Maddy in her Winnie the Pooh jammies, and me barefoot-casual. What a show!

WHOA!

WOO!

WOW!

In Maddy's joyous shrieks and gasps I heard the music of America. All the color and sparkle of our amazing country were reflected in her dazzled, uplifted eyes.

This is freedom. This is how it feels. This is what God wants for us — the peaceful, prosperous lifestyle He ordained.

Everybody honked their horns when it was over. Hey, Maddy, how was that for a birthday celebration for 'Merica? She replied: "Humungously great!"

That's what our country is, and that's how we want the Fourth of July to be. We want a worthy observation to remember all the wonderful things our predecessors fought to create and sustain . . . their blood, sweat and tears . . . their battlefield valor.

Whenever I watch fireworks, I think of and pray for our military all around the world, for my dad and other relatives who fought for our country, and all the patriots going all the way back to our founding. They did what they did so that a little girl in her jammies and her sleepy, barefoot mom could enjoy the splendors of liberty on a dark and starry night.

'Course, there was one celebration I heard about that didn't quite fit the profile of an all-American great time. Guess it's the exception that proves the rule:

It was at the fanciest country club in the region. In those days, the price for the Fourth of July party was staggering: $13.98 per person. But you got a lot for that: fun and games in the pool, an all-you-can-eat buffet, and then that club's signature fireworks show.

The first few pool games went fine, and then – disaster! The club had ordered hundreds of live goldfish, and dumped them into the pool so that the kids could swim around, try to catch them, and have a whee.

Trouble was, they didn't realize what chlorine would do to those poor little goldfish.

They died instantly. All the giggling little kids found themselves in a mass watery grave with hundreds of disgusting, dead fish! AAAIIIEEE!!!

The kids scrambled out of there as if escaping the "Baby Ruth" in that crazy "Caddy Shack" movie. Instead of sending lively little fish home in plastic bags for each family, the lifeguards spent the rest of the afternoon scooping the little piscine corpses out and throwing them away in front of the tearful young audience.

Then it was dinnertime. The crowd lined up for the all-you-can-eat buffet.

Trouble was, there were more diners than expected, or they took larger portions than they should have. The lavishly-prepared food disappeared fairly quickly. Those at the end of the line were out of luck. They had all they could eat, all right – of cocktail olives, parsley, roofing tile and whatever else the harried chef could round up.

Oh, well. Who cares about fancy food on the Fourth of July, anyway? It would soon be fireworks time! Fireworks are the main event! God bless America! This is our birthday party! The party-goers expectantly awaited the show. Daylight turned to dusk, dusk to dark, dark to pitch dark . . . but still no show.

Finally, 'waaaaay off in the distance, if you had binoculars and squinted really hard, you could see the orange poofs of a few pop-bottle rockets going off. I mean, like 27. And a few Roman candles. And that was it.

It seems the fireworks stand out in the country where this club had always bought the fireworks for their signature show hadn't opened up that year. The club employee in charge thought it would be easy to find really great fireworks at half price at a roadside stand on the afternoon of the Fourth.

But noooooo. When they finally found an open stand, they had hardly anything left. So pop-bottle rockets and Roman candles. That was it.

The bad news is, the party planning was pretty substandard. A little more forethought and preparation, and it would have been a much better event.

The good news is, the kids had a great time just being together, anyway. And the cash bar stayed open the whole time. So lots of the grown-ups had a bang-up Fourth after all.

Is this a great country, or what? †

79. Thanksgiving: Another Slice of Gravy

***And beside this, giving all diligence,
add to your faith virtue; and to virtue knowledge;
and to knowledge temperance; and to temperance patience;
and to patience, godliness; and to godliness brotherly kindness;
and to brotherly kindness charity.***

— 2 Peter 1:5-7

Many years ago, our family had Thanksgiving at the home of some relatives. They had invited the wife's father and stepmother along with a bunch of the same old, same old relatives. So it was a new blend. Everybody kind of, sort of, knew each other, but it was just a little bit awkward. Our hosts were young. I doubt they had ever had a big feast at their home before, for so many people.

As usual, everybody brought something, and then sat around for a couple of hours 'til the last-minute rush. Then, every woman in the house crowded into the kitchen to fix her contribution and get everything out on the table.

Our hostess was too busy to make the gravy. So she asked her stepmother. The older woman held a high-ranking professional job and had an IQ of about 400. But her cooking IQ was closer to her shoe size.

She confessed later that she had been put on the spot. She was too proud to admit she didn't know how to make gravy. So she winged it. Meanwhile, we all watched, and agonized.

She started well, with the turkey drippings, butter, a little flour and the gizzard water. But it was too thick. So she added more gizzard water, and a little milk. Then it was too thin. So she added more flour, and some salt. A LOT of salt.

Then it was too pale and salty. So she added more milk and some kind of meat tenderizer stuff out of the spice drawer. She splashed on some Worcestershire, too. Ewww!

We exchanged worried glances but no one said a thing. She set the gravy boat out on the buffet table much earlier than the other food. Out of sight, out of mind. Gradually the turkey and all the side dishes got put out there, too.

After we said grace and everybody went through the line, I took a little gravy, despite my misgivings, just to be sociable. Actually, it was OK, though a little thick and gloppy. It was cooling off rapidly. But it was doable.

Well, came time for seconds. Our host, a proud young man, wanted more gravy. He had NOT witnessed the last-minute cooking rush, nor sensed the tension and consternation. He did NOT realize who had made the gravy. He assumed that his lovely WIFE had.

Our host is one of the most respectful, kindest husbands in the world. But at that moment, he saw an opening for a one-liner, and he jumped on it.

With a flourish, he held up the lovely porcelain gravy boat. With a twist of the wrist, he ceremoniously turned it upside down.

AND NOTHING CAME OUT!!!

The gravy had congealed into a gelatinous blob. It was stuck in the gravy boat in a solid state.

With a wicked grin, his voice dripping with humor and sarcasm, our host loudly asked his wife:

"Say, Dear. Would you CUT me another SLICE of GRAVY?!?!?!?"

The men all roared.

The women's faces drained to white, especially the stepmother's and our hostess'.

Tactfully, she told her husband that his stepmother had made it, and wasn't it great? And after a quick reheat in the microwave, it would be great for second helpings. She leapt up from the table and got right to it. "I'll go help," said the stepmother, the corners of her mouth turning up.

I believe two those shared some gentle hilarity and a hug in that kitchen. Hope so, anyway.

In our host's embarrassment, his face emitted more radiation than 100 microwaves.

It's hilarious now. But back then, it was a supreme Doo-Dah moment.

Yeah, we had a Thanksgiving turkey that year. He was the one with the beet-red face, sitting at the head of the table. †

80. Harry for Christmas

Behold, I bring you good tidings of great joy.

— Luke 2:10

It was back in the 1930s, when people were reeling from the Great Depression. Everything was a lot simpler and cost a lot less then, including, most of all, Christmas.

My grandmother's family just loved the Christmas season. They were very close, and they had a lot of fun. There were six children, lots of aunts and uncles, and various cousins once or twice removed. The family home in Council Bluffs, Iowa, was warm and boisterous, mixing the generations in happiness and harmony.

My grandparents were young marrieds then, with two children. They both worked hard: she was in the index department at Mutual of Omaha, and he was a salesman. They owned their own home and a car. Life was good.

Nobody had much money. But to their family, Christmas was a big deal. Everybody looked forward to the family gift exchange. Everybody tried to come up with gifts for each other that were really, really special.

They would buy out the tie department at the old Nebraska Clothing Co., knit one and purl two on beautiful homemade sweaters, and hustle and bustle everywhere to find just the right gifts for each other to pile under the tree.

But that year, my grandfather announced that he and my grandmother would NOT be participating in the gift exchange.

The relatives were stunned. They tried to hide their pity. Money that scarce? Times that bad? How terrible, to neither give nor receive gifts.

But my grandparents had a secret:

They were giving Harry for Christmas.

Uncle Harry was the one family member who lived far away. He was a violinist in a small orchestra on the West Coast. He hadn't been home for years. He simply couldn't afford it.

Everybody missed him. There was a great, big hole in the family.

Well, my grandparents decided they wanted to fill that hole. They sent Harry their Christmas money, every dime. And Harry bought a train ticket home.

He arrived at the old Union Station in downtown Omaha on Christmas Eve.

My grandparents hid Harry in the trunk of their old Overland to get across the river. They couldn't let the toll-bridge operator see Harry, because he was a friend of the family. He would blab it all over town.

Their secret was too delicious to let out a minute too soon.

Harry spent the night with them and their children. On Christmas morning, they made Harry get back into the trunk to ride over in secret to my great-grandparents' house.

They were the last to arrive. They popped the trunk, and went in.

Everybody was already downstairs in the party room with the Christmas tree, eagerly awaiting the start of the gift exchange. They looked with curiosity and a little sadness at my grandparents, coming in empty-handed.

Suddenly, Grandpa asked for the floor. Grammie stood next to him, rubbing a tiny Aladdin's lamp. Everyone was puzzled.

Grandpa talked about the joy of Christmas, and how they'd wondered what the family would really like to have that year.

What would be the best?

What would mean the most?

Then Harry walked slowly down the stairs, playing the sweet notes of "Silent Night" on his violin.

There wasn't a dry eye in the house.

Everybody mobbed him, crying, laughing, hugging and chattering. Harry! How'd you get here? When? It's so good to see you! Oh, Harry! You came home!

Finally, they understood that a great gift had been given after all. It was a strong sacrifice, a loving statement about what was really important.

"It was a happy and a teary Christmas," Grammie recalled. She still got misty-eyed over it decades later, mainly because it was all Grandpa's idea, that sweet rascal. He sure earned his stripes with his in-laws that year.

His gift was good tidings. Great joy.

And a reminder that everything we need for Christmas, we already have.

We have each other. We have ways to bring joy. The best gifts we can give, that mean the most, don't cost much, if anything at all.

Most of all, we all have a song of love that we can sing to those around us, and play in our own hearts, 'til we join the greatest family reunion of all time. ✝

81. Spiritual Guide Dog

Well done, thou good and faithful servant.

— Matthew 25:21

I was getting out the Christmas decorations. I came upon the oversized dog bone "stocking" that my mother had made for our beloved black Lab, Shadow. It hung for years from the mantel alongside the children's stockings.

But it wouldn't be up there anymore. Shadow had died of bone cancer that year. She was 12.

We had left the urn with her ashes up on that mantel for months, with her trademark red collar encircling it. In the same way, her faithfulness had encircled our lives in all the years our children were growing up.

Shadow was a meek, mild, sweet, loving dog. She had wonderful bloodlines as a hunting dog, but was gun-shy. So she was sold to us as a pet.

As I held that stocking, tears flooded my eyes and memories flooded my heart:

Shadow was a "horse" when our daughter, at 3, decided to be a naked Lady Godiva riding her across the back yard as the neighbor boys hooted next door.

Shadow was a "reindeer" for one of our Christmas cards, patiently wearing felt antlers, silver bells and a red plastic nose.

Shadow was "Dolly Parton" one Halloween in a tangled blonde wig.

She was dubbed "The Black Sausage" when she got a little chubby later on. Like Mother, like "dog-ter."

She was "Shadow the Wonder Dog" in honor of the time she swam a quarter of a mile after a canoe load of family members trying to paddle away from land in a northern Minnesota lake. First, she ran back and forth along the shore, avidly and loudly barking to persuade us of the "danger" that only she could see. Then she heroically plunged in and swam after us. We kept thinking she would turn back. But no way was she going to slack in her No. 1 job of protecting our family. We had no choice but to turn back and let her lead us back to the dock with her steady dog paddle.

She was "Shadow the Card Shark" once when someone rang the doorbell while we were playing cards. She arrived at the door with a fanned-out hand of cards arranged perfectly in her mouth, delicately taken from the edge of the table. See? Like Mother, like dog-ter: always had something in her mouth.

She never barked at visitors, but always retrieved a "gift" for them: a toy or a sock or, that time, a solid gin hand.

She was a reminder of how we all should be: steady, loving, giving, accepting, at peace.

Shadow never chewed up anything, never scratched, never bit. As a retriever, she was bred to be "soft-mouthed" so that she wouldn't ruin a bird as she brought it back to the hunter.

Sigh: if only humans could be "soft-mouthed," too.

One other lesson stands out:

It was the morning of Christmas Eve. I had been on my traditional Christmas toot: shopping, baking, entertaining, and participating in all the rest of the holiday buzz. I was exhausted. I had stayed up the night before, wrapping, 'til the wee hours. Now it was the last day to get things done. I had a ton of things to do, including a quick trip to a nearby town to visit a lonely, old, shut-in relative.

The alarm went off 'way, 'way too soon. I ignored it and turned over. I wasn't aware of Shadow on the floor at the foot of the bed.

Mmmm. This bed is so cozy. I'm so tired. Why don't I just skip that visit today? I could sleep for another two hours. I could just go see him next week. It's a shame to let him down, but boy, I could use more shut-eye.

I was just drifting back asleep when all of a sudden, Shadow's tail thumped loudly:

Thump, thump, thump!

Thump, thump, thump!

Thump, thump, thummmmmp, thump, thump!

What? Hunh? "Jingle Bells"!?!

Shadow's tail had just played "Jingle Bells"! Clear as day!

My eyes flipped open. I grinned, threw off the covers, and sat up bolt upright.

"What am I THINKING? This is Christmas Eve! It's the best day of the year! That old guy needs some Christmas cheer! Let's get this show on the road!"

Shadow looked up at me, her big, brown eyes sparkling, her long, pink tongue curled up like a bow, her collar tags jingling. Her tail thumped some more.

And I heard the rhythm of Christmas in each merry thump of her tail.

Thank you, Spiritual Guide Dog. You really were our best friend. We miss you very much.

But we hear your collar tags in the bells at Christmastime. We see the sparkle from your eyes in the tree lights. We know you're up there retrieving harps for the angels, and thumping your tail to their songs of joy.

We'll see you again someday, Shadow the Wonder Dog. Wherever the light of love shines, it always leaves a shadow: a true and faithful friend.

Howleluia! ✝

82. Hunks of Hide

Am I my brother's keeper?

— Genesis 4:9

Know why Osama bin Laden got so mad at the world? According to the *Wall Street Journal*, he was the 17th of 51 children.

Ooh, nothing but hand-me-downs! Ooh, the fights over who got the last meatball! Ooh, the jockeying to change the TV channel. Think how long he had to wait for his turn to ride in the front seat!

Sibling rivalry is rampant and powerful. Thank goodness its root cause, aggression, doesn't often explode into something like terrorism. But it's certainly a universal problem among brothers and sisters.

Childhood can be like a blend of old sitcoms: the Smothers Brothers line, "Mom always liked you best!" and Batman: "BIFF! POW! BAM!"

Two sisters I know once came to blows over who could make their nostrils flare the widest. Two brothers had to put on boxing gloves to settle their differences without a trip to the ER. Parents consider fire hoses and tear gas to break up squabbles.

Our Dad used to pack us in the car and drive around and around Boys Town in west Omaha. Why? To warn us humorously where we would go if we didn't shut up and learn to get along.

Now that I'm a mom, I see why that's so important. But the fighting goes on here, too: even in our back pasture.

It started when we gave our horse Zippy a baby brother, Billy. He came with a set of diapers. Diapers? For a horse? "Neigh!" you say.

No, the diapers were to wrap around Billy's shins in case of cuts. Why might there be cuts? Because they're both geldings. And boys will be boys.

They have plenty of food and plenty of space. There are no girl horses around to impress, although that's a "fuhgeddaboudit" for geldings anyway. But we still figured they'd fight.

Right off the bat, Zippy put his neck over Billy's. Protecting his younger brother, his "mane" man? Not exactly.

The neck-over-neck treatment continued for a week. They walked side by side. They grazed with heads just inches apart. Zippy began to nudge Billy constantly, and herded him away from neighbor horses and passers-by.

These two males were so close, I thought maybe we had a "situation."

But then my daughter Neely, a teenage veteran of peer pressure wars, saw it for what it was. "Zippy is trying to keep Billy for himself," she said. "He's bossing him around."

The nudges turned into nips. Zippy would rear back and "pretend kick" with his sharp hooves.

One morning, a wide strip of Billy's skin and hair was missing across his forehead. It looked like a Native American headband of exposed skin. Ouch!

Zippy stood off in the corner, looking guilty. After scolding the 1,200-pound naughty boy, I gave him a "time out" in another paddock. I even turned on Christian radio in the barn, hoping it would soothe the savage beast.

But the next day, there were more hunks of hide ripped from Billy's shoulders. And the next, hunks were missing from his hips. He was literally being ripped to shreds. Death by a thousand nips!

Then one day, new hunks of hide were missing. This time, they were missing from Zippy! Now it was Billy off in the corner, in trouble.

They took turns ripping skin off each other senselessly for weeks.

Then it hit me: I've done the same thing, lots of times. All of us have. We try to herd each other to show who's boss. When we don't get our way, we rip hunks of hide out of each other with cutting remarks and verbal jabs. Sometimes, the fight turns physical.

When humans carry out acts of mass murder and terrorism against each other, we see aggression which far surpasses anything animals would ever do. It's a shameful reminder of how far short we've fallen from the goal of taking care of each other.

Zippy and Billy are horses, not humans. They go by instinct, not reason. But guess what? These big, strong brothers don't fight anymore. They worked it out. They learned to live with each other in peace.

So what's our excuse?

None. Maybe that's a lesson for each of us, in our herds, with our sisters and brothers. To be their keepers, not their attackers.

Instead of ripping hunks of hide out of each other, let's learn to . . . hold our horses. †

83. Finding Lexi

There shall no evil befall thee,
neither shall any plague come nigh thy dwelling.
For he shall give his angels charge over thee,
to keep thee in all thy ways.

— Psalm 91:10-11

Up in heaven there's a humoungus office for the angels. It consists of countless air-traffic control stations, with an angel at each one. It stretches as far as the eye can see, in all directions. Millions and millions of angels are all staring at screens, each focused on one human being. They watch over us and look out for us. They keep us on their scopes. And when we need it, they send help, somehow, some way.

You doubt this? Harrumph! In no case is this more evident than when it comes to children and their dogs. There was an example of it just last week.

See, my good friend Bev is an animal lover par excellence. It's a kick to visit her country acreage outside Lincoln, Neb. Over the years, my kids have gotten to pet horses, watch a pond full of koi, give tummy rubs to her dogs, chase her chickens, and one time she even saved a couple of goose eggs for us. I knew she meant for us to EAT the eggs, but daughter Beamer thought she meant for us to INCUBATE the eggs. She insisted! The study light on Beamer's desk didn't quite cut it, though. After a few days, it was painfully apparent that Bev had provided her with a good lesson on animal husbandry. The odor went away after about a week. Yikes!

But when you love animals, and live with them, those are the kinds of memories and experiences you enjoy.

So, the other day, this wonderful animal-lover friend of mine had a doctor's appointment in the big city. Her husband was driving her in their van along a busy highway, and had just turned off onto an equally busy city street. Bev noticed a black Labrador retriever standing on the bike path by the creek.

Hmm, she thought. Looks like Lexi. But it couldn't be: the happy black Lab that belongs to her adult children and grandchildren was safely in her own yard on a small farm, miles away. They visited the young family all the time. They knew the dog well. There was invisible fencing for the pets, and it worked well. Lexi had never broken through and run away.

So Bev didn't even mention it. She looked straight ahead as her husband drove on.

But then her husband glanced in his rear-view mirror, and happened to see a dog running lickety-split behind their car. It was a black Lab. He had a moment of concern about a dog in that very busy street but just kept driving.

He kept glancing in the rear-view mirror, though, and the dog kept coming. He mentioned it to his wife as they crossed the railroad tracks. "Honey, there's a black Lab that appears to be chasing us."

Bev gaped at him. "Oh, no! I just know that it's Lexi!"

"Lexi?!? Hunhh? Are you sure?"

She turned around and gaped. "Yes! That's Lexi!"

Well, you know, they all look alike. But she just had an inkling. The dog must have recognized their car back on the bike path, and started following them! There was no other explanation for why a dog would be running after them like that.

She made her husband turn around. They saw a couple of cars swerve and stop to avoid hitting the dog. It was a miracle that didn't happen, in that busy traffic.

As the car parked by the side of the road, Bev could tell by the way the dog was moving that she was "lost." There were cars approaching from both directions. The dog was out in the middle of traffic, tail between her legs, looking frantic and frightened.

Bev still wasn't 100% sure it was Lexi. But her heart pounded. As the dog came close, she knew.

"Lexi! Lexi!" they both called.

She hopped right into the van and smothered them with her kisses.

Bev bowed her head. "Thank You, Lord Jesus, for providing safety for Lexi." She was so glad her grandchildren were spared the devastation of losing their beloved dog, or having her run over by a car.

Grandpa was happy to dog-sit while Bev had her doctor's appointment. They returned Lexi and found out that the battery on her invisible fencing collar had died. That's why she got out. The family didn't even know she was missing.

What are the odds? How likely is it that someone who knew Lexi would happen by at that exact moment, miles away from home?

Well, remember that enormous corps of air-traffic controlling angels? Whenever you have that unmistakeable feeling of being in the right place at the right time, or there's a lucky coincidence, or you escape calamity by inches or seconds . . . think of those angels, watching over you for your good. You're on their scope!

And you can be doggone glad about that! ✝

84. MEOW-velous Midwife

But the salvation of the righteous is of the Lord:
He is their strength in the time of trouble.

— Psalm 37:39

New to the acreage lifestyle, and wanting to add an animal to her daughters' life experiences, my neighbor thought she'd start with something small and easy: a cat.

She drove to a whole 'nother town to pick up a free calico cat that she'd seen advertised. The price was certainly right. The farm lady declared that this little cat must be extra lucky, since she'd rescued her as an abandoned kitten, nearly dead. So my neighbors named the cat "Lucky Karma."

Yeah, well, SOMEONE had gotten lucky. This little cat was P.G.!

An unwed mother! And now there would be kittens to care for, too.

They didn't find out about it 'til a couple of weeks after they brought Karma home. Isn't that just always the way? Whenever you think you're keeping things simple, come to find out, you're not.

Undaunted, the neighbor thought a cat pregnancy and delivery would be a wonderful experience for the Brownie troop she was leading for one of her girls and her little friends. She's one of those mothers who just sucks it up and blazes through.

She called the veterinarian and got the prenatal health-care lowdown, all the signs of cat labor, what kind of a kitten layette she should prepare, and so forth.

Now, she asked the vet, should I bring her in to you when she's ready to give birth? Can the girls and I watch? How about some of their friends? I want to make this a learning experience for them, but I've never done anything like this before and didn't know how you'd feel about having so many people in the birthing room with you.

There was a silence. Then he laughed. No, he did not midwife kittens. There was no need for it. It was a stay-at-home, do-it-yourself kind of deal. "There's nothing to it," he assured her. "Just let Mother Nature take over."

Mother Nature: she was pretty doggone experienced and competent. OK. That sounded doable.

So Mother Nature's Helper set up a box in the storage room with some ratty towels. The little girls were excited. They and their friends monitored the pregnancy enthusiastically. All systems were go. Everyone looked up to our neighbor as this great Earth Mother, providing them with such a nice life memory.

When the great moment arrived, her kids called the Brownies and every friend, neighbor and soccer pal around, to come on over and witness the miracle of birth. The crowd of little girls all looked at the neighbor . . . excuse the pun . . . expectantly.

"This is going to be great," she told herself. "Piece of cake. Mother Nature's got this."

Before long, the first tiny, rat-like kitten arrived. The neighbor waited to see the kitty mom spring into action, cleaning and chewing off the cord, just as the vet had promised.

Nothing.

The kitten stayed connected to the young mother cat, the cord still in evidence. The children, clueless that this wasn't right, were still rapt with excitement. Soon enough, another kitten popped out. Same thing: no cord severing, minimal licking. Now there were two. The neighbor started to get a little upset. The mother cat was still passive, out of the loop, except for two cords coming out of her.

The rat-like kitties were squirming around all over, and as they were joined by more litter mates, one after another, it became apparent that the still-intact cords were getting all entangled. It wasn't a nice life memory. It was a great, big MESS!

With visions of her daughters' new friends going CAT-atonic over dead kitties connected by oozing cords to their unloving, unwed mother, she frantically called the vet. He told her to get some dental floss.

DENTAL floss?!?!

Yeah, to tie off the cords.

Tie off the . . . .

Ewwwwww!!!!!

With the formerly beaming and now increasingly frowning and grossed-out young faces looking on, she pretended to be confident and sprang into authoritative motherly mode. She was SUPER VET, tying, talking, cutting, and cleansing five tiny, squirmy, hairless, entangled newborn kittens.

In the end, the young and dazed mother cat took over her natural duties, sparing the neighbor from nursing and licking fur as well, much to her relief.

They all lived happily, though squirmily, ever after.

I think she had to go into a 12-step program to recover from the stress, but my neighbor survived it, and now it's funny, looking back.

That's motherhood for you. We moms are "MEOW-velous." Look how "FUR" we go for our kids! ✝

85. Montana Messenger

Behold the fowls of the air: for they sow not, neither do they reap, nor gather into barns; yet your heavenly Father feedeth them. Are ye not much better than they?

— Matthew 6:26

Our friends let us use their family's longtime cabin on a crystal river in south-central Montana. It faced a spectacular rock cliff. The deck stuck out right over the water. You couldn't see anything man-made in any direction. Deer came from nearby mountain meadows. Chipmunks chattered. They call the place "Rockhaven." How true. What a haven.

Most of all, I loved the birds in this diverse habitat. There was a young bald eagle and a red-tailed hawk. There was a tiny blue hummingbird, shimmering in the sunlight, and a spectacular goldfinch in his yellow and black tux. We heard Canada geese and woodpeckers, and saw wild turkeys and a mama duck and six.

I would take my coffee out on the deck in the early morning and watch the flickers and the swallows work the trees and bushes on the face of the rock cliff. My spirits soared with them.

But one afternoon, just before we left, my husband and I were sitting out there feeling flat, frustrated and emotionally flightless. We had been discussing a very difficult problem that was coming to a head. It was a toughie.

No easy answers were surfacing. Not even the beautiful setting with the magnificent rock across the river could keep tears from spilling down my face. Not even the wide arms of the old Adirondack chair, worn soft by generations of heart-to-heart talks, could keep me from slumping in both body and soul. I was slipping into despair.

Just then, a plain, brown sparrow lighted on my husband's knee. His little head bobbed all around, checking us out. We froze. In a moment, he hopped onto my head. I could feel his tiny feet shifting positions. So little, and yet so bold and carefree. After a few seconds, he flew off.

My husband grinned. "Nothing like that has ever happened before." He looked 10 years younger, surprised and delighted. "I'd forgotten how much I enjoy being out in nature."

I instantly thought of the Bible's promises that God cares for the smallest sparrow as well as every one of us. A sparrow is mentioned in Matthew 6:26, and again in Matthew 10:29. The Bible says that God knows when a sparrow falls, and He knows when we are struggling. He doesn't just watch; He acts. This time, he sent a winged messenger to let us know that He was with us, and everything would be all right.

It wasn't a robin. It wasn't a wren. It wasn't a starling. It was a sparrow, the one with the Biblical credentials. Suddenly, our problem didn't seem very big any more. Suddenly, I couldn't remember why I had been crying.

What, me worry? I'm a blood-bought child of the living God. He can do anything! He can send a cute sparrow to cheer up the worrywarts in the Montana wilderness. No problemo! He has His hand on every last thing in creation, all over the world and beyond. He knows what's going on with our situation. He will make it work out fine, for our good. Do your part, of course. Do what you know you should. But then quit fretting! Fuhgeddaboudit! Relax! Smile!

It was as if that bird flew off with my all my worries in tow. My spirits once again were lifted up lighter than air.

As the old song goes, His eye is on the sparrow . . . and even way out in the Montana wilderness, I know He watches over me. †

86. The Feel Club

But whoso shall offend one of these little ones
which believe in me,
it were better for him that a millstone
were hanged about his neck,
and that he were drowned in the depth of the sea.

— Matthew 18:6

Pedophile scandals and human trafficking knock me to my knees, they're so horrible. I give thanks to the Lord that I came from a family that taught me how NOT to be helpless – how to stay aware, and what to do to stay safe and NOT get victimized.

My dad once walked my sister and me down our quiet suburban street as he explained that there were bad guys in the world who might try to touch us or grab us in ways they shouldn't. He didn't go into any gory details. But we knew what he was warning against. I felt so loved and cared for.

He taught us that if some boy or man ever tried to touch us where our swimsuits usually covered, we were to knee him in the groin, hard, and run away.

Dad demonstrated on an imaginary assailant. My sister and I practiced, with zeal, as we walked along. My knee launched upwards with nuclear-powered force. I would've kneed any groper's groin to the MOON!!!

I was ready, willing, and able to protect myself. Thankfully, the need never arose. But that's OK. In fact, that's great.

I'm one of the vast majority of people in this mostly beautiful world, who have never had to deal with any kind of physical or sexual abuse, harassment, assault . . . nothing like that. THANK YOU, GOD! But I know some people who've gone through those forever-scarring horrors – rape, domestic violence, incest, sexual exploitation, and all the sordid rest. Nothing makes me more furious than to hear about children who have suffered sexual abuse.

I admire parents who carefully instruct their children how to protect themselves. It makes all the difference in the world. If someone cares enough about you to help you anticipate what could go wrong, and how to respond so that you aren't harmed, it's a tremendous boost to your self-esteem.

I think a lot of the broken and chaotic families in today's world aren't doing that for children. Sadly, it shows in the abuse and neglect statistics. We have too many victims, and not enough people doing everything they can to promote prevention.

Let's celebrate all those families and helpful adults who do fulfill this basic task, though. They really are all around.

One of Maddy's little preschool friends, Andrew, was obviously in that category. He was a serious, responsible 4-year-old with enormous blue eyes. One day, he was telling me a long story about how he would get in a car with his mommy, and he would get in a car with his auntie, and he would even get in a car with me . . . but he would never, ever, EVER get in a car with somebody he didn't know, no matter how nice they were, because they would be a . . .

. . . SSSTTTRRRAAANNNGGGEEERRR!!!!!

You have never heard an English vocabulary word pronounced with such intensity and drama. His voice dripped with dread and antagonism. Wow! I told his mom that Andrew had a future as a prosecuting attorney or maybe the host of the late-night TV horror flicks.

No need to worry about Andrew. He's the type who can protect himself, always looking out for others, too. That's good parenting.

Besides diligent parents, isn't it great to know that there are many teachers looking out for kids who are being victimized, too? The more school sex abuse cases that come to the fore, the more teachers are learning about detection and prevention. They want to protect kids and keep their profession pristine. So it's good. Educators see kids every day, so they can develop perspective over time, recognize the symptoms of abuse, and tap into their sixth sense – that intuitive flash when you just know something must be wrong.

I'm glad Nebraska has a mandatory reporting law about this. If a teacher, doctor or other youth-serving professional has a reasonable suspicion that a child might be suffering abuse or neglect, and they don't report it, it's a crime.

But one time, that same law almost gave me a heart attack.

See, our third daughter, Eden – nicknamed "Beamer" because she smiles all the time, like a sunbeam – had the world's most enthusiastic and loving kindergarten teacher. Beamer was flourishing in the busy, colorful kindergarten program under this master teacher's energetic programming.

She was already reading, was writing amazing and imaginative stories, loved her classmates, and bounced home from school every day with a happy smile and lots of engaging chatter.

Her dad and I looked forward to the spring parent-teacher conference. Finally, the day arrived. We came in and sat down in those itty, bitty chairs.

But what was this? The wonderful teacher across the table was silent and unsmiling – highly uncharacteristic. What?!? We were confused. Was Beamer in some kind of trouble? With as well as we thought Beamer was doing in school, the teacher's cool demeanor was totally unexpected.

Then the teacher leaned forward. With a highly apologetic and yet gravely concerned facial expression, she said:

"I am required by law to ask you something. I really hope that with your answer you can clear up what may very well be a misunderstanding and a false impression."

(HEART ATTACK!!!!! HEART ATTACK!!!!)

She continued: "Beamer says that you take her to something called 'The Feel Club.' That sounds like some kind of perverted sexual abuse ring. She says there are other children and adults there. Sometimes she takes off her clothes there, and sometimes she doesn't. She always gets a root-beer float if she's 'good.'

"But she's not showing any symptoms of abuse. She's the happiest, most productive student in the class. I can't BELIEVE you could be mixed up in something like this.

"What IS this thing you take her to, called 'The Feel Club'?"

(LAUGH ATTACK!!!!! LAUGH ATTACK!!!!!)

We exploded with relief and laughter. We quickly explained.

It's the FIELD Club! Fiel-DDDDD!!!!!

Our country club! It's where we golf and swim!

It's not "The Feel Club." It's the Fiel-DDDDD Club!

Beamer may take off her clothes there . . . if she's changing into her swimming suit in the girls' locker room!

She often gets a root beer float at the snack shop after swimming!

The only groping that goes on is if she can't find her towel and has chlorine in her eyes!

The Fiel-DDDDDD Club is a really historic, classy old country club. We don't belong there any more, but at the time, Beamer's dad was club president, and we were always taking our daughters there for Junior Golf, swim team, swimming play dates, family dinners, the annual Easter egg roll on the front lawn, the annual brunch with Santa, and sledding on those great fairway hills in the wintertime

This was totally wholesome and family-friendly fun! Not at all what the teacher was imagining – which we could only imagine – and thank God, it was only imaginary!

A good, hearty laugh was had by all. No report was turned in to the D.A. We didn't have to take a lie detector test. We didn't get our mugshots in the paper. We didn't get thrown in the slammer. We all lived happily ever after.

But you know what? We told that teacher that we were GLAD she had the guts to ask, and clear things up.

Would that everybody who connects with children would be diligent like that. To bravely err on the side of caution. To risk embarrassment and all the problems that might ensue if you guess wrong. And yet still have the common sense to give the parents the benefit of the doubt.

We want every child to be in the real Feel Club. It's a club where every child enjoys the innocence and delight of childhood. It's a club where every child can enjoy the birthright feelings of love, joy, peace, hope, worth, safety and security. †

87. Spinning Her Wheels

Pride goeth before destruction, and a haughty spirit before a fall.

– Proverbs 16:18

One day in junior high math class, the janitor stood for several minutes outside our classroom door trying to scrape masking tape off the glass. We all sat there and laughed because the tape was on the INSIDE.

How well I know the feeling. I've stood many times in the produce aisle struggling to get the little plastic sack open and feeling as though I have the brains of the Roma tomatoes I would put in it, if I could get the dang thing open.

Every time I leave a tag showing at the back of my neck all day, can't find my car in a parking lot, forget to plug something in and think it's broken because it won't work, or forget the secret password that controls access to our entire financial fortune (what there is of it, after four children), I feel stupid. And that's even without a snickering audience of know-it-all junior-high kids.

Nobody likes to look dumb. But everybody does dumb things. You know what the secret is: a sense of humor. If you don't laugh, by golly, you'll cry.

It took a REALLY dumb thing to make a friend of mine get this.

She's one of those outrageously gifted people that you just want to slap. She has an IQ of 9 kazillion and a dress size of 2. She never messes up, never snorts accidentally or on purpose, never loses anything, and never has the hair on one eyebrow pointing ridiculously up while the hair on the other eyebrow points the regular way. Rumor has it she didn't even lay down to give birth.

If you are gleaning from this that she is my diametric, antithetical, polar opposite, you would be correct.

If you tell her you have made an exciting, new, gourmet dessert, she has already made it, with two cherries on top, not just one, and served it to the Queen of England at her last soiree.

If your child walks into school proudly carrying an igloo made of sugar cubes, HER child brings an authentic scale model of the Louvre as it looked in 1793, complete with a replica of the Mona Lisa that the child painted holding the brush between her toes while singing "La Marseillaise" . . . in French.

You always leave an encounter with her full of admiration, but also feeling as though, compared to her, you are spending your days scraping masking tape off the wrong side of the glass.

But one cold winter night, us lesser mortals got our sweet revenge. There was a big meeting of school volunteers. Everybody who was anybody was there. Old business and new business were addressed and disposed of, chop chop, all the way down the terribly efficient agenda, typed, I suppose, by Mrs. Perfect right after she ghost-wrote the inaugural speech of some Third World president.

We all went out into the icy night together. Mrs. Perfect had a big, beautiful SUV. It was awesome. It was powerful. It cost more than my house.

As some of us chatted on the sidewalk, Mrs. Perfect started up the Perfectomobile and revved up the engine preparing to back out of the parking space . . . but it wouldn't budge. She was just spinning her wheels.

She revved it some more with her expensive leather boots, and the wheels spun and the ice chips flew backwards like a rooster tail, but it wouldn't back up. Wouldn't pull forward, either.

She announced to all of her admirers on the sidewalk that she must be "stuck on the ice." It was a perfectly flat parking space, but winter does dastardly things around here.

Several of us went over to see if we could help. Mrs. Perfect had us pushing and pulling. She even put the floor mats under the front tires for traction. We strained and struggled. No go.

Finally, she pulled out her cell phone and called her husband. You could hear the irritation in her voice, that there was something wrong with this fancy big car and a bunch of pinhead women couldn't budge it, either, so he'd better get on over there. Chop, chop.

Several of us waited with her. He arrived. He got in the car, and . . . don't miss this, it is key . . . RELEASED THE PARKING BRAKE . . . and backed up several feet, then looked at her. Voila.

In the streetlight, the look on her face . . . the look on HIS face . . . the look on my fellow pinheads' faces . . . it was surreal.

But then Mrs. Perfect did what none of us expected. She burst out laughing. It was a full-throated, jolly, helpless, sincere laugh. "Oh . . . my . . . God!" she chortled. "I can't believe I did that."

We all joined in, surprised and relieved. She had made a mistake in front of people, and she could laugh about it! She made a lot of friends that night. I always felt a lot more comfortable around her after that, and reminded her of it many times, to our mutual delight.

It's no fun up on a pedestal. There's no one to play with.

When pride has you stuck and on thin ice, humor and humility can get you going again. †

88. The Song of the Turtle

The flowers appear on the earth;
the time of the singing of birds is come,
and the voice of the turtle is heard in our land.

— Song of Solomon 2:12

Here's what I wish for children as every school year opens:

Learning that's unexpected, spontaneous, free-flowing, and fun.

We saw how important that is from a turtle named Louisa.

It all started when my husband was walking across his office parking lot, and a green rock moved. Intrepid explorer that he is, he picked it up. That was no rock: that was a turtle.

BB-gun dings were apparent in the turtle's shell. It seemed distressed. If he left it there in that industrial area, it would likely get pancaked by a semi.

So he brought the turtle home. We set up a temporary habitat in an old plastic wading pool, pleased that the pool's decorations were such a great fit: Teenage Mutant Ninja Turtles.

Fascinated by this up-close-and-personal encounter with wildlife, the kids fed their curiosity about turtles, going far beyond any school assignment.

They surfed the 'Net for turtle sites. We went to the library and checked out books on reptiles and turtles. We talked to a pet store guy. A local nature center put us in touch with a wildlife rescue team. A bunch of us went out there to meet the Turtle Guru.

She nursed sick birds back to health, trained squirrels without tails how to move from branch to branch, and had already rescued a herd of little yertles like our turtle. She taught us a lot, and referred us to a veterinarian for more. We learned:

- We had found a Southern box turtle, hundreds of miles north of her native habitat. If we released her around Omaha, she'd probably freeze to death in the harsh winter.
- She was a female, so we named her "Louisa," since my husband's childhood pet turtle had been named "Louie."
- She was a couple of years old, with a life expectancy of 30 years.
- Based on the distance from her native habitat, the BB dings and her drab coloring, she apparently was a malnourished, neglected pet who had been "dumped." She needed turtle TLC, ASAP.

So the kids built a more suitable habitat for her, a big, screened box. It had a reptile light with just the right wattage, and a shallow water basin at just the right angle for quick dips.

They built a chicken wire enclosure outside, "Spa Louisa," for her daily sunbaths.

They talked to a family friend who was born with a learning disability, and got low grades in school, but he had an amazing, encyclopedic knowledge about turtles, so he completely schooled us, and that was good for his self-esteem, too.

We shopped for the finest nutritious romaine. No plain iceberg lettuce for Louisa! We served up sliced cantaloupe and slivers of luscious tomato.

At the pet store, we bought crickets at eight cents apiece and broke their legs so they'd be easier for her to catch. The things we do for love! We were proud of her head-jabs when she "hunted."

We bought her mealworms, loved watching her slurp them up like strands of spaghetti, and kept confusing the containers of Louisa's mealworms with our own leftovers in the fridge.

To our delight, orange and yellow spots gradually appeared on her shell and legs. That's because of her improved nutrition, guys!

Look: she has five toes in front, and three bigger ones in back. Hmm. Wonder why. For digging? We researched it. That's right! She needs more muscle power to push the dirt away from the hole.

And then one day we heard a musical little rasp. We were thrilled to hear her voice. Her "voice"? Turtles can sing? Magical! Who knew? Yeah, well: who was listening, before?

Funny: the TV sat idle, those weeks. We were too busy learning from Louisa. The kids shared her with their classes. Everybody gained.

Then, as if on cue, my husband and I got invited to a weekend at the Lake of the Ozarks in south-central Missouri. It was within her normal range of liveable habitat.

"Hooray!" our girls rejoiced. "Now Louisa can go free, get married and be a mom!"

So we took her down there with us, rigged up a funny little wedding veil out of some tulle, and released her in a likely spot.

The bride wore green, with orange and yellow spots.

Now, the kids joke that we got a postcard from her a year later, living in an Ozarks trailer with Bubba and their 47 young'uns. LOL!

Louisa, wherever you are, thank you. You taught us well. We're glad you're free.

If only school could be like that all the time: full of wonder, freedom and peace. No bureaucracy, no big expenses, no constant pressure about standardized tests, no big politicized hubbubs.

We got a taste of what homeschooling must be like: learning at your own pace, even if it's as slow as a turtle's, so you won't miss the delights and rewards of the unexpected.

That's when you can listen for the song of the turtle . . . and see where it leads. †

89. Violin Lesson

And the servant of the Lord must not strive; but be gentle unto all men, apt to teach, patient. . . .

— 2 Timothy 2:24

Some people can sew. Some can design bridges. Some can keep a hula hoop going. Some can sing bass. Some can throw TD's. Some can do trigonometry. Some can dance hip-hop.

I can't do any of that. But by golly, I can spell. Spelling is my life. I'm only half-kidding about that. It's one of the few things in life that I can do, and do well. When I run into a misspelling by someone who should know better, it's like getting slugged in the stomach:

"Recieve." BIFF!!!

"You're turn." BAM!!!

"Best of it's kind." POW!!!

But with parent-teacher conferences coming up, I need to share a tale of what NOT to do if you find yourself in a Spelling Situation, as I did years ago.

One of our kids had a teacher who was a rilly pore spailer. She sent home a weekly note to parents with a misspelled word or grammar howler in nearly every sentence. Several times, she circled words on my child's paper as being spelled wrong, when they were spelled right. This teacher's spelling skills were far below the grade level at which she was teaching.

Moreover, the spelling words she gave each week were ridiculously easy. A wise friend explained that if most of the kids got

100% on the tests, the teacher could use those scores to offset the poor scores of the handful of struggling students, and make herself "look good on paper." Nobody would learn anything, but she would be acclaimed as the spelling teacher whose kids all got A's.

She refused to let the advanced kids out of the regular curriculum. She refused offers from parent volunteers to come in to class and work with kids on more challenging spelling words.

Because I'm so spelling sensitive, each incident felt like a judo chop. My distress grew.

Finally, came time for our parent-teacher conference. It started off fine. She bragged that, because she was our school's union representative, she was being sent to a weeklong writing conference at a luxury resort in a faraway state.

Ironically, I had brought her a gift: a copy of the famous writing manual, *The Elements of Style* by Strunk & White. She had said before that she had never heard of it, so I thought she would be happy to receive a copy. But nooo. She was offended and pushed it back across the table at me. I could feel myself blush with anger. Then I went too far. I said it had only cost $4.99, but she would get more good out of that little book than the thousands of dollars her combination free vacation and writing conference would cost taxpayers.

Her face got beet red.

Whoops! Better justify myself. Speaking rapidly, I told her about the misspelled words on her letters home, the words on my daughter's papers that were mistakenly "corrected," and the artificially high class grade average that exposed the too-easy curriculum.

And now she was hopping mad.

She sputtered that her own dad habitually misspelled her own first name, and that she was the first person in her family to go to college, much less gain a respected job like teaching. She'd been teaching for over 20 years. She was single; her job was important to her. She was doing the best she could. Was I saying she wasn't a good teacher?

I finally understood. She was very hurt. I might have been right. But I sure wasn't being kind. And that's never right.

I hurriedly apologized, and rushed into the rainy October night to go home. I started my car. Inexplicably, because I didn't normally have the car radio tuned to that station, classical music blared out of the car radio, at three times normal speed and volume.

DADADAHHHHHHH!!! DADADADAAAAHHHHHH!!!! DADADADADADADADAHHHHHHHHH!!!!!

It was so fast and so loud! It was painful!

It felt like the violin bows were jabbing out of the radio and stabbing me in the eye!

I punched at the buttons wildly. Make it stop! Make it go away!

Finally, it fell silent.

I sat in the dark car, with the windshield wipers beating a gentle rhythm. Finally, at last, I thought things over. I sank my forehead onto my clenched hands on the steering wheel, and cried.

The way that music had sounded to me, I had sounded to that teacher.

Too fast! Too loud! Too painful!

I hadn't helped. I had hurt.

And God was showing me what a lousy teacher I'd been. For her.

I cried for being mean and prideful, and for not using my most important communication skill. That's not spelling, but THINKING. With empathy, I would have helped her see how to get a better spelling curriculum and instructional strategy in place. Instead, I'd made a mess. The chance of educational improvements for those kids in that classroom? Zilch.

That was years ago. Since then, I've tried very hard to remain strictly Mrs. Positive with teachers. When I see an academic shortcoming, I have refrained from confronting the teacher directly, but have tried to use indirect channels and methods to make things better for kids in a quiet, respectful way.

That's the kind of lesson you learn when you let the Lord Jesus hold the violin of your life. He'll let you run the bow over the strings, back and forth, not too hard, not too soft, but just right. He'll help you get into the right relationship rhythms and patterns so you can make beautiful music with other people.

There's no misspelling in music. Or love! †

90. Flunking the Bar Exam

But as for you, ye thought evil against me;
but God meant it unto good,
to bring to pass, as it is this day, to save much people alive.

— Gen. 50:20

A friend of a friend wasn't sure she would ever be able to have children. Early in their marriage, her husband had to have surgery to remove a cancerous testicle. So when their one and only daughter was born a while later, they celebrated as if they had had a miracle from on high.

Which, of course, they did. She was the cutest of all babies, of course. They poured themselves into raising her. She was very, very close to her parents, especially her mother. She wanted more than anything else to make them proud of her.

She had a great childhood, studied hard, and became the valedictorian of a top-ranked Nebraska high school. She was deeply involved in just about every facet of her school, including athletics and extracurricular activities.

She made it into a prestigious West Coast university, and followed that up by attending a prestigious West Coast law school.

I doubt she ever got anything but an "A" in any class she ever took, in her 13 years of public school, four years of college, and three years of law school.

Finally, her "season" of education was coming to an end. She was in her final year of law school.

Her parents were so proud of her, and she was happy, except for one little thing. Probably because she had been such a gunner all through school, she had never had a serious boyfriend and had actually had very few dates. She was beginning to get a little nervous about finishing law school and beginning her legal career without any love life in sight.

Was work all there was going to be for her?

Then she came home to Nebraska to attend one of those iconic Cornhusker football games at the University of Nebraska-Lincoln. After all her hard work through all those years of school, her parents were thrilled to see her relaxed and laughing with some of her old high school friends. And sure enough, someone introduced her to a handsome and charming young man.

And even though he was from "boring" old Nebraska and she was now a California cool cat, they hit it off really well.

She returned to California to finish law school, kept in touch with the young man by texts and phone calls, saw him again at Christmas and over spring break, but was resolved to take a job with a top law firm in California and work 24/7 to "be" somebody out there. She was graduating at the top of her class. All that stood between her and that dream job was the California bar exam.

Which she took, after she had graduated and spent most of last summer studying for it. Test anxiety? Not her. She was a great test-taker. Everybody told her it would be a piece of cake.

But, for the first time in her life, she failed at something. She flunked the bar exam.

What? Nobody could believe it. She was devastated. All that studying, all those years, for nothing? It would have been easy to sink into bitterness and despair. It was by far the most terrible thing that had ever happened to her.

Rather than stay out there and try again, she came home to Nebraska, full of shame, to take what she thought would be an easier bar exam, and go right back out there to California and start her high-flying career.

But the minute she got back to town, the young man came right over, took her in his arms, told her he was glad she had flunked that dumb bar exam because it brought her back to him, and told her he loved her and wanted to spend his life with her.

Wow!

Very soon after that, she found out that her mother had not one but two kinds of cancer – thyroid and breast – and needed her one and only daughter by her side as never before.

The daughter didn't even blink. Of COURSE she would stay in Nebraska and see her mother through this trial. Her mother's friends all agreed that she was the most wonderful daughter in the world, to sacrifice like that and interrupt her career at the drop of a hat.

The husband and father was there for the sick woman as well, with a quip. Remember how he had lost one testicle to cancer more than 25 years before? Now his wife was going to have a mastectomy. They'd each be missing one body part special to their respective genders. But he told her, with a warm hug and a smile: "We've always been a matched set!"

As their one and only child saw her parents' tears, realized what a blessing it would be for her to be there for both of them during this difficult time, and saw that her chance at true love was right there for her, too, all of a sudden, failing that bar exam looked like the most wonderful thing that had ever happened to her.

Thank You, Jesus. Thank You that she failed . . . so that she could succeed in the "exam" of life . . . which is all about our relationships.

Right now, the daughter is getting ready for the Nebraska bar exam, living at home to care for her mother post-surgery, and spending a lot of time with the young man, making sure he is "the one."

In closing arguments here in the "court of public opinion," I think the verdict is unanimous that there will be a trip very soon to that other iconic place in Nebraska besides the football stadium where everybody loves to go.

I'm talking about Borsheim's, the famous jewelry store owned by Warren Buffett – where young Nebraska couples have often gone, over the decades, for an engagement ring.

That diamond will shine bright. But nobody's smile will shine brighter than the loving parents of the bride-to-be. She failed, and that allowed her to succeed. †

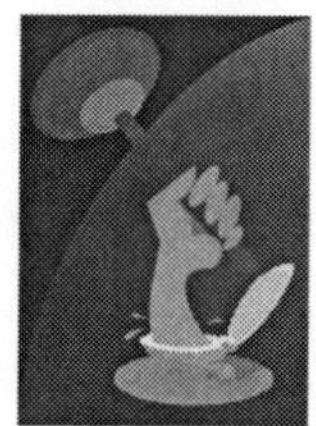

91. I Fought the Clog, and the Clog Won

He shall deliver thee in six troubles:
yea, in seven there shall no evil touch thee.

—Job 5:19

Last Friday night, the kitchen sink backed up and cascaded onto my beautiful maple floor, cupping the planks and splattering down into the basement toy room.

Then the laundry-room sink clogged, too. I had to hurl bucket after bucket of water out onto the driveway from both sinks.

I'm recovering from a rib injury. Lugging all those buckets of water was painful. I had to bend over sideways and waddle crookedly like a deranged duck.

The neighbors must've gotten an eyeful as this frowning, crab-like creature regularly kicked open the door and burst out onto the driveway, hurling buckets of water and emitting peculiar grunts, like an over-the-top pagan ritual.

In between hurls, I pumped the plunger and dumped drainer goo. But the flow still wouldn't go no mo'.

The sinks kept refilling. Where was all this water coming from?

What was clogging the pipes?

And why had our water pressure been so puny? It took an hour to fill up a pan, and all I had to shampoo my hair was steam.

But I didn't want to call a plumber. Who's got $4,000 an hour?

Meanwhile, my spouse, who wears the logical/mechanical pants in the family, was inconveniently out of town. So I was stumped.

Suddenly, the overflow stopped. I stared suspiciously at the standing water for hours. Finally, I collapsed into bed.

Next morning, the sinks were empty! I rejoiced.

Too soon! Eerily, 24 hours later, the overflow was back.

Again, after an hour of crab-like scurrying and bucket hurling, it stopped. Again, next morning it was allllll better.

My spouse arrived home from softball Nationals in Georgia with our daughter late that night. I described the clog. He brought up the Shrimp Peel Holocaust from our newlywed days. You can't put anything down the disposal, remember? Did NOT! I don't even put WATER down the disposal anymore!

Meanwhile, his suitcase had sat, forgotten and forlorn, on the tarmac in Atlanta in a thunderstorm. When it finally arrived in Omaha, everything was drenched.

So the next day, again crab-walking, I lugged three sacks of wet, stinky laundry to the cleaners.

I also had to take the dog to get spayed. HER plumbing needed attention, too.

The four daughters all had crises going on. TLC Alert!

Then, suddenly, my email startup page disappeared, with my irreplaceable contact lists. I was stumped.

Then the clog came back.

And our basement storage room flooded in a torrential downpour, so I had to wet-vac, bent over sideways, both whining and grunting.

No laundry, no dishwasher, no showers, and it smelled too plumbing-y to cook or eat in the house. Desperate situation.

Finally, the plumber came. He worked for two hours and couldn't get anywhere. He said to call Roto Rooter.

Roto Rooter worked for seven hours and couldn't get anywhere. They said to call the plumber.

This time, two came, with nuclear detonators, and finally fixed it.

Not really. The weight of the water in the line apparently just pushed the clog forward and out. Presto! It unclogged itself, basically. This, for $4,000 an hour. (Well, not really, but it was costly.)

They said the clog formed because the water line turns seven times through our house. It should be making a straight shot. It's because of my basement remodeling decisions. I was determined to avoid low-hanging pipes in the basement rec room. I wanted the tall, dark and handsome boys our daughters would date in the future not to bonk their heads on the pipes, or they'd never come back, and we'd be stuck with super-short sons-in-law.

But now, we have seven changes of directions for our pipes. Problems will continue to ensue. Solution: brace yourself. It's a $1.29 detachable screen mini-basket for our kitchen drain. It will keep potato peels and such from conglomerating in those twisty-turny pipes.

Hark! A light in the wilderness!

Other huge problems started to resolve, too.

The computer guru recovered my email, salvaging my self-esteem by saying the problem was stupendously unusual that I had nothing to do with.

Phone communications were restored.

Everyone got their TLC.

The dog feels fine, now a "Ms."

The laundry is fluffed and folded.

Once again at peace, I sat down, and philosophized:

Life is like a plumbing clog: mysterious, hidden, with twists and turns. Sometimes it hurts, or stinks, or makes us look silly.

Most things in life work fine without our intervention, like plumbing. But when things go wrong, if you hang in there, keep your sense of humor, and get help, eventually problems will work themselves out.

That's my story, and I'm sticking to it.

This morning, though, my bathroom sink took a long, long time to drain.

I started to panic. I could feel the urge to crab-walk. But then I got a hold of myself, set my jaw, and told that clog:

"Don't mess with me. This, too, shall pass." †

92. Earl the Pearl

And they will deceive every one his neighbour,
and will not speak the truth:
they have taught their tongue to speak lies,
and weary themselves to commit iniquity.

— Jeremiah 9:5

I should've known better than to trust a home remodeling flyer left in our door. Who does that? Everybody knows you spin around three times and then point to a listing in the Yellow Pages when you need to select a home remodeling contractor.

But I went by this random flyer. That was my first mistake.

Fingers crossed, I placed the call. The man who answered had the communication skills of a United Nations interpreter, the confidence of an NFL quarterback, and the grace and charm of a five-star hotel maître d'.

His name was Earl. He said he could do the plumbing. He could do the electrical. He could do the carpentry. He could do the tile work, the carpeting, the mirrors.

He could do it all! And he SOUNDED so NICE on the PHONE.

This, to me, was enough.

I got him over to look at the hideous guest bath. It really did look like something out of Alcatraz. It needed a complete re-do.

Earl took one look, scratched a few numbers, gave me a quote that sounded very cheap, and we shook on it.

I called my Beloved. "He can do the plumbing! He can do the electrical! He can do the carpentry! He can do it all! I call him . . . Earl the Pearl!"

My Beloved, as usual, was skeptical. But, as busy as he was, he thought it would be fine if I wanted to run this job. Just make sure never to pay him until AFTER he has done the work, he advised me. Stay on him! You've got to hold his feet to the fire!

What? Not this guy! He will get it all done, chop-chop! It will be perfect! He will never let me down! He was Earl the Pearl!

Earl the Pearl showed up just after dawn on the first day. I bust my buttons over his promptness. He brought in all his own tools in a beat-up old plastic shoebox. That's my Earl the Pearl! The picture of cost-efficiency! Who needs a fancy, store-bought toolbox? He was no-frills and all-business. Atta boy!

He had that old bathroom completely torn out by lunchtime. What a pearl!

He asked for a small checkie-poo to cover expenses at the hardware store, and said he would be right back with these materials after lunch. I had no misgivings, compunctions or reservations whatsoever. I cut the check.

Voila: he left, but came back with a bunch of stuff. He showed me the receipts, and worked through to the end of the afternoon.

I was in heaven! This was progress! Earl, my heaven-sent Pearl!

Yeah, well remember the Bible expression, "pearl of great price"? Riiiiiiight.

(Cue the ominous organ chords)

The NEXT day, Earl arrived at about 8:30 a.m. It was not exactly dawn, but still acceptably early. He asked for another checkie-poo, this one fairly major, to go buy more construction stuff. I figured it was already time for the big stuff, so I was OK with it. Off he went, mumbling something I couldn't quite hear.

Now imagine the hands of the kitchen clock whizzing around. Ten. Two. Four.

Oh, no, Earl! You must have been in a terrible accident! That's the only explanation for your absence! Or you were kidnapped! Or the bridge collapsed! Or you had a massive heart attack! Don't worry! I'll find out which hospital, and I will send a nice bouquet.

Suddenly, here Earl came, at 4:52 p.m., with a silly smile, slurred speech and one overall strap fastened with two twists.

He dropped off a small quantity of supplies, much less than what that major checkie-poo would have covered. But before I could engage him in purposeful conversation, he spun on his heel, mumbled over his shoulder something unintelligible, jogged to the driveway, and laid scratch in what I now realized was about a 1949 Ford pickup with bad tires and a rusted-out door that didn't close all the way.

The dust kicked up by his bad tires formed a word over the driveway:

S – U – C – K – E – R !!!!!

The next day, Earl didn't come at all. The lonely cricket chirping in the busted-out guest bath was my only companion.

He didn't answer his phone. He didn't stop by. He didn't come at all the next day, either. Or the next. He was AWOL for over a week.

The luster was wearing off my Earl the Pearl.

He did arrive on a spotty basis over the next few weeks. But he wasn't half as cheery or confident. I kept overhearing him having furtive, stressed-out telephone conversations with "someone" on the other end. This person was apparently coaching him on how exactly to do the plumbing, the electrical, the carpentry, etc.

Do you know how it feels to have forked over a major checkie-poo to a guy who stretches your kitchen phone into your nuked-out guest bathroom and you can overhear him whispering fervently on the phone, "C'mon, man, you've gotta help me. What do you &(#&% mean? What are those? I have no %&$*@ idea how to do that. Couldn't you just use ^&@*$ duct tape?!?"

And then he would waltz out of there to put the phone back, with a phony smile. I'd ask, "Anything wrong, Earl?" He'd mumble something I couldn't quite hear that sounded like, "Oh, nooooo! Not at all! Everything's fine!"

Oh, boy. There goes my "cred" with the Mister. He'll never let me do any remodeling ever again!

Oddly, whenever Earl would ask for another checkie-poo, I could always hear every word he said, loud and clear. But when I sought an explanation for the delays or lack of progress, a linguistic gulf the size of the Grand Canyon developed.

Slowly, it dawned on my pea brain that this poor man knew as much about bathroom remodeling as I did. And I was too naïve to see it! He needed a job so badly, he thought he could bluff his way through. And since he had a dope like me for a customer, so far, it was working.

He had me over a barrel, anyway. This job was already taking so long, our little daughter who was jouncing around in her crib on his first day here would be planning her high-school graduation party before he was done. The bathroom was about half completed and a big mess. If I fired him now, the yahoo I would find to take over the job would charge me triple, just because of the "sucker!!!" pheromones wafting thickly through the air.

So I gave Earl what, for me, were serious threats. Let's quit messing around. Let's get 'r done. Let's see some visible progress. Or no more checkie-poo's.

He didn't show up for another several days. In the meantime, someone delivered a big box of floor tiles. I put them in the garage.

These were what us geezers call "linoleum" tiles, made of fake whatever, and fairly rubbery. I was happy to see that Earl was to the point where maybe if he could get the floor done, we could actually see the end of the project, at least with a highly-calibrated telescope.

It was the dead of winter. When Earl arrived that next rare morning for work, I told him about the floor tiles, and pointed him toward the garage to bring them in. He did. He took one out. It was stiff. Of course it was stiff. It had been in the garage for a week because he hadn't been here.

"Well," Earl the Pearl said, "I can't put these in. They're too stiff and cold." He turned on his heel to high-tail it out the door, mumbling over his shoulder. "I'll leave them here in the house to warm up and come back next week."

"OH, NO, YOU WON'T!!!!!" I literally grabbed him by the scruff of his plaid shirt's collar.

"You come right back here, Earl. You can put these tiles in the microwave a few at a time, and warm them up enough to be flexible. THEN you can leave. Here. See?"

I demonstrated by placing a tile in the microwave and zapping it for 15 seconds. Took it out, and bent it to and fro with awesome flexibility.

He gaped. I startled myself with my new-found assertiveness. Aha! The old "high technology" defense. It had never occurred to him that a ticked-off housewife would stoop to using the kitchen microwave – something! anything! – to get that job done and get him out of her hair.

I think I waved his original flyer in his face, too, and mentioned key vocabulary words such as "city licensing office," "municipal prosecutor," "Better Business Bureau," "our attorney," "our friend Knuckles the Professional Persuader," and other concepts, which spurred him on to hyper-speed completion of the project.

I don't remember anything else about the job, except of course that My Beloved made a few well-chosen remarks from time to time as he surveyed our bank balance dwindling.

But it finally got done. Even though high blood pressure emanations over our house were still being picked up by radar at the Strategic Air Defense Command outpost, I was relieved.

After all these adventures, as he was leaving for the last time with his crummy shoebox of tools and the very last kiss-off checkie-poo, Earl the Pearl lingered on the step. He cleared his throat. And then he asked if he could use me for a reference.

Dark thoughts flooded my mind. What for? "America's Funniest Home Videos"?!? The Better Business Bureau's Public Enemy No. 1 list?

I mumbled something that could've been a "yes" or a "no," and gently shut the door. I leaned against it on the inside, started chuckling, and outright laughing at the silly ordeal. I think I got a little delirious. Eventually, tears ran down my face, causing me to go into my beautiful new guest bathroom for a tissue.

I noticed that, despite the stress, the room turned out fine.

Though Earl the Pearl might have exaggerated a bit on his flyer, and got a little sidetracked in the process, overall, in the long run, he turned out to be a jewel after all. I shouldn't have been so impatient. It takes a long, long time to make a pearl. And 'til it's done, you might as well clam up. †

93. RumDum Cake

Favour is deceitful, and beauty is vain:
but a woman that feareth the Lord, she shall be praised.
Give her of the fruit of her hands;
and let her own works praise her in the gates.

— Proverbs 31:30,31

My friend is a tremendous, faithful Christian. She also has been a tremendous cook all her life. In fact, she wrote a cookbook, had it published, and sold it from coast to coast. Like many people, I think of her as a culinary expert, a real kitchen guru.

She's not all swolled up about it. In fact, she shares stories of cooking blunders just like the rest of us. It's nice to know the pro's occasionally have kitchen clown acts, too. Here's her latest:

It all started at the Bag and Save. Betty Crocker cake mixes were on sale for 89 cents. My friend couldn't resist that price. She also had a hankering for the Rum Cake recipe from the cookbook she authored. It had been her mother-in-law's favorite, always a hit. She knew the ingredients by heart, and picked them up. She was good to go.

Her adult son was coming over for dinner. He always kids her by walking into her kitchen and lifting the lid off the heirloom covered cake plate she keeps on the counter, a beautiful, swirled glass number from the 1950s. He lifts the chrome lid with the black Bakelite handle with a hopeful smile on his face, and then elaborately sighs when there is no cake underneath.

She'd surprise him this time with the Rum Cake. Sweeeeet! Literally!

It was a busy day. She was getting ready for a garage sale, and had piles of stuff all over the kitchen counters. A roast was browning in a pot on the stove. She took it off the burner and popped it into the oven. A few minutes later, for lack of counter space, she placed the glass cake plate on the burner . . . but had forgotten to turn off the heat.

POW! The glass exploded. Sharp slivers rained into the hot rum and butter glaze that she had going in the nearby saucepan.

It was, well, shattering. After the glass cleanup, she started over on the glaze, leaving it to simmer.

A while later, she and her adult son and his wife were in another room with the door closed, preparing for the garage sale, when he came out to put something on a pile and saw that the house was filled with smoke.

The forgotten glaze was ablaze!

A lid took care of the blaze, but not the smoke, the black crud on the bottom of her pan, and the overwhelming odor of burnt sugar. They opened all the windows and doors, hoping a silent alarm wasn't being sent to the fire station.

She started the THIRD batch of glaze. By now, there was not nearly enough rum left. Her son ran out for some more. They all thought the best idea would be to drink the rum and forget the glaze. But she nailed her feet to the floor in front of the stove so that she could not leave and screw it up again.

Meanwhile, the disasters had left her with no time to make potatoes from scratch, to go with the roast. So she pulled out her tiny, hidden stash of instant potatoes that she keeps, a la Queen Esther, "for such a time as this" (Esther 4:14). Unfortunately, her husband walked into the kitchen when she was opening the foil bag. He grew up in poverty, and had O.D.'ed on instant potatoes. He made a face.

So she tried to doctor them up with a few leftover "real" potatoes she'd stashed in the fridge from a few nights before. She stirred them into the fluffy mass. That's funny! It became more liquefied, rather than stiffening up.

Hmmm. She ran her finger inside the leftover potatoes container . . . and tasted cream cheese frosting.

Ewwwww!

So they had peaches and green beans with their roast beef, and no potatoes. Decidedly un-American. Substandard for a cookbook guru.

They compensated by having not one, but two pieces each of Rum Cake for dessert. She figured the cost at $53.89. Oh, well. It was delicious!

That's how it goes with cooking. You take your lumps, smile, and go on. Yo, ho, ho and a piece of Rum Cake. †

94. The Magnificent Rhubarb

Seest thou a man wise in his own conceit?
There is more hope of a fool than of him.

— Proverbs 26:12

I had a Big, Bad Birthday coming up. Time to reassess. All the goodies that come with youth were gone. What was left? Experience, stealth, cunning, and the theme song lyrics to dozens of corny 1960s sit-coms. They would have to do for my old age.

But when you reach a milestone like this, it's nice to be able to point to SOMETHING for which you've developed skill over the years. For me, that's gardening.

When the going gets tough, the tough first go to Dairy Queen and get one of those great new Brownie Batter Blizzards, and then go out to the garden to work it off. Blood, sweat and tears: my garden has gotten them all from me. We have a three-acre monstrosity of a yard and pasture. I always have a new project going on.

One year, it was a big berm out front with "bubbling boulders," a wacky water feature that sets our house apart. From the indoor switch, it also allows us to play naughty practical jokes on unsuspecting passers-by. You know: you hold up your rake and shout, "Water! Come forth!" and your accomplice inside flips the switch. I now know how all those pagan witch doctors got the people to worship them without breaking a sweat.

When we lost about half of the trees between our yard and our dear neighbor's, weeds were springing up. It was a real maintenance nightmare. So I made a gigantic shade garden for us both to enjoy. I used the overflow from both of our yards – hostas, columbine and perennials galore — and a meandering flagstone path. It's 20 degrees cooler there on hot summer days, a real haven for skeeters and people alike.

Last, but not least, when we got rid of our horses, we turned the two paddocks into a sort of Disneyland of garden space. It's now a grid of garden beds, complete with tough black plastic walkways separating Flowerland from Strawberryland and Veggieland from Herbland. When there are weeds, count those beds as "Tomorrowland" – because I never have time to remove them today but will always have time . . . you know.

My loved ones "enabled" me. My Beloved brought in countless trailerloads of primeau compost and constructed a bunny fence reminiscent of the Berlin Wall. My brother-in-law gave me bombastic, tall tomato cages that are the envy of the neighborhood. My cousin made me a dozen super-strong veggie cages that would withstand a nuclear blast. Mom gave me all kinds of garden gear. Our daughters gave me a spectacular garden hat, cute gloves, and darling stakes. One even painted the names of herbs on smooth river rocks for an Etsy look that I love.

Now men let my husband win on the golf course just so they might score a jar of my famous habanero pepper jelly. Those of Italian descent say my arrabbiatta pasta sauce is a world-beater with homegrown tomatoes, hot peppers, onions and herbs.

I loved growing the flowers for our daughter Eden's wedding, and from the overflow of their descendants last year was able to raise a good deal of money in bouquets for my inner city friends' Christian mission.

So yes, there is pride in my heart about this gardening gig. And you know what cometh after pride:

Last year, I added only one plant, a rhubarb seedling. My Beloved loves rhubarb pie, so it seemed a worthy new pursuit. I put the baby rhubarb in an out-of-the-way spot by the asparagus, where I knew the soil was super fertile. A hasty check in my reference book showed that all you do the first year is let it grow. Ooh, those big, curly leaves! This would be fun!

Sure enough, this spring, the seedling came back and grew huge! Gigantic! Mondo!!!

I swaggered out to check it from time to time. Mmm-HMMMM!! Was I the bomb at gardening, or what? I side-dressed it with more compost, patting myself on the back with my dirt-stained gloves.

Of course, the long stalks were white as snow, not lusciously red. But I figured that must come later in the summer as the plant matured.

It wasn't even June 1, but the rhubarb was getting taller and taller, the stalks got longer and longer, and the leaves got big enough for a rain cover for the College World Series ballfield! I would be able to make a HUNDRED rhubarb pies!!!

What a magnificent rhubarb plant! What a great gardener am I!!! I was thinkin' state fair. Heck! NATIONAL FAIR!!! INTERNATIONAL!!!

My chest puffed out and all the buttons popped off.

Then one day, my darling neighbor's equally darling daughter asked me over the fence, "Hey, Sus, what's that BIG plant in your garden? Mom has one just like it and we wondered how it got there."

I told her it was a rhubarb plant, and wasn't it marvelous? But I hadn't kept the tag so wasn't sure of the variety. It didn't go to seed last year and I hadn't cut any off. So how could it have spread? Well, lucky day!

A few more weeks went by, and SWOOSH!!! These really tall spikes with thousands of seeds thrust up from my magnificent rhubarb plant. I broke a few spikes off, because I didn't think you were supposed to let it go to seed, but just wasn't sure. Now it was still a magnificent rhubarb plant, but a lopsided magnificent one.

But hmm – the long stalks were STILL as white as snow. I could see the plant's crown in the ground, which looked like a scary, white, giant alien BRAIN . . .

. . . and I suddenly realized, that's no rhubarb plant.

THAT'S A DANG WEED!!!!!!!!!!!!!

Somehow, it had displaced the real thing, and just happened to look a lot like it. I think this weed is called "burdock." All I know is, no delicious pies can be had from it.

My dear neighbor, and her equally dear daughter, quietly confirmed the diagnosis with a twinkle in their eyes.

Now I have the task of going out and digging the thing up. Doubtless has roots growing halfway to China. Going to need my strongest spade, biggest trash can and a LARGE-size Brownie Batter Blizzard.

Oh, this gardening. It'll cut you down to size. On the other hand, it produces a good thing to grow in your heart.

Guess I'll be making pie this season after all. Humble pie! ✝

95. Bittersweet

***The full soul loatheth an honeycomb;
but to the hungry soul every bitter thing is sweet.***

— Proverbs 27:7

Ours may be the only home around with a whole bunch of dead, creepy branches coiled up in the bathtub, soaking. No, I'm not getting in there with them and taking some kind of weird new environmental bath. That "woodn't" be very glamorous.

No, they're grapevines from our backyard. We have an area under huge pine trees that is supposed to be a shady garden wonderland. But I let it go this summer. It became a thicket of unwanted vines, volunteer trees, weeds and my old nemesis, poison ivy. Two afternoons last week, I "manned up" and went out there and collected five garbage cans, five yard-waste sacks, and a pickup truckload of the bad stuff. Boy, does it look better.

How did the grapevines get in our yard? Our neighbors had purchased some fancy European grape plants some years ago. They cultivate them on some makeshift "T's" and have their own mini-winery. It's cool! Well, the birds occasionally feast on their grapes. Then nature happens as they fly over our backyard. And we had grapevines aplenty.

Even though it was a pain to pull the stiff vines off the trees and out from under the soft layer of needles, I now have about a mile of the stuff. You know grapevines: the ones with the funny little springs sticking out? All kinds of character. I'm so excited.

I'm soaking them so they'll be pliable. As soon as I get a chance (this week? this year?) I'm going to try to make wreaths and garlands out of them to give as presents.

What I thought was going to be a chore – weeding – turned into a fun adventure. Now I'll have something tangible to show for my bad back and aching arms.

There's more: I picked up a ton of pretty pine cones that would make great winter decorations, but they were sticky. The answer: you bake them in the oven for a couple of hours at a low temperature to kill off the bugs and get the sticky resin to ooze off.

The good news was, our house smelled fabulous. The BAD news was, I didn't think to put foil in the pan. It got dotted with countless hard blobs of resin and took a lot of work to clean off. But I love my new pinecone arsenal and am looking forward to doing fun things with them.

Still another benefit: I didn't even know our neighbor had a black walnut tree back there until I started spotting all these half-gnawed walnut shells, and plenty of the hard, green, mini tennis balls that are the unshelled nuts. Now we have a half-bucket full, and my mouth is watering over all those great holiday desserts I can make.

I could've paid some burly man to do all this for me. But then I wouldn't have had an adventure! I could have bought grapevine wreaths, pine cones and black walnuts at the store, very inexpensively. But they wouldn't be a tenth of the blessing they are, since I foraged for them myself, on a gorgeous Indian summer day in my own back yard. The hard work was well worth it.

But then the phone rang, and it was my mother. She is doing great, but she has battled lung cancer and now brain cancer in recent years.

She remembers giving away boxes of holiday decorations last year, when she didn't think she was going to make it. Thankfully, she was wrong. Now she needed her Halloween stuff back for Bridge Club, which she is hosting next week. She thought she had given it all to me. Since it is Indian summer, could she be an Indian giver and get it back?

"But Mom, I don't have it," I protested. I had just been rooting around in our holiday closet, and hadn't seen the ceramic jack o'lanterns and other decorations she described. Could she have given it to the Goodwill? She didn't think so, but she sure didn't want to have to go get all new stuff.

She said with a sigh, "Maybe I can just go out and buy some bittersweet and use that for my table."

But I had been out and about, and hadn't seen any bittersweet in any of the garden stores. We had just been to Nebraska City, the apple orchard capital of our state with all kinds of autumn decorations for sale, and I hadn't seen any bittersweet there, either.

I hung up. And teared up.

Poor Mom. I don't want her to have any disappointments or frustrations. But I can't help her. All these months as she has battled cancer, I've felt helpless. I'm not a surgeon, not a radiologist, not a nurse. And now, in a really easy area where I should be able to help – cutesy home decorating — I'm a bust, too.

Immediately, the phone rang again.

This time, it was the neighbor – the one with the black walnut tree. She has a spectacular yard with all kinds of plants and is getting ready to re-landscape.

"We're replacing the fence around the swimming pool," she said, "and we're going to have to take out our big, old bittersweet plant. Would you like to come over and take as much as you want?"

WHAAAAAAAAT?!?

Would I?

For 10 years we've lived here, and I've seen that big bush cascading over her fence. For 10 years, I had no idea what it was. The berries are kind of hidden underneath the foliage.

I told her what Mom had just said about bittersweet, and since this neighbor had gone to school with my mom decades ago, it was fun for her to be able to bless her so specially.

Wiping my tears, I toddled over there, met this dear neighbor for a hug in the sun, and clipped off a whole plastic tub of the long strands of golden berries. The "harvest" was enough to line our kitchen windowsill and make a wreath for our daughter's first apartment . . . saving the best sprigs for Mom's Bridge Club centerpiece.

The look on Mom's face was priceless. She was so happy and surprised! I knew it was yet another blessing from the Gardener, taking a bitter situation and making it sweet, for both of us.

This morning, those golden berries had burst into their fiery orange splendor, with the golden "coats" still on. I'm sure it's the same at Mom's house. The Bridge Club will be totally impressed!

Thank You, lovely Gardener, for the way You weave the vines of love around us and through us. Thank You for these little "coincidences" that comfort us with the knowledge that every need will be met, every hunger filled. Thank You for always turning what seems to be a bad situation into something good and precious and right, with blessings that burst open in warm colors in our hearts.

Can't wait to see what You come up with to help me clean my bathtub when the grapevine's out of there! †

96. Josita's Voice

And he said unto me,
My grace is sufficient for thee:
for my strength is made perfect in weakness.
Most gladly therefore will I rather glory in my infirmities,
that the power of Christ may rest upon me.

— 2 Corinthians 12:9

She's a wonderful, fun nun, a member of our extended family. The first time I met Sister Josita, we were at a wedding rehearsal dinner, and I was seated next to another relative, a priest.

He had his clerical garb on, plain as day. Despite the obvious clue, some other party guest asked me, "Is that your husband?"

I looked at Sister Josita. She looked at me. We both burst out laughing. From that day forward, we had a bond.

But I just found out something that makes her even more precious to me, especially now that it's the Christmas season.

See, Josita contracted paralytic poliomyelitis during her senior year in high school. It was during the polio epidemic of the early 1950s. She spent an entire semester in the hospital and had months of physical therapy, but still graduated with her class.

Even though she has had to deal with polio and its lifelong consequences, Josita has led an inspiring life. She graduated from college and worked as an elementary school teacher for 36 years. That career was followed up by many more years of service to her Notre Dame Community in "retirement" – as if — ha ha. Nuns never truly retire, you know. She's still working, to this day, in the development office of the Notre Dame Community. They do a ton of good, here and around the world.

The thing is, soon after Sister Josita retired from teaching in the 1990s, she developed symptoms of Post-Polio Syndrome. That's fairly common for polio victims. In her case, it attacked her voice. Her left vocal cord became extremely weak. She began to have difficulty communicating. Her voice dropped to a raspy whisper.

Now, Josita is a delight to talk to. She can communicate very well. But you do have to listen carefully.

Of course, friends teased her that the reason she lost her voice is that she yelled at her kids all those years that she taught. Not a bit of it! She says she told the students that she was NOT the type to yell and scream. Instead, she told them, she would use a reasonable voice, and "you will just have to listen, because I might say something important, like, 'Recess time!'"

Her engaging humor and great attitude also are shown by the fact that she loves those moments when she is meeting with people who don't know her well. After a few minutes of discussion, invariably somebody will ask, "Why are we whispering?"

Her gracious attitude, like her whispering, is contagious. And that's a good thing. Would that there were more people in this world who never talk loud, and who make you want to listen. Josita chooses to look on the bright side, staying positive and appreciating blessings of all kinds, no matter how subtle.

And here is the best blessing of all:

In 2007, her elderly, widowed mother was quite ill in a nursing home. But miraculously, all eight of the adult children and most of their spouses were able to come from all around the country to celebrate her birthday with her as she reached the big milestone, 99. It was nearly Christmas.

There was birthday cake, and a party. But for the most part, their mother stayed quiet, kept her eyes closed and just squeezed her children's hands, letting them know she loved having them there. But her condition weakened.

One son, an archbishop, celebrated mass in the nursing home chapel, and brought Viaticum (Holy Communion given to Catholics who are on their final journey). The siblings split up the night vigil.

The next afternoon, all of the family sat or stood around the bed, praying a little. Then a brother suggested that, since it was almost Christmas, they should sing "Silent Night," the way they did when they were children.

Josita opened her mouth to sing, no doubt expecting only a weak rasp to come out.

Much to her surprise, though, out came a strong voice, in the alto harmony that she always sang to "Silent Night."

She began singing the song, and the rest joined in, astounded, as she was. "They all just kind of looked at me," Josita said.

She said, "The miracle of that moment was that, even though there was a large cupboard behind me and I was backed up to it, I felt a warm presence behind me, as if there were some-one standing right behind me.

"It felt as though there were strong hands gently around my neck. The warmth put strength in my vocal cords I had not felt for 11 years."

Tears shining in her eyes, Josita sang the first and second verses of "Silent Night," belting out the chorus, overwhelmed with joy.

Josita said, "It wasn't anything I had planned. I hadn't wished that I could sing to Mother. But of course, that was the best birthday gift for her imaginable. I feel sure that it was Jesus, behind me, helping me. He would know the deepest desire of my heart even better than I would."

She also felt that, through some mystery, her late father was also in the room. He was the one who had continued her physical therapy after graduation, as she fought off the polio. They formed a very special bond. "He taught me how to cope with the physical pain and accept my limitations," Josita said. And now here he was, in spirit, showing her that, with Christ, there ARE no limitations.

As quickly as it came, though, the vocal strength passed. She could only whisper songs and prayers for the rest of the afternoon. "No voice – absolutely nothing," she said. "So I knew it was a miracle."

The room was peaceful. Just a few hours later, the siblings gathered around the bed, and the mother slowly breathed her last breath.

You know, the story just makes the point that the greatest blessings in this life can only come to those who are suffering. If Josita's voice hadn't gotten so weak, that moment of supernatural power could never have happened.

Josita puts it this way:

"We know that God is there constantly for us. Nothing will ever happen to you that you and He can't handle together."

You said it, Sister. What a message for today. Sing it, loud! Go tell it on the mountain, over the hills and everywhere, that Jesus Christ is alive and well and in this world.

And come what may, with His incredible power, He will give you a song to sing, strongly, beautifully, and full of grace. †

97. Heaven-Scented Departure

But I have all, and abound:
I am full, having received . . .
the things which were sent from you,
an odour of a sweet smell,
a sacrifice acceptable, well pleasing to God.

— Philippians 4:18

A friend's mother was diagnosed with a terminal illness at age 81. She went to her daughter's home to die.

There would have been enough money to put her in a nursing home or retirement center. Nobody would have thought a thing of it, if the family had decided to pay professionals to care for their loved one, ease the transition, and conserve their time and energy.

But my friend wanted to be her mother's final caregiver. She wanted to do it, even though she had no nursing experience and had never done anything like this before.

Doctors said her mother didn't have long. So my friend determined to make the best of a bad situation. She switched to part-time on her job, and transformed her living room into, well, a dying room.

It was to be a cheerful dying room, make no mistake. The hospital bed was surrounded by chairs, for lots of expected visitors. There was a lot of light in the room, just steps from the kitchen.

My friend's whole family helped make it happen. Everybody pitched in as best they could. Still, most of the burden fell to the daughter: making meals, shampooing her mother's hair, lifting her, dispensing her medications, changing the sheets, questioning the medical people, handling the endless paperwork, and on and on.

The dying lady made just one simple request: she wanted her daughter to plant sweet peas outside the window, where she could watch them grow.

My 40-something friend is not an avid gardener. She had never done much more than watering pre-planted, store-bought pots. She didn't even know what sweet peas are. They're an old-fashioned flower you don't see too often in people's designer yards these days.

But, glad to have something tangible and easy that she could do to please her mom, she bought a sweet pea seed packet for 79 cents. She planted the seeds in plain sight of the window nearest her mother's bed.

With her mom's coaching, my friend coaxed the seeds to germination and kept the roots cool with a little mulch. She rigged up a string trellis for the vines to climb.

The weeks passed. Together, mother and daughter watched the vines spread out across the trellis. The tendrils were holding on tight . . . just like my friend and her mother.

The leaves unfurled. The vines grew. The trellis filled up. The illness got worse.

Finally, one summer day, the mother died.

My friend came home from the funeral exhausted. She saw her mother's empty bed. She grabbed the pillow and sniffed her mother's fading scent. Painful reality slammed into her. The good front she had put up suddenly collapsed. She threw herself on the bed, and burst into horrendous sobs.

"Mom! Mom! You're dead! You're gone! I'll never see you again!" She sobbed some more.

Finally, blinking through tears, she lifted her head and looked outside. Her cried-out eyes focused on the sweet pea plant. She saw that the first flower had blossomed.

It was big.

It was white.

It was perfect.

She ran outside and ran up to it. It had a beautiful scent that could only be described as *heavenly*.

She cried some more. This time, they were tears of joy.

Job well done, the flower was saying.

That's spiritual economics. The sweet peas had cost just pennies but gave her mother great pleasure in the midst of suffering. The daughter had given just a few minutes of effort to grow the flower for her mother in those last days, but the simple little acts of love are the ones that mean the most.

Doing what's right. Doing what comes naturally. Expressing love. Bringing joy.

It's the five-senses fullness of a summer morning, the promise of a bud about to burst wide open, the persistence of a vine climbing eagerly up, higher, toward the light.

Isn't that how the Gardener wants us to be?

Stretching toward the light. Growing. Expanding. And yet, still holding on tight.

Then, when you're ready, when it's time, you bloom.

Later, a friend told her that in the language of flowers, the sweet pea means "delicate pleasures and departure."

Departure! Yes. How fitting. But departure also leads to arrival. The flower signaled that her mother had arrived in a better place. She knew it was true. She knew she'd see her again one day, and they would be together forever. The flower was just the exclamation point on that promise.

That's the Gardener's perfect timing.

And you can count on it, Sweet Pea. ✝

98. The Yellow Rose

***Behold, I will put a fleece of wool in the floor;
and if the dew be on the fleece only,
and it be dry upon all the earth beside,
then shall I know that thou wilt save Israel
by mine hand, as thou hast said.***

— Judges 6:37

She's a sweet, gentle lady. Nothing bad should ever happen to her. But it did.

She had a daughter in her 20s who died of a drug overdose.

It ended a long struggle. The girl had been sexually molested by her father. She tried to commit suicide. She dabbled in lesbianism, and then got mixed up with a rough party crowd.

The daughter knew the things she was doing were wrong and destructive. She underwent counseling. She prayed. She loved God. She tried to get stable. But it was hard. She was overwhelmed with pain.

Drinking with friends seemed to help. She was over 21. The family couldn't stop it.

Her mother knew that after a certain point, all you can do is pray. So she did.

But the daughter drifted down, deeper into trouble. A health problem that added physical pain to her emotional distress led to the use of pain-killing drugs.

One morning, the mother walked in on her, dead of a drug overdose.

The mother was devastated. She cried out to God: "Why? Wasn't she asking for Your help? Didn't You hear our prayers?"

She was terrified that her daughter would go to hell. The daughter had promised to devote her life to Jesus and to trust Him for everything, but then she turned around and proved that she didn't trust Him at all, by doing what she did.

The mother was in agony. Like Gideon and his dewy fleece, she pleaded for a sign. "Oh, God," she cried, in those first hours of grief. "Give me a sign that she's in heaven with You. I won't tell another soul. I just want to know for sure."

Desperate, she proposed one. "Show me a yellow rose. Then I'll know that she's OK."

As the funeral bouquets began to arrive, she scanned them eagerly, expecting to see her wish come true. But the funeral came and went. There were no yellow roses. Not a single one.

Her daughter had "blown" her salvation? It can't be! She trusted you, God!

Then she felt guilty for "testing" God with her demand for a sign. God is loving, but He's not a short-order cook that you can boss around. She decided to be patient, and let Him be Him.

The weeks passed. She thought about her wish a little less often. Eventually, she felt up to resuming her life's routines. One of them was to go to an old folks' home once a week and read to an elderly lady.

She walked in, and her eyes riveted on something that was in a waterglass on the TV. A yellow rose!

"Would you take that for me?" the old lady was saying. "The aroma bothers my emphysema."

To the grieving mother, it smelled heavenly. Her heart leaped and she burst into tears. She took the rose home, elated, thanking God all the way. It was a holy moment that she kept to herself and cherished.

But that isn't all. One year later, her sisters both brought flowers to the grave on the anniversary of her daughter's death.

They each brought an armload of the same flower: yellow roses. But the mother had never told a soul about her "deal" for reassurance.

Some coincidence, eh?

A while later, a friend gave the mother a bookmark. It had a poem by Esther Lorenz: "My Yellow Rose of Peace." The message:

Accept my yellow rose
With love and peace
I pray that your joy in the Lord
Will never cease.
When He comes to take you
From this land
May He walk with you in eternity
Hand in hand.†

99. Sparkplug Epiphany

For though I am absent in the flesh, yet am I with you in the spirit. . . .

— Colossians 2:5

We were at our summer home on a gorgeous lake in northern Minnesota. It has been our refuge for over 50 years and four generations. We call it "The Last Resort."

There's a white cabin Grandpa built with Dad's help. There's an old red tractor named "Maudie." There's a big dock for the old fishing boat, the ski boat and "Eggie" the canoe.

Knew you'd ask: the canoe was new. We were buying letters to put on it once we thought of a name for it. My little brother, the worrywart, said we'd better get TWO bags of letters, because what if the name had TWO of the same letter in it?

Like what?

Like, uh, like, uh, "Eggie."

"Eggie"? For a canoe?

So "Eggie" it was.

There's Gull Rock, where we feed scraps to the swirling scavengers. There's the deepest outhouse hole in four counties, dug for us by a guy named Puny.

But "The Shop" is the heart of the place.

It's an old toolshed. It smells like marine oil and fish. It's stuffed with bobbers, buckets, pulleys, pipe elbows, nails, glazier's points, fishing tackle, and dozens of ancient sparkplugs lined up along the windowsill.

We had left it untouched in the three years since Dad's death.

Unlikely place for an epiphany, or life-changing burst of insight. But that's what I needed. I was emotionally untouched, like the Shop, since Dad's death. He was only 64. He had spent the last year of his life bedbound, struggling with pulmonary fibrosis. We were very, very close, and it was a terrible ordeal.

When it was over, for my mom's sake, I pretended to be strong. I barely cried. I stayed on emotional autopilot. I never fully grieved. Stuffed my feelings, as they say.

Well, that day up at the cabin, everyone else was off fishing, and I was puttering around doing "pro-yects," as Dad would call them.

Though he was a big-city CPA, he had been a farm boy, and he loved tinkering. He had "Rube Goldberg'ed" the place: our plumbing, wiring, mechanics, carpentry, everything.

First, he spent time "in engineering." The Engineering Department was a tattered director's chair overlooking the lake. He would gaze out over the water, stroking his unshaven "vacation chin," in decades-old duds and his father's ancient felt hat.

Then he'd jump up, go into The Shop, and do a "pro-yect."

He played with outboard motors and hacksaws, snagged reels and broken axles. He dipped in to countless Folger's cans of assorted nails, nuts, screws and bolts. It was Creativity Central. He solved problems, served his family, relaxed, and whistled while he worked. He was happiest then. Complete. It's how I remember him best.

So, all alone that day, I ran into The Shop for a screwdriver. Suddenly, I stopped cold, overwhelmed by the aroma of boat motor oil.

All around me were Dad's things: the four-foot lumberjack's saw. The age-old can of convertible top dressing. His jacket and chinos. His paint-spattered tools.

My knees buckled. I slumped down onto the worn, oak floor. "Dad is dead. Dead! He'll never use any of this. He's never coming back!"

Emotion overtook me like a Minnesota thunderstorm. I bawled like a moose in labor. Dad! Ohhh, Dad! I wailed, then sobbed, then whimpered.

Finally, as always, the Holy Spirit intervened, mercifully and tenderly, with humor.

My cried-out eyes spied a tall lumberman's ax in the corner. I tipped my head and grinned. Dad, never one to be Politically Correct, would call a fat lady "an ax handle and a half."

I laughed out loud. Oh, Dad! I haven't lost you, after all. Wherever I go, you'll be in my mind and heart. You'll always be with me. Even now.

On my knees, on that floor, I finally accepted Dad's death. And, more importantly, God's peace.

Got my spiritual sparkplugs changed.

Bet the Fisherman had the whole thing "in engineering" all along. †

100. Behind the Back Tire

And the dove came in to him in the evening;
and, lo, in her mouth was an olive leaf pluckt off:
so Noah knew that the waters were abated from off the earth.

— Genesis 8:11

There's a family man in Omaha who parked his truck in the driveway every night and went inside to his wife and daughter. He had cares, of course, but overall he was happy, healthy and living the American dream.

And then one day he went out to his truck, started it up and backed down the driveway . . .

. . . not realizing that his little daughter was playing behind the back tire.

The jolting bump.

The sight of her crumpled body on the pavement.

The implosion of his lungs and guts.

Yelling to his wife. The screams. Scooping up the limp little body. Rushing to the hospital. The sobbing, the guilt, the self-recrimination, the hopelessness, the shame.

They buried her in one of those little child's graves with toys all around.

He parked his truck over to the side on his driveway and vowed never to drive it again.

Time went on.

He punished himself. It was all his fault, he obsessed.

If he just hadn't been in such a hurry that day. If he just would have been a responsible enough father to know where she was, every instant. If he just would have taken a few seconds to teach her never, ever to play around a vehicle.

He felt horribly heavy, lifeless and alone. It was as if he buried his life in that grave, too.

More time passed. Still he grieved.

Why, Lord? Why did You take her away from me? Why did You let this happen? Didn't You see? Why didn't You stop me? Why, God, why?

Then one day he went out to his driveway, and right behind the back tire of his truck, right at the spot that was the source of all of his aching despair and pain, where his precious daughter had been, there was a snow-white dove.

Before his eyes, it took off, majestically, into the sky.

As he watched it fly up, it was as if the weight of the world was lofted up and away from him, carried away on the wings of that dove.

It was the picture of, "Surely he hath borne our griefs, and carried our sorrows. . . ." (Isaiah 53:4)

He thought of the dove of peace that told Noah that everything was all right, and that solid ground was just ahead. He knew it meant that his little girl was in her glory, still very much alive, just in a form he couldn't yet see. It was OK.

He watched the dove fly out of sight, his face uplifted to the sky. He left it that way for a while.

He felt peace. At long last, peace.

He fell to his knees, and sobbed. This time, he felt a healing release. It was as if his heart was resurrecting. He felt a renewed hope and certainty of the life to come.

He won't know for a long time how all of this fits into God's plan for his life. He won't know until the day in heaven when he holds his little girl again and feels her love and forgiveness. Above them in triumph will fly a snow-white dove whose message is peace and whose gift is joy.

Jesus Christ is risen, indeed. All is forgiven, indeed. God is love, indeed.

Alleluia!

Amen! †

Index of Bible Verses

Verse	Story #
Proverbs 27:7	95
Proverbs 28:11	72
Proverbs 31:30,31	93
Ecclesiastes 6:9	38
Song of Solomon 2:12	88
Song of Solomon 2:15	10
Song of Solomon 3:4b	22
Song of Solomon 6:3	48
Isaiah 7:11	24
Isaiah 11:6d	75
Isaiah 44:3	65
Isaiah 54:10	29
Isaiah 60:8	20
Jeremiah 9:5	92
Jeremiah 31:11	33
Zechariah 5:3	44
Zechariah 9:14a	9
Matthew 5:8	66
Matthew 5:24b	16
Matthew 5:25	27
Matthew 6:11	35
Matthew 6:12	18
Matthew 6:26	85
Matthew 6:28b-30	2
Matthew 10:30	5
Matthew 10:86	52
Matthew 14:36b	40
Matthew 18:6	86
Matthew 19:4	61